RUNNING AMERICAN BUSINESS

RUNNING AMERICAN BUSINESS

Top CEOs Rethink
Their Major Decisions

ROBERT BOYDEN LAMB

Basic Books, Inc., Publishers   New York

Library of Congress Cataloging-in-Publication Data

Lamb, Robert, 1941–
  Running American business.

  Includes indexes.
  1. Strategic planning.   2. Decision-making.
I. Title.
HD30.28.L355   1987   658.4'03   86–47732
ISBN   0–465–07150–3

for Nancy, Roland, and Helena

CONTENTS

CONTENTS

ACKNOWLEDGMENTS

This book could not have been written without the participation of eighty-nine chief executives who run or ran major U.S. corporations. During the twelve years I researched this book, these CEOs either allowed me to interview them and their staffs or they provided me with copies of speeches, internal reports, and strategic plans. A list of some of the CEOs who helped appears in the appendix at the end of the book. However, there were many additional CEOs who asked for anonymity because of the sensitive nature of their revelations about their industries, companies, colleagues, predecessors, and competitors.

The most important individual debt I owe is to Robert Teitelman who worked tirelessly for months on drafts of this book. His originality, enthusiasm, dedication, and judgment were invaluable.

For all their efforts on my behalf I want to express deep gratitude to my assistants: Panayotis Kontos, Spencer Ferdinand, Claudia Hansen, Robert Bull; to my colleagues: Richard West, William Guth, Oscar Ornati, Paul Shrivastava, Michael Porter, Henry Mintzberg, Alfred Rappaport, William Rothschild, Fred Gluck, Robert Kuhn, Charles Hofer, and Bruce Henderson; and to Basic Books: my editor, Steven Fraser, and also Martin Kessler, Jeanne Gottschalk, and Debra Hudak.

While working on this book I have benefited from suggestions from many of my colleagues and students at New York University, Wharton, and Columbia as well as from many other friends at Harvard, MIT, Yale, the University of Chicago, Dartmouth, Northwestern, Stanford, the University of California, Carnegie Mellon, the University of Georgia, McGill, the London School of Economics, Oxford, Cambridge, the London Business School, the Administrative Staff College, the University of Paris, Inmead, the University of Bocconi, the University of Venice, the University of Hamburg, and the University of Tokyo.

ACKNOWLEDGMENTS

Over the last twelve years there has been a virtual explosion in analysis of business strategies: at corporations, institutes, and at management consulting firms. I have benefited greatly from my discussions and work with colleagues at Alcar, General Electric, the Strategic Planning Institute, The Planning Forum, The Association for Corporate Growth, The Boston Consulting Group, McKinsey & Company, Booz Allen Hamilton, Arthur D. Little, Stanford Research Institute, Coopers and Lybrand, Management Analysis Center, The Conference Board; and finally, Pat Hogan and Nancy Pratt on the *Journal of Business Strategy*.

RUNNING AMERICAN BUSINESS

CHAPTER ONE

DECISION MAKING IN THE REAL WORLD

It was not long ago that the American management style stood, in the eyes of the world, as a mighty colossus—so formidable, so accurate, so impregnable—that all the rest of the world could do was to imitate its workings. . . . It is true that American business, which has generated wealth and prosperity for so many for so long, is in terrible trouble.

—WILLIAM F. MAY, former CEO, American Can Company

A corporation is the shadow of the man at the top.

—ARJAY MILLER, former president, Ford Motor Company
(with a gloss on Ralph Waldo Emerson)

Down in the Engine Room

How do chief executive officers (CEOs) actually run American businesses? A simple sounding question, but a most difficult one to answer satisfactorily. When I first pondered that question some twelve years ago, I gathered the usual piles of textbooks and studies describing how chief executives construct a strategic plan and then send it to a cadre of eager managers to be implemented. From those studies, it seemed as if most companies had a sort of strategic-planning assembly line: ideas come in here, trim and wheels and headlights are slapped on here, here, and here, and the plan rolls off onto the highway, in most cases a juggernaut—after all, this was mighty *American* business I was looking at—but with an occasional Edsel thrown in just to keep everyone honest. Simple, indeed. Then I went a step further and actually began to talk with chief executives, eighty-nine of them in all, and the picture that began to form was as different from the theory as an organizational chart differs from the thousand or so lives it encompasses.

One day, for example, I talked to Arjay Miller, the smoothly intelligent former president of Ford Motor Company, then Dean of the Graduate School of Business at Stanford University. In the midst of a long conversation, he began to talk about how basic strategy developed at Ford. What was so fascinating was not so much the actual content as the sense of complexity he communicated: he, of course, thought it was simple. Here is just a fragment of that conversation: "Right after the end of World War II, there was enough pent-up demand for our product both in the U.S. and throughout the world, that Ford really didn't need a product strategy. All we had to do was shift from military to civilian production as rapidly as possible. Early on, we decided that we were going to grow from within. A natural match existed between the generation of internal funds and the recruitment and training of people. At the same time, we established long range product and profit goals, including the shift from centralized to decentralized operations. Each division was required to make five-year plans, covering the first year in considerable detail. Of course, outlining essential steps to be taken is the easy part. The tough part is getting the job done— especially when success depends on influencing other people. Every month we evaluated our progress before the board of directors. No matter how well plans are made, unforeseen developments require changes."

Talking with executives such as Miller was like going down into the engine room of an ocean liner to peer into its highly intricate works. These interviews stimulated in me a whole series of questions. What, for example, was the real process of translating "essentially simple ideas" into what Miller called his three Ps: products, profits, and people? Is strategy imposed on the company by the chief executive, or does it bubble up from below, created by planning staffs or line managers and filtered through committees, only to land upon the chief executive's desk with a phone book–like thump? Are there particular types of strategic decisions that are more likely to be made from the top down rather than from the bottom up? Are there certain types of managers who are more prone to one form of strategic decision making than others? To what degree is strategy planned and to what degree does it represent a sort of muddling through? Is strategy merely a reaction to external environmental pressures, or does the corporation have control over its own destiny?

4

DECISION MAKING IN THE REAL WORLD

Certainly, in a series, these questions seem as dry as the instructions to an income tax return. But the reflections they elicited, which appear in the pages ahead, revealed a pungent, complex, and deeply contradictory reality to American business and American chief executives. Perhaps, I thought, my original question was off the point. A better question might be: how did Arjay Miller disburse Ford resources in the early 1960s? Or, how did John deButts of AT & T choose his successor? Or, what was the thought process behind Harold S. Geneen's diversification strategy? Mies van der Rohe was right: God *is* in the details, and it is those details, in the form of a number of action strategies, that are the foundation of this book.

A Landscape Strewn with Failure

A good part of American business has to do with that most un-American of ideas: failure. Where running a big company used to be like serving as captain of a ship on gentle, southern seas, today it is more akin to white-water canoeing—fast changing, fast moving, and full of hidden dangers, sudden twists and turns. Many firms have taken spills—AT & T, IBM, GM, and Exxon—and many of the most famous chief executives I interviewed—Roy Ash, Michel C. Bergerac, Tex Thornton, Peter McColough, even Harold Geneen—have experienced traumatic failures or have seen their corporate creations founder after their passing. Ash, for example, presided over the demise of AM International Inc.; Bergerac's strategy at glamorous Revlon Incorporated led to its acquisition by the prosaic, though profitable, Pantry Pride Incorporated; the intricate corporate machines assembled by Thornton at Litton Industries, Inc. and by Geneen at ITT Corporation fell on hard times; McColough's much vaunted focus on technology at Xerox Corporation nevertheless did not prevent certain specific failures in computers and office equipment. Others in this book, less well known, suffered as well: William C. Verity saw his company, Armco Inc., enter the valley of the shadow of death called the steel glut; it has not come out yet and is barely hanging on. Wallace N. Rasmussen, who had worked at Beatrice Companies, Incorporated for his entire career and saw it as his family, retired, only to have the company ripped apart by internal dissension.

5

So in many ways, this is a book about failure. The confidence of American business after World War II—it now seems almost a hubris—has been shattered, to be replaced by a more realistic view of the world. "I think it is fair to say, our halcyon days are over," said William F. May, the former chief executive of American Can, then dean of the Graduate School of Business Administration at New York University. "These are turbulent times . . . just about the only thing we can be sure of today is the certainty of change." The steel industry reflects that fall from grace like no other business. For decades, the giant integrated steel operators believed that if technology wasn't invented here—here being U.S. Steel Corporation or Bethlehem Steel Corporation or Jones & Laughlin Steel, Incorporated— it wasn't worth looking at. As a result, U.S. steelmen were rare visitors at the major international steel meetings, and even rarer licensers of foreign technology. But the Japanese were, of course, willing to learn from others, and by the 1970s had far outpaced most American operators, who were saddled with World War II vintage open-hearth furnaces and vast, inefficient facilities. American steel may never recover. And it is a bitter joke among steel engineers today that while U.S. steel companies used to not send their technical people to technical shows because they didn't care, now they don't because they can't afford it.

Indeed, despite the widespread realization of failure, the habits of a smug and comfortable management establishment—management by guesswork or management by inertia—persist. Those habits probably will always exist, as a sort of frictional force that no amount of lubrication or clever design can entirely eliminate. However, it is hopeful that today most chief executives can recognize that reactive planning or simply muddling through are not sufficient to meet the demands of the present or the future. Any company that does not consider its own competitive strategy and the strategies of its competitors will be left behind just as quickly as a firm that still sells vacuum tubes in the age of semiconductors, or as one that continues to stuff its dollars into mattresses in the age of sophisticated cash management. That realization is the start of a reformation.

Change has long been a part of American business. During the Great Depression, the New Deal, and the world war years, American industry was preoccupied with production because of the prevailing scarcities. Chief executive officers tended to be chosen from the ranks of production directors. In the postwar years of the 1950s, marketing skills became the critical resource, as corporations sought ways to distribute and sell a glut of products. As a result, certain marketing executives rose to the top. With the credit crunch of the 1960s came the realization in management that capital was becoming the scarce resource. Thus, financial skills gained in importance, financial managers were the primary people chosen to be chief executive officers, and students at business schools flocked to take finance courses. During this time, new financial mechanisms were invented and exploited in order to take advantage of a corporation's leverage or debt capacity. "Off-balance-sheet financing" and other hybrid types of securities were introduced, each helping to fuel a new wave of mergers and acquisitions and conglomerate enterprises which soon proliferated.

But the key historical moment for this book—and for current American business—is the double blow of the 1973–74 oil price shocks and economic recession, which wrenched most companies from their lethargy and thrust them into a darker, more threatening world. That experience only hastened the collapse of many conglomerates, and of their role as a sort of corporate avant-garde, as well as the decline of high-risk financial firms and speculators. This was a major watershed, and it convinced many chief executives that financial manipulation alone was insufficient as a management focus. Other hard lessons followed: of the need for productivity and quality control, the dangers of debt and high interest rates, the overall realization that natural resources were a critical requirement, and that dependence upon international markets and sourcing of materials and goods abroad had become facts of life. Troubled times thrust chief executives back to the fundamentals—the mundane but vital benchmarks like accounts receivables and inventory. Peter McColough, former chief executive of Xerox Corporation, describes the lessons of the 1973 recession: "Until 1973, very little emphasis was put on the balance sheet. We didn't ignore it, but we only gave it about 5 percent of our attention. We weren't in jeopardy of going bankrupt or anything, but the balance sheet got sloppy. We've had enormous efforts since then on accounts receivables. We realized that while the days outstanding in the United States was pretty good, 35 to 40 days, it was far greater in other countries. An average was 80 days, though it was 180 days in Latin America. So we had a concentrated drive.... Europe now has the same as the United States, and that, of course, gives you a lot of cash. Same thing with inventories."

McColough's response was typical. Chief executives came through the fire of 1974 sensitive to the fact that they operated in a world not of plenty, but of limits—in capital and financial credit, in new sources of energy and

7

resources, in efficient U.S. manufacturing capacity, in effective marketing, in new technology, even in management and operational talent. Although the stark Malthusian fears of the mid-1970s would give way to a more optimistic view in the 1980s—particularly as oil prices dropped and OPEC collapsed—a certain innocence had been lost.

The Role of the Chief Executive Officer

In the world of the chief executive, winning and losing are achieved in an arena called strategic planning and initiation. Corporate strategy is to a remarkable extent the creation of the chief executive officer. This does not mean that he necessarily details the strategy himself but that the strategy exists only if he fosters and nourishes it. On the other hand, even large departments of strategic planning can wither into superfluity if the chief executive is not interested in their work, anxious about their conclusions, or stalwart in his support. This has meant that most key strategic initiatives in companies are imposed from the top down, although some critical ideas and initiatives do bubble up from the bottom, from, say, planning departments or strategic business units. Yet it is usually the domination and leadership of the power structure by the chief executive that creates a climate of encouragement and direction that gives the strategic planners the sense that they are allowed to take bold strategic initiatives. Without this, most corporate strategy programs would not have been created or implemented. I am not saying here that strategic planners are expendable and that all that is necessary is a strong, single-minded chief executive. Nor am I entirely sure, as Arjay Miller is, that the corporation lies *entirely* in the shadow of one person. Rather, I am simply pointing to the fact that the chief executive, to a considerable extent, sets the planning agendas and, more importantly, that he or she does so by imposing constraints upon the planners' projects.

Most corporations do exist in the shadow of a single individual, the CEO. For good or ill, this executive controls the reins of power and determines the direction that the company takes. The signs of a failure to lead are obvious: a lack of direction, a sense of stagnation, corporate infighting, high turnover, small crises that can lead to full-scale disasters, and finally, financial difficulties. The fundamentals of leadership are far less tangible, despite the flood of self-help books on the subject that annually crowd the bookshelves. The CEO must sell his strategy to his managers, who in turn must convince their subordinates to act in concert. While coercion may work as a short-term tactic, more times than not it leads to dissatisfaction, lack of follow-through and coordination, and ultimately, failure. In the long run, managers will not follow a strategy they do not believe in.

Thus, a CEO is very much a politician. He must persuade others of the merits of his strategy, then involve himself actively in each stage. A strategy is only as good as its weakest stage, and the CEO who disregards a particular aspect runs a tremendous risk. A CEO must motivate his troops with a subtle mixture of carrots and sticks. And management must feel that the CEO has constructed a just system, in which rewards and punishments are meted out not by whim, but by a rational system of judgment that exists beyond him. Finally, the CEO must sell himself, his organization, and his plan clearly; ordering priorities; spelling out, for both high- and low-level managers, short-term and long-term goals.

All this is hardly easy, and truly superior CEOs are rare indeed. The CEO must blend many conflicting priorities, which may change over time. He must balance different centers of power within the company, and motivate a range of different personalities. And he must evaluate, communicate with, and balance a large number of external forces: institutional investors, major lenders, major customers, Wall Street analysts, and government figures both here and abroad. It was fascinating to watch the CEOs who figure so prominently in this book wrestle with those various constituencies, adapting their strategies or junking them outright, as the conditions changed. Success, in a product line or division, may convince a CEO to shift the company's strategic direction. Or, more commonly, failure, often culminating in a crisis that threatens both the CEO and the company, forces him to reevaluate the strategic direction. In both these cases, the CEO stands as the pivot. For better or for worse, he forces a change, or stays the course. If he is removed, another CEO takes his place, in the hope, of course, that he can throw a longer shadow.

In theory, this sounds simple. In practice, it requires a finely tuned sense of personal relationships and a strong feeling for leadership. This is a more amorphous area that I have chosen to call *manpower strategies*. "People make the difference," said Miller. "All corporations exist in the same environment. They all operate under the same laws, have access to the same raw materials, and face the same customers. The *only* difference among corporations is the people. The vastly different success rates among cor- porations, even in the same industry, result from these 'people differences,' starting at the top."

Thus, while organizations and even cultures can differ, the tools of lead- ership are surprisingly similar. Miller was discussing several books on Jap- anese management practices he had just read. "I found it interesting that as the authors went deeper into the study of Japanese style, which is es- sentially the bubble-up or consensus approach, they found out that even in Japan the top man really had a game plan. He just didn't reveal it. It was always in the back of his mind. He knew what he wanted to accomplish, but he had to make it appear that it originated lower within the organi- zation." John deButts, former CEO and chairman of AT & T, elaborated on the ambiguous nature of chief executive leadership: "In the final anal- ysis," he said, "the chairman makes the decision. I seldom make a decision until I'm pretty sure I have overwhelming support. There have been times when I refused to go along with the committee; there have been times I've had to reverse them. But that very seldom happens." Later, I shall look at the top-down and bottom-up approaches to planning more closely.

The Light at the End of the Tunnel

Because chief executives establish that top-down or bottom-up frame of reference, strategic failures can often be traced to a limitation in the chief. These people, after all, are only human, and they are as dogged by the same sort of weaknesses, either internal or external, as other people. These limitations regularly lead to what I refer to in this book as *tunnel vision*, meaning that the planner's vision is frequently circumscribed within very narrow confines. Many of the problems of U.S. companies can be traced, I believe, to executive constraints that foster a myopia among managers faced with a rapidly changing, competitive world. The limitations of the chief executive's training or outlook, as well as the traditions of the company or industry, can impose blinders upon the range of strategies that a particular company will consider.

Consider the case of the chief executive of a major chemical company. When I spoke with him, I asked whether he had a strategic plan when he became chief executive. His reply was illuminating and indicative of many companies during that period. "No, I did not," he said. "I think as with most corporate executives, of our corporation at least, I was a career employee. I graduated from college and knocked on the door of the employment lobby—even at that point in time I didn't have a clear idea of my assets or what I could do in a company and I was totally dependent on them for a career path. Fortunately, they put me in an area where I had an interest and could use the skills I had. I grew up in the organization. We all seemed to know each other pretty well. I'd probably have to say that I was molded in terms of my attitudes toward certain things and what the principles of the company should be and what was, perhaps, important. These were just imbued in me in the beginning, and so by the time I reached the chairman's job the philosophy I had probably agreed with my predecessors'."

Later, I asked that same chief executive how he had decided to diversify into the cosmetics business. "The cosmetics thing was fortuitous," he said. "The company said that maybe if we do something else, cosmetics might be a logical extension of our activities. . . . It did utilize the same production base and you could stretch your imagination to the time when research and development might make a contribution." But this old-line company had never been an aggressive acquisitor, so the proposed strategy languished. "We didn't have the guts to really initiate anything. . . . [their bank] came to us and said, 'Why don't you buy?' And so we were forced to make a decision."

This should not imply that such a company has suffered unduly because of its conservative strategy; for many of the very largest companies, conservative management has proven to be quite a successful way of doing business. After all, these companies were traditionally involved in preserving lucrative markets; more than one chief executive subscribed to the notion, "If it ain't broke, don't fix it." There is some wisdom to that, but like all aphorisms, it is simplistic. Few markets are static, and few companies can continue to preserve a status quo. In fact, today, pharmaceutical companies are faced with a variety of threats, from generic drug manufacturers, to the aging of many of its drugs and the new technological challenges posed by biotechnology. It is getting more difficult to prosper by reacting to events—a lesson that many companies and their chief executives have learned the hard way over the previous decade.

Most corporate strategy resembles that of a medieval lord hiding behind his castle wall more than, as myth would have it, that of a crusading knight on a white charger. Defensive financial strategy can mean not only an unwillingness to take on more debt, but an unwillingness to try new financing techniques or hybrid securities issues, a refusal to borrow abroad, or the failure to finance new projects or fully capitalize old projects. It can also mean conservative accounting practices, excessive built-in reserves, excessive coverage against loss, or contingencies abroad against foreign exchange deficits. Again, let me emphasize that defensive strategy, in the right situation, may well reflect sound business sense. And aggressive strategies involving the launching of new products, expansion abroad, or the undertaking of numerous acquisitions may be simply foolhardy.

Defensive strategies, such as those that protect existing assets, customer bases, or distribution channels, can take on a variety of forms: providing customer service to make customers dependent upon one's engineering or maintenance experts; helping an alternative supplier to get into the business so as not to be dependent upon one source; extending longer credit to hold customers, or shedding customers who cannot pay their bills. Perhaps the most significant defensive strategy, however, stems from management's focus on short-term results. From my interviews, it became glaringly obvious that most U.S. chief executives consider the short-term perspective to be the safest and most rational approach to doing business. Furthermore, they frequently consider any long-term business planning to be impractical, counterproductive, or dangerous because of the tendency for long-term plans to go awry.

This shortsightedness is gradually becoming recognized as a failing; nonetheless, maximizing short-run returns continues to be the standard by which most chief executives judge themselves, their managers, and their competition. Virtually all of the chief executives I talked with were fully aware that this short-term perspective ran counter to the strategic emphasis of European and Japanese companies. Again and again U.S. executives mentioned that foreign companies, especially when backed by their governments, could afford to take a longer-term strategy of slow growth with almost no growth in year-to-year or quarter-to-quarter earnings. This option simply is not open to U.S. chief executives. Said one CEO, "If I did that I'd be fired."

Many admitted that they were aware of the tension between their role as day-to-day corporate managers oriented toward short-term results, and their role as long-term strategic planners. Many were concerned, for instance, about the exclusively short-term focus of their subordinates in both their business decision making and the construction of their personal careers, particularly the tendency to job hop. They condemned this trend, blaming it for the problems involved in implementing long-term strategies and for what they viewed as a decline in corporate loyalty. Many of these chief executives recognized that their subsidiary managers' constant focus on short-term results and job hopping tended to jeopardize the companies they worked for, milking each business for its short-term payoffs at the expense of long-term health.

These chief executives also recognized that short-term maximization was often counterproductive, and this troubled them. Many of them were experimenting with their pay and reward systems to try to develop some incentive for long-term achievements. But it is still a long way from recognizing the problem, and tinkering with the strategic plan is not the same as actually altering it.

Creating a Strategic Plan

Although chief executives' assent is crucial in the building of a framework for corporate strategy, they often have little to do with the actual planning process itself. Most large companies are simply too large and complex with too many strategic initiatives going on at once for the chief executive to be directly involved. Imagine, for example, the strategic planning required by the Eastman Kodak Company, the $10.6-billion Rochester, New York, giant that has seen its camera markets slowly eroding and has been desperately searching for growth in acquisitions, joint ventures, consortia, and new ventures. "In 1985 alone," said Kodak's chief executive, Colby H. Chandler, "Kodak acquired a half-dozen new companies, invested in seven joint ventures, moved aggressively forward with its new businesses in the life sciences, and continued to further its mainstream business in photography, chemicals, fiber and plastics, electronic imaging, information management, printing reproduction . . ."[1] And many of these businesses are worlds apart. For example, while Kodak bought a small producer of magnetic media, Spin Physics, in California, it also has joined the Microelectronics and Computer Corporation, a consortium that will be looked at later in more detail. At the same time, Kodak is participating in joint ventures with four biotech companies—Amgen, Cetus, Immunex, and Cytogen—and watching its equity investments in Sun Microsystems, a manufacturer of advanced workstations, and Interleaf, which is strong in electronic publishing. To harness all of this requires tremendous discipline and flexibility.

Chandler could never master the details of all of these companies' different operations and technologies. Most chief executives are like movie directors: the conception is theirs (though they may have hired someone else to write the script) but the process of filmmaking is a collaborative one, requiring the employment of a variety of people with a variety of skills. Most chief executives take responsibility for planning certain aspects of strategy, such as determining whether to start operations abroad, deciding on mergers and acquisitions, and choosing their successors, thereby influencing the ongoing strategic shape of the corporation. But then they delegate to their strategic planning departments or line managers the task of setting out and designing most details of the company's strategy. The chief executive who is the grand designer of corporate strategy exists, but is rare. Harold Geneen is one, but even he had to devise a sometimes ruthless, often unwieldy system of regular, marathon meetings to keep himself informed and the mechanism functioning properly.

Chief executives of smaller companies are more likely to take a detailed interest in strategic planning, simply because the scale of operations is more manageable. As a result, corporate founders often seek to involve themselves deeply in the details of this or that plan even after the company has grown to a size that renders it impractical. Stories abound of founding chief executives wandering the headquarters at night turning off lights, or counting the workers who arrive late, or simply demanding the right to approve every decision right down to who gets the parking spots and what kind of office equipment to buy. Moreover, founders as a group often tend to depend on an intuitive understanding of business—seat-of-the-pants strategists—rather than on systematic planning and the use of modern management methods. As for most chief executives of established companies, their strategic options tend to be confined by company tradition and peer pressure, except in cases when an executive has come in to try to engineer a turnaround. Then, under crisis conditions, the chief executive usually has carte blanche to make any changes necessary for survival.

The most obvious limitations are those imposed upon a chief executive by outside forces: economic conditions such as a recession, or a rapid period of expansive economic growth. We have already seen the historical trends in management over the last fifty years shift the emphasis from production experts to those with marketing and financial skills ultimately to strategic planners. Likewise, the competitive condition of an industry also has a profound influence upon a chief executive's strategic options. Hence, as I found in my interviews with chief executives and their strategic planning staffs, it is vital when examining strategic options to focus not on plans that are isolated from real-world economic and industry conditions, but on the context of the economic and industrial conditions now and in the foreseeable future.

But there are a number of other less ascertainable, but still quite powerful, external influences. Chief executives are strongly influenced by their peers and by their predecessors. Business is a community—a phantom club of CEOs, as I call it in the next chapter—with all sorts of unwritten rules and hazy traditions, a pantheon of heroes, and a blacklist of villains. Many of the chief executives I spoke with mentioned the value of such business organizations as the Conference Board, the Business Round Table, and a number of other forums where they can make their voices heard and others that serve as advocacy groups. What became increasingly apparent to me was that such chief executive groups, clubs, and associations serve as socializing vehicles, providing a vital external influence on one's conception of acceptable, workable, and rational strategic options.

The chief executives I interviewed spent from 35 to 55 percent of their time on activities outside their firms—among them, the associations already mentioned, a wide variety of involvements with government regulatory authorities and community organizations, and a web of corporate boards. My figures are corroborated by Henry Mintzberg and his team of researchers, as well as by several other major investigators of chief executive work patterns and decision making. These clubs are particularly important in influencing even the formulation of a chief executive's strategic management. In terms of peer pressure, chief executives often follow the strategies that are in vogue. They often formulate a strategy that parallels those of chief executives in other firms. External peer pressure appears to influence chief executives in their standards for judging good strategy, good consulting firms, and the proper form, sequence, speed, and goals of strategic implementation. At times, these external views are given more consideration than the opinions of internal managers, board members, or stockholders.

Let us touch quickly on two areas where this club or community provides important services to chief executives. The first has to do with influence. Throughout this book there are a number of discussions about two highly influential "clubs," one centered around Tex Thornton and a group of

15

U.S. Air Force officers he brought together during World War II called the "whiz kids," and the other comprising the enormous number of executives who worked for Geneen at ITT and then left to operate their own companies. Both groups left their legacies. The whiz kids popularized and disseminated a method of planning called *systems management*, a highly rational (at least on the surface), quantitative approach to strategic thinking. Geneen, the great promoter of financial results and diversification, popularized the "no surprise" school of management featuring weekly and monthly reports, an attempt to hold in harness companies of wildly different characters.

Second, this community of chief executives provides an important source of information—although it may not always be accurate. For example, during a conversation I had with John deButts in the late 1970s, he declared confidently, "There is no indication of recession," "I talked with the current CEO of General Motors the other day. Do you know what he thinks? He thinks growth in 1979 is going to three and a half percent, and the automotive business, especially General Motors, is basing its manufacturing plans on it. They are going to make more automobiles in 1979 and they're going to sell them. Where's the recession? Inventories are under better control than in ten years . . . industrial production is up. Housing is holding up. [The chief executive of] Chase said the other day they had topped off their interest rate and Bill Miller [chairman of the Federal Reserve Board] confirmed it." DeButts and his high-level informants were, of course, dead wrong. The recession of 1980 was right around the corner.

If peer pressure, objective economic conditions, and the individual limitations of the executive pose external constraints, many chief executives have found their options limited internally by the traditional practices of the company. The rigid culture of a corporation, after the legacy of the founder or the founding group, forces a kind of conformity to certain rituals, routines, and dogmas about appropriate and inappropriate managerial options, styles, or structures. The extraordinary tunnel vision in some rigid companies spills over into the ranks of those aspiring to become chief executives. As a result, when they do rise to the top, they have been conditioned for years into thinking along a narrow, limiting path.

This narrow vision of what strategic options are possible for the company generates an enormous organizational or bureaucratic drag when any new chief executive tries to shift to a new strategy. DeButts said that by far his hardest task at AT & T was to force managers to stop thinking of themselves as old-line telephone men in a government-regulated utility and, instead,

16

to start acting as tough competitors. Charles Brown, his successor, said almost exactly the same thing after he had been in office for a year. For years, the submerged weight of traditional behavior patterns and psychological habits and attitudes persisted, and they still persist. The result, said deButts, whom many chief executives echo, is that it sets limits to the strategic agenda; to what strategies will be discussed and tried; to the form of the strategic plan; to what strategies will be deemed successful; to the yardstick used to judge success; and to what strategies will be rewarded, fully funded, quickly developed, aggressively pursued, or given top priority.

Examples of the weight of internal corporate tradition as a constraint on the chief executive's ability to formulate, carry out, or alter strategy is a very common phenomenon. For example, at Beatrice, there was a tradition of virtually no debt. Wallace Rasmussen, then chief executive, had joined the company just after high school in a job hauling blocks of ice in a dairy, and had risen through the ranks over a period of forty-six years. During his tenure, Rasmussen demanded that his headquarters staff start work by 6:30 A.M., just as he had done in the dairy. So while Rasmussen clearly was somewhat more circumscribed by tradition than were other chief executives, he also represented a particular financial philosophy. "I simply can't increase the debt ratio of this company. That Triple-A rating that we have is almost unique among American corporations. We've had it for forty years." [Rasmussen's successors did not feel the same loyalty to the debt rating and the debt level of Beatrice soared after its leveraged buyout.] But Rasmussen was also traditional in other ways. He sought out acquisitions, like Tropicana Products Inc., that were strictly within the food business because, he said, "it fit with our traditional acquisition policy."

David Rockefeller gave me many examples from his experience at The Chase Manhattan Bank of the same rigid constraints imposed by the bank's internal traditions. He indicated, for example, that the old-line loan officers who ran the bank when he first arrived were unable to think of it as a company or a business. "We had no yearly budget," said Rockefeller. "We had no organizational structure. We had no five-year plan. No plan. We had no strategy and no set of goals."

In contrast to AT & T, Beatrice, and Chase, it might appear that the new electronics firms, such as Hewlett-Packard Company, Texas Instruments Incorporated, the Digital Equipment Corporation, and Control Data Corporation, young though they might be, have each changed their traditions and internal cultures to keep pace with the rapid shifts in techno-

17

logical advances, foreign competition, new product development, and increasing cost pressures. But this is not true. Indeed, like their older cousins, these companies tend to establish traditions and keep to them, regardless of changes in the strategic environment. Internal growth has been far more important at these firms than acquisitions. In most of these new electronics companies, managers are reluctant to make mergers and acquisitions even when they have grown to over a billion dollars in revenues. Likewise, their financial, marketing, and human resources strategies frequently appear to be locked in from the earliest days of the company's development. But even a tradition of innovation can be limiting and dangerous. Sometimes a market is simply not prepared for innovative products.

Strategy as a Process of Discovery

Actual strategy is not a written plan; nor is it the unfolding of a single design. Rather, strategy is an interactive process in which various participants discover, adapt to, and accommodate to a shifting reality. As a process, strategy resembles a snowball, growing and developing meaning and shape, gathering supporters and muddy detractors, altering its shape as it hits various obstacles. Strategy also involves experimentation and the interdependent development of various parts of a corporate organization. And each strategic experiment involves a confrontation between strategic goals, hypotheses, and actual circumstances—an adjustment of a theoretical policy to reality and all of its confusions and contradictions. I am therefore defining strategy not as a company's simple written strategic plan—what Michel Bergerac facetiously called "the official history"—but as what a company actually does. In short, the plan is only the beginning of the strategic process; the actual events are the end. Most of the chief executives I interviewed had come to this realization, sometimes painfully. *Plans are not strategy. Strategy is what a firm actually does.* Or, in Lenin's words, that "practice is a hundred times more important than theory."

Thus, we find that a company with no written plan and no avowed strategy can still pursue individual action strategies—marketing, technology, new ventures—with very real strategic consequences for competitors, creditors, stockholders, and suppliers. This conception of strategy—actions, not plans—flies in the face of those who would limit the concept of strategic decision making to conscious grand designs and full-blown plans. Many chief executives and their staffs simply draw a trend line through whatever activities the firm is engaged in at present, extrapolating that trend line into the future and defining that line as their strategy. To purists, this, too, is not strategy. It bears no relation to a careful portfolio analysis of a corporation's different divisions, businesses, products, assets, strengths, and weaknesses. But while it is true that such inactive management can be disastrous, it is also true that aggressive and fantastic plans can go awry—to quote Roy Ash, "an error of commission rather than omission." Inertial decision making, in some situations, is not necessarily bad strategy.

Another way to gain a perspective on the world of the chief executive is to try to untangle the undergrowth of rational and irrational impulses that go into initiating and implementing strategies. Later, I shall examine a decision by Harold Geneen to build a telephone cable plant in San Diego, a decision that, on the surface and from the testimony of his own planners, was palpably irrational. But to Geneen, who had political considerations in mind and who felt the need to locate more facilities in the United States, the decision was the height of rationality, and he grew irritated when I suggested it was not. Who was right? Well, we do know that the plant was a financial failure, which leads one to suspect that the decision was irrational. All of which suggests a corollary to my earlier dictum associating strategy with action: successful actions tend to be tagged "rational," while those that fail are often considered to have been irrational.

Hindsight is not always needed, however, to determine the rationality of a strategic decision. I must say that time after time when I asked chief executives how this or that strategy failed, I heard them speak of a variety of emotional reasons and personality conflicts underlying the decision. Moreover, decisions rarely arose from more than a handful of alternatives, so that only a tiny fraction of the true options were considered. What was taking place, I discovered, was a narrowing process that all but eliminated the vast majority of choice. This narrowing does not mean that the two or three choices considered were not chosen rationally; rather, it means that a sort of bounded rationality was taking over. What are the symptoms of this form of limited analysis? The blithe and unthinking acceptance of assumptions and hypotheses by both the chief executive and his planning staff. The tendency to replace facts with emotions or biases. The adoption of vogues—acquisitions, for example, such as those that built conglomerates in the 1960s and those that drove the hostile takeover boom of the 1980s, both of which resulted a few years later in a trail of divestitures rattling behind them like a string of tin cans attached to a car. Another example is the packs of companies that went abroad, then returned to these shores just as suddenly as they had left, dragging their losses behind them.

As we have seen, chief executives can also be divided into two camps: those with a tendency toward grand designs, who actually try to plan and implement a strategic plan, and those with a propensity to muddle through. Both of these descriptions take in a remarkably varied collection of phenomena—some successful, some not. The muddlers, for instance, try to blend common sense and a seat-of-the-pants approach with opportunism and ad hoc entrepreneurial decision making to come up with what ultimately becomes that company's strategy, although as I've said, there is no theoretical underpinning to it. Such muddling managements often have no clear long-range goals to which the CEO and staff adhere. Rather, they manage by fighting fires on a quarter-by-quarter basis and react to external and internal crises rather than anticipating them. Many such managers are far more concerned with personal security, comfort, and minimal business growth than they are with maximization of profit.

Although almost all of the chief executives with whom I talked professed that profits are the key goal of their corporations, most sought solutions that had little or nothing to do with profit maximization. Instead, the interviews made clear that corporate safety, organizational growth, personal accomplishment, and maintenance of minimum corporate momentum toward sales goals appeared to be the preeminent goals, with maximization of profits a kind of window dressing for the shareholders, Wall Street analysts, financial press, and the public.

The Chief Executive as Role Player

Over the past few years, various studies of chief executive decision making have suggested that strategies might be viewed as role playing. That is to say, specific corporate strategies articulated by chief executives appear to correspond to chess moves, war games, or a theatrical performance, and chief executives emulate roles that they believe other chief executives expect them to play. Each individual strategic move, therefore, stems less from any inner conviction or character trait than from the rules and practices of a game or masquerade. This fundamental issue has been approached by game theorists, war strategists, psychologists. Perhaps the best-known study is by Michael Macoby of Harvard, in his book *The Gamesman*.[2] Macoby concludes that the most successful of today's managers is the gamesman who is not personally committed to any one set of beliefs but who is able to shift gears quickly and play a variety of roles in rapid succession, depending upon changing circumstances.

Corporate strategic decision making in this view is subject to infinite flexibility in order to plan for an infinite number of contingencies and uncertainties. The chief executive's strategic moves must be seen as an endless series of temporary thrusts or feints in one direction, then another, as in fencing or chess or a military exercise. Macoby argues that the gamesman wins out over the entrepreneur, the organization man, the craftsman or jungle fighter each of whom are too rigid or constrained to operate in today's rapidly changing world.

But do chief executives truly fit into such categories? My twelve years of interviewing convince me that while there are extremely different styles and a variety of psychological types among chief executives, such stereotyping is simply not useful. What is wrong with the gamesman stereotype? First, gamesmen tend not to go into corporations at all. Those so-called gamesmen who do enter business gravitate toward nonmanagerial roles such as securities trading, arbitrage, and futures trading, where the payoff is quick and the markets more attuned to game behavior, and where each player is judged purely on his or her own decisions and performance. Further, most so-called gamesmen do not choose to be judged by the protracted outcome of years of often poorly rewarded effort in obscure locations, serving interlocking managerial layers, and participating in a series of committees, as is the case in many corporate managements.

Second, instead of four or five clear character types in business, I have found a seemingly infinite variety of psychological types, from introverts to extroverts, from the well adjusted to the neurotic, the paranoid, and even the psychotic. Third, chief executives demonstrate a combination of different character traits and behavior patterns over time which result in a range of different strategic decisions. Thus, to be truly useful, a psychological study of chief executives must go into considerably more analysis. The gamesman is thus not a clear, identifiable, or useful categorization in corporate management.

A final note: in each of the eighty-nine or so interviews that make up this book, I asked a series of questions that provides the context for the chief executives' replies. Exactly what determines a particular strategic decision? Is it primarily the result of the individual, or external factors such as the economy? Is it the result of a trend, or does it constitute fresh, decisive thinking? What are the roles of others in the decision? What role does the company organization, or tradition, play? How do industries differ in terms of strategic decision making? What determines the weight or influence of all of these factors and constraints upon the outcome of the decision?

While reading the chapters that follow, it is important to remember that in analyzing the interviews I tried to avoid the simple or the stereotypical, and labored to project the unvarnished complexity of the chief executive's role. That is one reason why I allowed these executives to talk at length; only by hearing them talk through a particular incident or crisis or maneuver can we obtain an idea of the range of options and alternatives open to chief executives. What was the total range of factors, and how did each of them affect, or fail to affect, that decision? The answers to these questions make up a complex and multicolored tapestry. There are no simple prescriptions offered here, no easy panaceas for the ills of the American corporation; success in business, even in the best of times, will always be tough to achieve and confoundingly difficult to pass on to others. Some of the chief executives you will hear from in this book have found that success; others have not. Few indeed are untainted by some failure, if only retrospectively. The voices you will hear and the situations they will describe will be as complex, contradictory, and individual as the real world of business. And that, above all else, is what this book should suggest.

CHAPTER TWO

THE PHANTOM CLUB OF CEOS

Once the club was locked, he got control of the people.
                    —ROY ASH, former CEO, AM International, Inc., and president,
                    Litton Industries, Inc., describing Tex Thornton and the whiz kids

The Many Rooms of the Club

The working life of a chief executive is preoccupied by what I call *action strategies*—assembling new ventures, developing marketing and financial strategies, paving the way for a successor, and so forth. We will look at those specific strategies in some detail in subsequent chapters. For now, let us take a step or two backward and look at a more general concern: the environment in which chief executive officers operate in, or what I like to call the "phantom club" of CEOs.

Of course, it is not really a club; nor, as some Marxists would have it, is it a conspiracy—at least not usually. Instead, it is a free-floating, shifting collection of informal and formal relationships that CEOs build throughout their careers. As I interviewed chief executives over the past twelve years, I gradually realized that I was entering into the precinct of a very exclusive organization, with its own rules and limits. I think it is helpful to explain how I got involved with this project. It really began in 1976, on my first day as an associate editor of *Fortune* magazine. No sooner had I arrived, been shown to an office, and hung up my coat, than I was assigned to a *Fortune* project surveying the political affiliations and beliefs of CEOs belonging to the *Fortune* 500 companies. My first subject was Henry Ford II, who was then still actively running the Ford Motor Company. Around that time, Ford, an Independent, had arranged along with others for a number of CEOs to meet with presidential candidate Jimmy Carter. His first words when I called him on the telephone capsulized the personal nature of his venture: "I understand that you want to hear about how and why I decided to get some CEOs together to meet with Jimmy Carter. It's simple. These CEOs are friends of mine. So I thought these top corporate leaders needed to hear what the candidate is planning. And they needed to tell him what ought to be his top priorities to improve the business environment, if he gets elected."

And so I began. From Ford I went on to some twenty other Democratic/ Independent CEOs, from Irving Shapiro, then CEO of E. I. duPont de Nemours & Company, to W. Michael Blumenthal, then running Bendix Corporation and later slated to be the secretary of the treasury under Carter. The interviewing was a revelation. Not only did this group of CEOs all know each other and refer to each other by their first names, but they had worked together before, often in more than one association. And much of what they said resembled the others' statements. Said Ford, about his political affiliation, "Because I'm an Independent, I'm considered a maverick by other CEOs." Shapiro, a lawyer and the first non-duPont to run the giant chemical company, added, "I guess I could count on two hands the Democratic CEOs I know. I realize we're kind of unusual." And Blumenthal: "I guess it's not hard for Democratic CEOs to know each other. There's just not many of us altogether."

What then of the far larger number of Republican CEOs associated with president Gerald Ford's reelection committee? Well, it turned out they too had known each other over a period of years and through a variety of meetings, associations, committees, and boards. It soon became clear that politics was only one link in this complex web, and that a variety of other ties—trade associations, boards of directorship, charities, simple competitive pressures—brought CEOs together.

With that realization, I began to undertake more quantitative research to analyze the extensive interpersonal ties between CEOs. I started by compiling CEO membership lists—some thirty-seven years of statistics from the Business Round Table, the Conference Board, Business International, the Young Presidents' Association, the Association for Corporate Growth,

24

a host of presidential commissions, university boards of trustees, even fund-raising dinner panels. Then I tried to assess what attributes, if any, could be said to characterize the members.

The most obvious distinction I found is between those CEOs who join such associations and the smaller number of those who don't. "Some guys are just joiners," said one CEO, who was emphatically not one himself. "Somehow they need these CEO clubs, maybe to make themselves feel important, or to feel as if they've arrived at the top. I know other CEOs who actually believe that their job requires joining that sort of thing. They think it's expected of them by other CEOs. Or they kid themselves that this is necessary to show their own managers the right example of CEO corporate responsibility. Personally, I regard most of this joining of CEO groups as showing [that] these guys [are] on a total ego trip." Is there some distinguishing feature separating the joiners from the go-it-alone CEOs? Says our critic, "I tend to go my own way. But then I'm an entrepreneur who started my own company. I've never been much of a club man or a joiner."

And yet, while many entrepreneurs are loners who avoid the types of associations of more corporate-bred CEOs, the issue is more complex than just that. For example, it did turn out to be the case that long-term company men were more likely to join CEO associations. Psychologically, these men are simply used to joining and participating in groups, and so they take it for granted that the next step beyond achieving the chief executive officer's office is to mix with others of that rank in a variety of associations. On the other hand, I had assumed that CEOs with introverted personalities would shy away from those groups, while the extroverts would rush to join them. That simply wasn't true; the personalities of the CEOs had less to do with it than I had expected. "I kind of had to force myself to be outgoing at these Business Round Table meetings because it's really not my character," one CEO told me. "But I consider the work we do to be truly important. So I decided I'd better be willing to participate regularly." In fact, it turns out that very few CEOs are real loners; even the critic quoted earlier, it seems, knows quite a lot about his fellow CEOs. That impression was reinforced by the in-depth interviews I then undertook. Not only did most of these chief executives know many other CEOs, but they could speak to each other through a variety of channels.

In numerous cases throughout this book, I will discuss manifestations of the phantom club. For example, there is what I call the "ITT Alumni Club"—a group of chief executives who had worked under Harold Geneen at ITT. These include Harry J. Gray of United Technologies Corporation, Edward L. Hennessy, Jr., of Allied-Signal Incorporated, Michel Bergerac of Revlon, Donald M. Kendall of Pepsico Inc., and of course, Rand V. Araskog of ITT. There are anywhere from two to four hundred alumni of ITT working as chief executives, chief financial officers, or founders of other companies, according to Steve Yesenosky, founder and publisher of *EXITTERS*, a newsletter aimed at the alumni group. What links the members of this club? Many of them have taken the lessons of corporate diversification preached by Geneen and adapted them to new situations. Hennessy, for example, has taken Allied, which used to be a basic integrated chemical company—a business that has been steadily declining since its days of glory in the 1950s—and, through skillful acquisition, built a strong, far-reaching empire, a latter-day conglomerate without the irrational acquisitions that similar companies have engaged in. When I asked Bergerac what strategies he learned at ITT that applied to Revlon, he thought a moment, and in his French-accented English said, "They don't." Then he laughed. "But I do not believe that I ever implied not having learned a lot with ITT, because I did." He elaborated: "One of the first things I had to do when I came here was to decide what was good and what wasn't so good. The name, the franchise, was extraordinarily valuable, like Pepsi or Coke." When Bergerac joined Revlon, most of the company was in the beauty business, with a tiny fraction in health care. He elected to diversify into pharmaceuticals, and to use the Revlon name to try to sell more and different cosmetics. Certainly, Bergerac was dealing with a different situation, a different company than ITT, but his diversification strategy was similar to ITT's.

Still, belonging to the ITT alumni club does not mean that these executives try to imitate Geneen in all ways. In fact, for them, Geneen triggered deeply contradictory responses. After I spent some time with Geneen, I interviewed seven other CEOs who had worked for him. Without my even mentioning his name, all made repeated references to things they had learned under Geneen's tutelage. While many of them admired his ability to focus absolutely on the rate of return, they frequently stressed what they viewed as serious faults, particularly his propensity for constant, marathon meetings. "Geneen was authoritarian, dictatorial, and absolutist in his demands," said one former ITT manager. "I dreaded those meetings," said another. "Today," said yet another, "I'm careful as hell not to terrorize top management guys or spy on them all the time the way Geneen did."

Geneen, not surprisingly, disagreed. "We did a very good job of keeping a very nonpolitical, open atmosphere where anybody could argue with me," he recalled. But one former ITT manager, now a CEO, saw it differently: "In those meetings, we were terrified when Geneen attacked us. Geneen made us squirm like a fish on a hook. He knew that and he liked it that way. That was his idea of what a good manager did."

Despite all of the mixed feelings, the Geneen style—daily, weekly, or monthly reports and a close watch on the numbers, particularly financial figures—is now commonplace, in good measure because of this vast and influential club. As *EXITTER* publisher Yesenosky said, "It's the 'no surprises' requirement. Even if you didn't like it—and most people didn't—you copied it. The legacy of the Geneen management style is so powerful because people revert to it and use it and depend upon it." A further note: Geneen's alumni have gone on to operate a bewildering variety of companies, from consumer firms to high-technology firms to conglomerates. Geneen was interested in performance; he didn't particularly care what kind of business produced it.

Other companies have spawned more focused networks. IBM, of course, has produced entire legions of executives for the computer business, including Dr. Gene M. Amdahl, who founded Amdahl Corporation and Trilogy Systems; Hewlett-Packard, where Steven P. Jobs once worked, has been credited as being the breeding ground for his Apple Computer, Inc. and other Silicon Valley companies. In a smaller way, Abbott Laboratories, the Chicago-based health-care supplier, has seeded the biomedical field. Former Abbott executives are powers in three of the top-tier biotechnology companies: James Vincent runs Biogen N. V., Kirk G. Raab is the president and COO of Genentech, and George H. Rathman is the founder and CEO of Amgen. The connections, or pedigrees, are fascinating. In 1972, Vincent left Texas Instruments to go to Abbott, bringing with him a group of executives. At Abbott, Vincent took over a moribund diagnostics program. But Vincent had a vital insight: that technology was making diagnostic tests in medicine the analogue to the semiconductor in data processing. He also had a brilliant diagnostic research head named George Rathman. Vincent went into action building Abbott tests that were run on very easy-to-use automated hardware that could be "added on"—that is, new tests that could be run on the same machine without additional cost. By the early 1980s, Abbott began to dominate certain diagnostics markets; and by 1985, under the direction of Jack W. Schuler, a Vincent protégé and another Texas Instruments alumnus, Abbott had driven a number of competitors out of the market and had become the dominant player.

By then, of course, Vincent had left the company. "He was a guy who had to run his own show," said one former Abbott executive. Eventually he got his wish, at Biogen, and Schuler took his place at Abbott. Rathman had left as well, to set up Amgen; Raab, who had been the president of Abbott, went over to mighty Genentech. Are there any ties that link these former Abbott execs? Like IBMers, these executives share a sort of esprit de corps that comes from graduating from a well-known corporate "school." They are bound by a sense of how technology and marketing fit together, and by a kind of entrepreneurial spirit that can thrive even in the precincts of a large company.

But arguably the most influential of phantom clubs over the last thirty years has been the Tex Thornton–led whiz kids, who propagated not only a management method, like Geneen, or a set of skills, like IBM and Abbott, but an all-embracing business philosophy called systems management, developed when the group's members served in an Air Force statistical control unit during World War II. The alumni of that club—Thornton, Ash, Robert S. McNamara, Miller, and others—represent just the tip of the iceberg. Once these men scattered after World War II, some to Ford, some to Hughes Tool Company and Litton, then into the government or to other companies such as AM International, they recruited and molded a new generation of executives, scattering them like seeds across the corporate landscape.

As Roy Ash describes it, one of the characteristics of the whiz kids, who left the war with a "mission" to reform corporate America as they had on more scientific grounds in the Air Force, was a sense of their own superiority. That came, in large measure, from the stringent entrance requirements imposed on the group by Thornton. Said Ash, "When Tex was given this job of setting up this management control function [in the Air Force], he said, 'We've got to have a way to bring business management principles to the Air Force, because the Air Force is much more like business than the army, with scarce resources.' His first stop was the Harvard Business School to talk to Ed Learned, who was a professor there at the time. They merged forces and decided that both purposes would be served: the business school was running out of students with the war going on, and like any business wanted to survive by operating an officers candidate school; and Tex had an opportunity to draw from the background of the people there who had something in common with the problems of the Air Force. Somehow—and I'm not sure how—Tex got into Army regulations, and even if you have four stars you can't operate against the regulations, that you cannot be a 6402, a statistical control officer, unless you are a graduate of the Harvard Business School Officers Candidate School. He locked the club, right there. He kept it pure; you could only come in through one funnel. There was a temptation for generals in the field to take some favorite colonel and give them a great desk job.

"Once the club was locked," said Ash, "he got control of the people. Then he watched that gate very carefully. They got a process established, where the statistical control unit at Harvard got the first claim on the top 10 percent of every Air Force Officers Candidate School in Miami Beach, halfway through the course. These were the days of the 'ninety-day wonders'—the course took ninety days—so six weeks in there was a half-term grading, when the names of the top 10 percent were sent over to the interviewers at statistical control who had first claim on any of those that wanted to take their second six weeks at Harvard. He really was able to purify and get the people he wanted. It was, looking back, very important. That's how the whole statistical control function got started and how they were able to man it with such high-powered people, and how no one, no matter how many stars he had, could fiddle with it. And Tex was only beholden to his superior, not to the local commander who didn't understand what we were doing and often didn't like these smart young guys who were trying to tell him how to run the Air Force."

When Ash and his colleagues left the Air Force, they carried that same sort of zeal for recruiting who they thought were the "best and the brightest." Years later, when Ash returned to the government, he tried to use the personnel strategy that Thornton had pioneered. "In the government, most of the people are civil servants. But the top layer can be appointed only by the president. At the Office of Management and Budget I could appoint maybe the top six or eight people. When I went out to get those top guys, I fell back on my earlier experiences. I wanted an entrepreneurial-type person. I set some criteria: forty years of age or younger, a fast-track guy who's already making at least $100 thousand a year. That limits the world right there; obviously we couldn't pay them $100 thousand. I told these guys, 'I don't want you for four years, I want you for two. I realize you're going to make a sacrifice, but this could be the most exciting time of your life, coming down here to be an entrepreneur in government.' They were a pretty good bunch of guys." In essence, Ash was re-creating the whiz kid environment—molding a group of executives, then sending them out to do the same.

A final mechanism of this kind of corporate socialization ought to be mentioned as well. By the time Thornton and his gang left Harvard, they had left their imprint on that powerful institution. Harvard became a prime promoter of the systems management approach to thousands upon thousands of students who, in turn, became powerful and influential executives—magnifying enormously the reach and influence of the whiz kids. Was it a club? Certainly, though it might actually be better described as a club within a club within a club, like some Masonic lodge, where one ascends through the hierarchies to a final mystery or source.

The Pecking Order

Generally, the strongest ties of chief executives, and their most searing experiences, are with their immediate predecessor, often a mentor, occasionally an antagonist. Most chief executives have strong opinions about their predecessors. We have already heard Ash's praise of Tex Thornton, and later in this book Peter McColough expresses an almost reverential attitude toward his predecessor, Joseph Wilson, founder of Xerox. Others were not so kind. Declared one newly appointed chief executive about his predecessor, "What a jerk he was. A total idiot. Christ, he left the company in total shambles." Another chief executive (who shall remain nameless, for good reason) confided to me that his predecessor had embezzled millions of dollars. "If it weren't for the tremendous amount of bad publicity that a court case would generate," he said, "I'd love to see that bastard behind bars." Other chief executives reflect the ambiguity of most successors: while they refer to their predecessors with respect, they often question some of their policies. That was clearly the case with Harold Geneen and some of his managers.

While the relationship between junior and senior chief executives can be equally as charged, and as ambiguous as that between parent and child, there is a remarkable unanimity of opinion by the members of the phantom club toward certain members. "There's no question that Tom Watson [of IBM] was the leader of this whole industry," a chief executive of a computer company told me. "We all looked up to Walter Wriston and what he did at Citibank," said a bank CEO, summing up the feelings of a number of bank chief executives I interviewed. Reputations can rise and fall like a rollercoaster ride. Roy Ash was considered a brilliant manager at Litton and Hughes, though always in the shadow of Thornton. At the OMB he finally carved out his own identity distinct from Thornton's, but his government post was considered a different sort of role. By the time Ash left the government, Litton had slipped a bit, as most conglomerates did in the mid-1970s, and his reputation was less glittering. Then, as he tried to prove his worth as a chief executive at AM International, his reputation sank even further. Is it fair? Of course not, but some judgments of others have been even harsher. For instance, many CEOs I interviewed had something bad to say about David Begelman, who was convicted of embezzlement while at Columbia Pictures Incorporated. And regarding competitors, the responses ranged from downright nasty—"All those vicious, underhanded tactics the guy uses should be outlawed"—to a rough sarcasm about their misjudgments or a grudging admiration for their successes. Still, to go public with such candid opinions, as Frank Borman of Eastern Airlines Corporation once did in the *New York Times*, is considered taboo among most members of the phantom club.

All clubs present to their members a pantheon of heroes and villains, and the club of CEOs is no different in that respect. Some chief executives can remain powerful role models—for good or for bad—long after they have left office. Henry Ford, with his assembly line and low-cost strategy, and Alfred P. Sloan, with his legendary segmentation strategy for General Motors Corporation, to this day continue to dominate the automobile industry. In the 1960s, corporate pied pipers such as Harold Geneen, Jimmy Ling of Ling Temco Vought (LTV), and Tex Thornton led many a CEO into the deceptive Eden of the conglomerate. Today, the likes of T. Boone Pickens, Jr., (of Mesa Petroleum) and Carl Icahn (who took over TWA) are influencing a new generation to the rewards of takeovers. A *Forbes* magazine article quoted a soon-to-be-graduated business school student who insisted, "I can do what Carl Icahn does." When told that not everyone thinks of Icahn as a role model, the student shot back, "If management isn't doing its job, it deserves a hostile takeover."[1] Yes, these strong chief executives do generate a faddish imitation; but others, notably Sloan, manage to span generations and industries, affecting generations of chief executives.

If many CEOs are faddish about their role models, they are also fickle.

When CEO heroes fall into either disagrace, as John Z. DeLorean (who founded DeLorean Motor Corporation and was arrested for selling cocaine) did, or stumble a bit, as did Donald C. Burr of People Express Airlines when he faced potential bankruptcy or Steve Jobs of Apple Computer when he was forced to resign from the company he founded, many chief executives who had formerly fawned over them take it as a personal betrayal. The switch from hero to villain can be as sharp as a knife blade. "Burr's a total egomaniac. I don't know how we could have all been so taken with his People Express egalitarianism," said one chief executive. "I really thought John DeLorean was going to build a new corporate dream," another bewildered CEO told me. "In fact, I put $200 thousand into that bastard's car company. For the life of me I don't understand him. People ask me how I could have been so dumb. Let me tell you, I ask myself the exact same question." (Since then, of course, DeLorean has been acquitted of selling cocaine because the jury believed he had been entrapped.) Nonetheless, once Humpty Dumpty falls off his wall, no one can put him back together again.

Such mistakes in judgment, or a tendency to follow the fad, lead many chief executives to imitate the *wrong* parts of a hero's strategy. CEO imitators often fail to see that a corporate strategy is an organic set of policies that combines an integrated network of financial, marketing, and technological strategies. Many CEOs simply appropriate what they *think*, often without thinking very hard, was the strategy of a CEO hero, and try to make their company fit the strategy. Unfortunately, neither life nor business strategy is that simple. Nonetheless, when their strategies backfire, many CEOs go after their erstwhile heroes with a big stick rather than look inside themselves.

Finally, as in any club, there is a definite pecking order in the phantom club. Much depends on the size of the companies involved—as in bank accounts, the bigger the better. Traditionally, CEOs of large companies looked down on those of small-fry or "cowboy" companies, and regarded each other as peers or "major-bracket CEOs." All of that became jumbled in the early 1980s, when smaller firms started to gain leverage and to take over their larger cousins. In the ensuing denunciations about leveraging and junk-bond takeovers, there were legitimate concerns. But there was also the kind of fear one feels among an insecure class, an outrage that such small-fry companies could dare to threaten the major-bracket guys. "Those little bastards have no experience running a company this size, they have no experience in the chemical business, they have no track record in this business," ranted one threatened corporate chieftain. "Who the hell are they? Why the hell are these banks willing to constantly lend these know-nothing CEOs of tiny companies billions of dollars against nothing but the assets of the company, so that these little pipsqueaks can take us over? It's all greed. It's short-sighted selfishness on the part of the banks and the major institutional shareholders who jump in to take part in these high-cash, hostile tender offers. God, it makes me furious."

Such is the murmuring of any threatened ancien régime.

The Ties That Bind

Chief executives' styles or strategies are clearly formed through contact with their peers. A multitude of links bring them into direct contact, particularly through the common practice of serving on each other's boards of directors. In such forums, chief executives get a close view of the practices and beliefs of their peers. A bit later, we will look at the role of boards. For now, let it suffice to say that while serving on boards is a fairly public role, there are other, more discreet links that are perhaps just as powerful. For example, after talking with a number of CEOs, I began to trace the connections between chief executives through consulting firms such as McKinsey & Company, Booz, Allen & Hamilton Incorporated, Arthur D. Little (ADL), General Electric Consultants, and the Boston Consulting Group (BCG). What makes these links so fascinating is the distinctive strategic character of the advice offered by these consultants.

For example, the Boston Consulting Group specialized in a strategy model called a "growth share matrix." I was able to trace that strategy through a number of companies, many of whose chief executives had participated in weekend retreats sponsored by BCG. The choice of a strategy model was often based less on rational analysis than on a variation of hero worship. Almost invariably, these CEOs told me that they had chosen such a model either because of a personal contact with another CEO who was using it, or out of respect for what another CEO had been able to do with it. Said one chief executive, "I knew Joe had used McKinsey and he'd been pleased." "I sit on various other company's boards," another CEO said, "and I've seen how and why their CEOs had used BCG, Booz, ADL, McKinsey, and others. So I've been able to assess which consultants got

33

results and made meaningful improvements in business, and which ones were really a complete waste of time and money."

Again, such intuitive or personal decision making provides fertile ground for the faddish and the imitative corporate strategy. Strategic consulting firms first appeared on the scene when Bruce Henderson set up the Boston Consulting Group. Henderson was the catalyst that sparked the first multi-industry model for strategic planning, and he became highly influential at a variety of companies. His success spawned a whole collection of firms whose "cookie-cutter strategies" tended to be applied indiscriminately to a wide range of companies. A great deal has been written about the influence of consulting firms on thousands of companies. Let it suffice to say here that such concepts as BCG's growth share matrix or McKinsey's business attractiveness matrix—complicated lingo for relatively simple ideas—seemed to many CEOs profoundly simple and convenient ways of summing up all of the factors that went into the business onto a single blackboard. Eureka, they would say after a presentation; now I know what my business is all about. Of course, they really didn't. And it has taken twenty years for some CEOs to realize that these models often were too simple, required too many staff and too much paperwork, and in many cases, involved the wrong goals and strategic objectives.

Not all was lost, however. Even failed exercises occasionally forced chief executives and their staffs to look at their companies more carefully. And it sometimes forced them to become more sensitive to the strategies of competitors both here and abroad. Most important, the consultants did open many chief executives to the novel idea that there were new concepts of strategic planning loose upon the land. The proof, I suppose, of that new consciousness is that nearly every chief executive I interviewed chattered on about his strategy—some seemed to have discovered them very recently—whether they had one or not.

Sharing the Wealth

In 1985, the board of directors of Philip Morris Companies, Incorporated, the sixteen-billion-dollar cigarette and consumer goods company, met to wrestle with a major decision: the proposed acquisition of food-processing giant General Foods Corporation. While Philip Morris had made other acquisitions in previous years, this one had a special urgency for the company's chief executive, Hamish Maxwell, who must have felt increasing pressure not only because of archrival R. J. Reynolds Industries, Incorporated acquisition of Nabisco Brands, Incorporated just a few weeks earlier, but also because of a number of lawsuits that were threatening the company's highly profitable cigarette business.

A key participant in the intense discussions around the Philip Morris boardroom table was a young, fresh-faced outside director named John Reed. It had been barely a year since Reed was chosen to replace Walter B. Wriston as the chief executive officer of Citibank. Although surrounded by successful people, most of them older than he, 44-year-old Reed brought to the discussion a wealth of insight and information, part and parcel of his role as leader of the world's then largest and most powerful bank.

Citibank, after all, was no stranger to corporate takeovers. In the 1960s and 1970s, under Wriston, Citibank had led the charge into financing corporate acquisitions. Reed also had sat in on earlier Philip Morris discussions of other food company acquisitions. He was a board member of other companies, and his most senior managers, each often holding one or more directorships, were fanned out across the landscape of corporate America. Reed could also tap the wealth of information on corporate balance sheets from Citibank's extensive lending network. Finally, he understood the complex undergrowth of bank policies and protocols that governed his actions in such a situation. Just as important, he knew the protocols, lending policies, and financial condition of his big-league competitors: The Chase Manhattan Bank, N.A., BankAmerica Corporation, and Manufacturers Hanover Trust Company. Which banks lent to which companies? How far could they prudently go out on a limb? What were their other sources of capital? And what were the personalities—the foibles, the tendencies, the flaws—of the chief executives involved in the deal? Reed was able to offer informed opinions on all of these questions. Indeed, some said the acquisition took place, thanks in part to Reed's expertise.

While Reed is somewhat unusual in his breadth of information (there are few companies that reach as far as Citibank does), he illustrates the complex, interrelated world of many CEOs at large American corporations. Information is power. And financial institutions such as banks and accounting firms tend to form hubs of vast information networks about a variety of companies and strategies. Each top bank officer sits on a number of boards and deals with a variety of corporate clients, constantly judging the merits of particular strategies and initiatives. Likewise, a bank is tied into a vast network of correspondent banks which do business with an even greater network of companies, and of suppliers, creditors, and customers. Finally, corporate clients will use a major bank for so many functions—loans, letters of credit, commercial paper, as a custodian of various funds, as syndicated loan managers, even as coordinators of stock sales or leveraged buyouts—that few secrets can be kept from a bank. A similar case holds for the Big Eight accounting firms which, theoretically at least, get a glimpse into the internal financial operations of a company (although recently, a number of audits have been challenged for what they did not reveal—or did not know) or of an industry at large. Touche Ross, for instance, has been specializing in retailing for so long that it has both a breadth of insight into individual companies and a deep knowledge of the past as well as the present.

This kind of strategic cross-pollination was most striking when I spoke with David Rockefeller at Chase Manhattan. Rockefeller was intimately aware of the specific strategies that client companies were pursuing, and was often informed when the firm was considering any sort of change. Often, he said, such warning was legally mandated in the contractual agreement between the bank and the client, particularly when a major loan had been made or other financial arrangements such as letters of credit extended. Often, Rockefeller, who of course was also tied into a vast web of family, social, and political interconnections—a tribute to the power of his family name—said to me that such information was passed on to him purely as a matter of courtesy, although in his case, such courtesy is a mannerly cloak for the rules of the phantom club: courtesy today, good relations tomorrow. As one CEO said, "I informed David what my corporate strategy was in order to cement good feelings with him and the bank." Another CEO confided, "I told David [in order] to continue a feeling of intimate trust, and to smooth future commercial dealings between our corporation and the Chase bank."

Such strategic sharing of information can cause difficulties; the rules of the club are often hazy, and sometimes clash with the larger body of rules in the outside world. For many years, my stepuncle, Thomas Lamont, was the vice chairman of Morgan Guaranty Trust Company, and therefore routinely sat on the boards of a number of companies. One of those was a company called Texas Gulf Sulphur which made a large ore discovery in Canada. Over a number of weeks, the reports of the metallurgists filtered throughout the company, and soon its stock began to rise. Within a short time, the Securities and Exchange Commission (SEC) moved against Texas

Gulf's board, its chief executive, and a number of others. The charge: that they had passed along inside information and thus profited personally from their knowledge of the discovery.

Texas Gulf became the first and most famous insider trading case, at least until the Boesky imbroglio. Lamont never made a penny personally and was eventually exonerated but not before he was dragged through the courts and deeply embarrassed. Texas Gulf Sulphur was caught in an unfortunate position: the rules of the game had changed. As he said to me as the case worked its way through the courts, "I did absolutely nothing wrong. I did absolutely nothing that is not universal practice in corporate boards of directors and in banks."

In this age of megamergers, with the SEC ever vigilant against insider trading of any sort, the role of a banker or accountant at the hub requires enormous discretion and overall good judgment. There is always the potential for the passing of inside information, but I would like to emphasize the necessity of these cross-links of strategic information. Such information provides not only a vast pool of strategic experience for CEOs, but a necessary source of data on the ever-shifting conditions of the business environment. The system could not run without it.

Ethics, Peer Pressure, and Taboos

While bankers and accountants might control the crucial hubs where information flows, most CEOs also command an enormous amount of strategic information on specific companies and individuals, particularly within their own industry. Nonetheless, members of the phantom club have an unwritten, even unspoken, code when it comes to talking about members to outsiders such as journalists. Corporate blackmail, particularly when it involves unsavory personal habits, is taboo—at least for the record—in this club where personal appearance is most important. Chief executives like to see themselves as dignified, respected, full of probity and fair play. Scandal-mongering does not belong in that image. One CEO, for example, told me about his efforts to kill rumors among those in his company about a competitor's adulterous relationships. "Hell, I don't want that adultery business being waved around by guys in this company. I told my staff to kill that talk real fast," he said.

Such rectitude has its limits, of course, particularly when the company is threatened in a takeover. Then, it is not at all surprising to see personal attacks between phantom club members smeared across the media. In the chapter on takeover strategy, I will describe the use of damaging information by The Mead Corporation in its attempt to beat back Occidental Petroleum Corporation; a similar tactic was used by Harold W. McGraw, Jr., of McGraw-Hill to defeat a takeover attempt by American Express Company. Such retaliation can get nasty indeed. When William Agee, formerly of Bendix, approached RCA Corporation about a takeover, Thornton F. Bradshaw, RCA's normally reserved, even gentlemanly, chairman, immediately launched a scathing personal attack on Agee. "Mr. Agee has shown himself to be unable to be successful managing his own personal affairs, not to mention his unsuitability to run this company." Bradshaw, of course, was referring to Agee's much-rumored affair with his young aide, Mary E. Cunningham, whom he eventually married.

But while most chief executives refuse to talk to club outsiders about their colleagues, there is a tremendous amount of peer pressure to conform to certain generally accepted rules of behavior. For example, one CEO said about the practice of sabotaging a competitor's operation: "We all draw the line at that." Others expressed a repugnance for political initiatives such as the alleged involvement of ITT in Chile. Likewise, insider trading is criticized, although this is as much due to the bad publicity to the business community that it would prompt as to its inherent wrong. For instance, many CEOs cited the bad publicity generated by Paul Thayer, former head of LTV Aerospace Corporation, a board member of a number of other companies, and the number-two man in the Defense Department, who was convicted of passing along inside information to his mistress, among others. While most CEOs knew insider trading was going on all the time, most told me they thought it should be stopped. "All the CEOs I know agree it's essential that we at the top of our corporations must set an example," said one chief executive. "I've stated that such insider trading will not be tolerated among my staff. When I catch it, I come down like a ton of bricks. Instant dismissal. I've warned the whole company of that, in no uncertain terms. If you tolerate rot, it spreads."

Times are changing, however, and the rules of the phantom club change too. Personal behavior that might have seemed shocking a generation ago is now accepted out of hand. For example, in the early 1970s, most CEOs looked upon hostile takeovers as ruthless and immoral; by the 1980s, many of these same CEOs were prepared to view it as just another form of strategy, one that a CEO should not only prepare against but know how to use. Industrial espionage is also more accepted. In 1975, chief executives would become almost hysterical at the mention of espionage; today, they have mellowed considerably on the subject. One reason for this change in attitude is the Hitachi Limited case, in which employees from the Japanese company were caught stealing plans from IBM. Fear of the Japanese provided the excuse to change a lot of CEO minds—quickly enough to make one suspect that many chief executives were looking for a rationalization. Said one CEO, "Hell, I saw that if I didn't get busy beefing up our counterintelligence efforts, then pretty soon this company wouldn't have any secrets worth protecting." Self-defense quickly became an offensive strategy. Indeed, one CEO told me, "Over the past two years, I've recruited three former CIA agents and two former FBI agents who were former military counterintelligence officers into our corporate staff. I hired them to beef up our own in-depth competitor analysis and to strengthen our internal efforts to ward off our competitors' industrial espionage against us."

A similar shift in attitudes applies to raiding among companies for executives. In the early 1970s, chief executives who raided their competitors were sharply criticized; by 1985, it had become as common as spying. In fact, head hunters had proliferated as thickly as consultants in the corporate undergrowth. And with it, no surprise, came another rationalization: chief executives now tell me, somewhat piously, that raiding another company for executives—euphemistically called *external staffing*—is essential to avoid inbred management and to keep new blood flowing into the company. One CEO summed up the change this way: "Years ago, I never would have raided a competitor's executives for talent. Now they're raiding my staffs, every week; head hunters are on the phone to my guys all the time. It's a different age, so I don't feel that those traditional views of company loyalty that I grew up with in this company still apply. So to answer your question, 'Will I use head hunters to raid executives from other competitors,' the answer is, you bet. Reluctantly, it's a part of corporate survival in today's market. I've got to do it to replace the top executives who keep being raided from us. For this company to survive, I need to keep the top talent coming up, so either we keep growing our own stars or we get stars from someone else. It's as simple as that." Another CEO told me, "We used to blackball any CEO who raided another company's top executives. It's not like that anymore. Not at all. Perhaps our sense of morality is changing. Perhaps we're just all getting practical."

The Changing Role of the Board

Boards of directors have long occupied an ambiguous position in the formulation of strategy. As we shall see in the chapter on succession, chief executives really hold most of the power when it comes to the actual formulation of strategy. Boards are often either rubber stamps or advisors, save in crisis situations. However, from the perspective of the phantom club, the board of directors looms large. Perhaps in no other formal group do CEOs draw so regularly together to discuss substantive strategic questions. And in no other forum do the winds of change—some call them fads or fashions—blow the hardest.

A good example of the kind of role a board can play was described to me by David Wallace, the chief executive of Bangor Punta Corporation. Wallace was trying to turn around the conglomerate assembled by the founder, Nicolas Salgo. Salgo had retired, but he continued to wield power from his position on the board. As Wallace made more and more changes, and as he warned the board about problems within the ramshackle, far-flung structure of the company, Salgo grew more and more agitated. "The board became increasingly supportive of me after they got over the shock of some of the things that I said about this or that division not being worth a damn," said Wallace. "You must remember that Mr. Salgo was also the largest shareholder. . . . I didn't have any basis of support except logic and results." Finally, it came to a showdown between Wallace and Salgo. When Wallace threatened to resign, the outside directors intervened, asking Salgo to resign. "The outside directors deserve a great deal of credit because they really stood up and were counted as far as the philosophy of the corporation was concerned," said Wallace. Similar situations also occasionally took place even at ITT, where Geneen, as a board member, continued to dominate the company.

Over the past decade or so, serving on a board has become more onerous. Stockholder suits have increased, and the liability of board members is much greater now than it used to be. Many chief executives told me that in the past, they would not hesitate to serve on the boards of CEO friends; it was a matter of courtesy. Today, many of these same chief executives told me that they do a careful analysis of their potential personal liability before they join a board; as a result, many are refusing to join boards. "I just can't take the chance that some unforeseen exposure from his company's legal problems might come back to haunt me at this company. I know he needs me, and I feel bad I have to turn him down. But my own business is pretty rocky right now and I really have to devote attention to it for the moment." Time demands on board members have also increased; instead of eight to twelve days a year, a merger or other crisis can mean weeks at one time. All in all, serving on boards has become a pain in the neck. "I joined Charley's board years ago when all we did was get together a few times a year. I did it partly to help him out. I did it partly to learn firsthand how another bunch of CEOs think—but now it's all a tremendous headache."

As a result of this change, external directors have become a far more potent and independent force. I saw how the outside directors of Manville Corporation had to decide the crucial issue of whether to go into Chapter 11 bankruptcy. I also saw how John deButts, and other chief executives, regularly consulted with outside directors to keep them informed about the progress of potential successors. While the outside director as a pawn of management still exists—just as the old-boy network still exists—chief executives can no longer count on such automatic support in a crisis. Some chief executives found this to be a profound shock, a sense of betrayal. One especially bitter CEO confided in me after losing a board vote on his proposed leveraged buyout: "Hell, I understand why he voted that way against me on the board. He had to because of the liability laws. But it hurt like hell. I've known him for thirty years. I never would have expected this from him. Never."

Why join a board as an external director? Many of the chief executives I spoke with sketched a series of relatively complex calculations, balancing the time loss and liability question against the pull of friendship, the desire for new business contacts, prestige, and cementing long-term business relationships, rather like the aristocratic habit of arranged marriages as a means of cementing national relationships. From the other side, from the perspective of the chief executive looking for outside directors, I found a similar set of factors. These calculations, however, tended to overlook such questions as the asset size of the potential director's company, or the geographic location, or the industry, or financial health. Instead, time after time, decisions were based on the existence of friendship and trust—proof, if nothing else, of the club-like nature of the board.

That having been said, boards can, on occasion, be a source of strength and wisdom. When Union Carbide was being threatened by takeover from GAF, the company's board, which was dominated by external directors such as Harry Gray of United Technologies, John J. Creedon of Metropolitan Life, McColough of Xerox, and William Sneath, former chairman and CEO of Union Carbide, told Warren M. Anderson and his managers to leave the room while they decided on a strategy. William May of American Can summed up the value of having other CEOs on his board. "Those guys really know what's going on. They've faced the music. They've served their time in the trenches. They're used to making hard decisions. They give me good advice. . . . shoot from the hip. . . . tell it like it really is." Said another chief executive, "They know my kinds of problems day to day because they're living with similar problems and screw-ups. I learn from them; they learn from us."

Many chief executives view these external directors as a peer group from which they must gain approval. When their business plans are approved by the external directors, many find it a great confirmation of their managerial and strategic abilities, and of their membership in the phantom club. "That's my really important performance rating," said one chief executive. "Those votes in that boardroom can be infinitely more important positive feedback for me as a CEO than the votes in public shareholders meetings I run each year, which are almost entirely stage-managed affairs." Another admitted that most of his company's annual shareholder meetings were really a farce. Ironically, most boards are nearly automatic rubber stamps, though CEOs do not view them that way. Virtually all of those I interviewed said their boards had voted almost unanimously on all matters that came before them. At the same time, they boasted of their boards' "independence." While some chief executives—notably, Geneen—saw the boards' acquiescence as a weakness, other CEOs insisted on looking at it through rose-colored glasses, as a sign of their own continuing success, despite any disasters the company might be undergoing. Time after time, chief executives, almost plaintively, reiterated that their boards did not disagree with their decisions, as if the board was all that mattered. Alas, for many CEOs obsessed with their standing in the phantom club, that may well be the case.

THE PHANTOM CLUB OF CEOS

The new liability laws that went into effect in the 1980s have roiled those formerly placid waters a bit. As a result, head hunters are now regularly called in to try to find suitable external directors for some companies, a break with tradition. That personal network is becoming sorely tested by takeovers and leveraged buyouts. Again, let us look at that Union Carbide–GAF battle. One strategy proposed by Union Carbide management to fight GAF was to take the chemical company private, through a leveraged buyout (LBO). That forced the board to ask which strategy would truly preserve the values of the shareholder: GAF's all-cash bid, the LBO, or an all-out defense. However, because management had blatantly injected its own financial interest into the conflict, through the LBO suggestion, the lineup of external directors described earlier had to make the decision themselves to avoid a conflict-of-interest charge. Here is how the *Wall Street Journal* described the deliberations: "The external directors quickly concluded that any effort on the part of the Carbide management to profit at shareholders' expense by allowing a leveraged buyout . . . was doomed. Likewise, although Carbide managers favored a poison-pill defense that would give Carbide holders rights to buy stock at a deep discount, thereby making an external takeover difficult or impossible for a hostile outsider, would also be seen to entrench existing Carbide management, and thus the external board members totally rejected the poison pill as a defense."[2]

Ah, life has not gotten easier for members of the phantom club. Foreign competition has actually forced companies to compete, shareholders have actually sued or rebelled, the government has imposed all kinds of different rules (though they have eased a number as well), new technologies have appeared out of nowhere, barbarians (of a sort) have raided and pillaged their operations. Now, even the sanctum sanctorum of the boardroom has been invaded by un-club-like sentiments. For all of that, the club still exists, and being fired, or taken over, or forced into retirement—to be forced from active membership—can be a crushing blow indeed to many of these chief executives. As one CEO put it: "It's not that I dread retirement. But you get used to a club-like relation between these CEOs you've worked with. I'll miss that."

CHAPTER THREE

TAKEOVERS: LIFE IN THE JUNGLE

U.S. executives aren't looking at takeovers as a means of enhancing shareholder value. They only look at takeovers as a threat to their salaries and their perks. And the reason they perceive it this way is that they generally own very little stock in their own companies. . . . When a potential acquirer makes a premium-to-market bid, these executives don't see it as making a substantial gain on their investment—they see it as a threat to their kingdom.
—T. Boone Pickens, Jr., chairman and president, Mesa Petroleum Company[1]

It's too general to say there shouldn't be unfriendly takeovers. Under normal circumstances, where a company is doing a good job of managing its resources, to have someone else come in is probably not in the best interest of society. That's a personal observation.
—J. W. McSwiney, former CEO, The Mead Corporation

From Taboo to Strategic Imperative[2]

Over the last decade or so, the hostile business takeover has gone from a faintly disreputable activity pursued by those in the margins of corporate America, to an activity as popular and common as selling common stock. With the rise of conglomerates, followed by the appearance of all-but-professional raiders—Saul P. Steinberg, Carl Icahn, Victor Posner, Irwin L. Jacobs, T. Boone Pickens, Jr.—a whole new world and a new strategic vocabulary has sprung up: "greenmail," "white knights," "leveraged buy-outs," "poison pills," and so forth. Today more than any time in recent American business history, CEOs have to be constantly aware of the take-

45

over, or the takeover defense, as an active strategy. And they must be aware of their own sometimes excruciating ambiguous position as both corporate manager and custodian for shareholder values.

This was not always so, at least not since the wild and woolly days of Jay Gould and Daniel Drew. Where once blue-chip firms shied away from any acquisition that might be construed as hostile, today, not only do many of them view an aggressive acquisition program as a prominent part of their strategy for growth and the enhancement of shareholder values, they receive the high-priced help of investment and commercial bankers and distinguished law firms. Moreover, an altered legal environment, particularly the lax enforcement of antitrust laws and a radical shift in antitrust policy by the FTC and the Justice Department, has meant that many of the traditional constraints on takeovers have relaxed. In fact, the distinction between a friendly takeover or merger and a hostile one has, in many cases, been blurred. Even if the management of a target firm is willing to consider the suitor's proposal, it is often in their own self-interest to fight the tender offer and extract a better offer. And that may turn the friendliest of takeovers into a bitter public battle. John W. Culligan, CEO of American Home Products Corporation, told me: "Takeovers, hostile or friendly, have become a reality. Each situation is different and each must be judged on its merits. It's the CEO's job to provide leadership to its board and its management to be certain that all decisions are made in the best interest of the shareholders."

Traditionally, takeovers were viewed as a kind of Darwinian process. An expanding, efficient company moves in and takes over a troubled competitor run by incapable, recalcitrant managers, and after making improvements, reaps the capital gains. While such takeovers continue to occur, the enormous multibillion-dollar battles of the last few years—Conoco versus Seagram, Bendix versus Martin Marietta, Gulf versus T. Boone Pickens, Carl Icahn versus USX—have considerably altered the notion of what a likely "target" company should be. No longer are the largest, or the most efficient, companies safe from the threat of a takeover. In fact, in this upside-down world, the company with a secure hold on a lucrative market, or one with its coffers full of cash, may be more likely than the stumbling, strapped operation to face a bid for control. "It's gotten a lot rougher," a chief executive told me. "I'm not sure my basic personality type is suited to this hostile takeover era. Today, the problem is to either prepare to fight them or join them. You just can't get on with the job of making your products and running your company the way you used to. You have to be constantly looking over your shoulder."

What are the new motivations behind the takeover? Over the last decade, there is no question that financial factors and economic turbulence have stimulated merger activity. High rates of inflation made real interest rates sometimes appear low, or even negative, making it easier for companies to purchase new assets rather than replace old ones. As a result, financial researchers have tended to emphasize the improvement in a company's valuation that can result from a takeover, or pure tax, and accounting considerations. But that is only one of a host of reasons CEOs offer for an upsurge in merger and acquisition activity. They often raise the issue of gaining market share or providing a counterweight for cyclical businesses. And then, of course, there are those omnipresent personal considerations— the drive for prestige, power, and higher salaries—that light a fire in the belly of many a corporate executive.

Let us look more closely at one famous takeover battle, the dance between Mobil Corporation, DuPont, Dome Petroleum Corporation, and Joseph E. Seagram & Sons, Inc. for Conoco, the Houston-based oil company, which throws light on the complex considerations behind a takeover. For perspective, let us turn to Edgar M. Bronfman, the chairman of Seagram and arguably the winner of the contest—even though, technically, it was DuPont that swallowed Conoco. Why would Seagram, a giant wine and spirits company, become involved in a battle over an oil company? Primarily as an investment, although to put it so simply is to gloss over the fascinating range of options available to Bronfman. It all began for Seagram some years ago, when Bronfman's father Samuel, who founded the distillery, paid $50 million to buy an oil company called Texas Pacific. Some time later, Edgar Bronfman, who had by then taken over operational control with his brother Charles, sold the company for $2.3 billion, probably unloading it at its height—a brilliant, or very lucky, piece of timing. He then put the money in the bank. Why did he sell? "If you looked at our stock, we were getting no credit for our enormous oil well," said Bronfman. "It was on the books for five-hundred-and-some million dollars, and it had earnings, but our multiple didn't reflect the underlying asset. Second, I was uncomfortable running a business I knew little about. Third, the price of oil was ridiculously high. So we made our deal with the Sun Company and suddenly we had $2.3 billion which, in those days of high interest rates, was worth another couple hundred thousand every day or so."

But Bronfman did not want to leave the cash in the bank forever, so he went shopping. He looked around for a consumer products company, but the prices were too high. He took a stab at St. Joe Minerals—"an asset play," he said—but eventually backed out when the price got too high. Then came the ferocious competition for Conoco with DuPont and Dome. Bronfman saw an opportunity for a friendly agreement. "Conoco was just so damned cheap. If we had taken over Conoco, we would have traded production of fifty thousand barrels a day [from Texas Pacific] for over two hundred thousand barrels—all with the same money. The oil business, I thought, was looking a little brighter. Conoco was cash self-sufficient." As the struggle continued, Bronfman realized, however, that DuPont's entry offered an even greater opportunity. "We were very conscious that we were coming in the back end [of the deal]. It worked out almost precisely as we planned. The shift in policy was to take something less than a majority position.

"After Dome made its bid for 20 percent of Conoco we decided it was a perfect opportunity for us. We went out to visit Bailey [Conoco's chief executive] and made our bid and he turned it down." Some time thereafter, Bronfman decided to make a public tender offer. Much of this time, Bronfman was in Europe, discussing matters by telephone. When the struggle intensified—when, as he said, things got "esoteric"—he returned, flying in from Nice to Montreal. At this time, Seagram had to decide to make a new bid. The question on the table at the time was whether it should be ninety or ninety-two dollars a share for 20 percent of Conoco. "Before the meeting started, one of Felix's [Rohatyn, of Lazard Freres] partners gave a ten-minute disquisition on why it should be ninety-two dollars, but I walked out at the beginning to meet with someone else in another room. On the plane over, he asked me why I decided on ninety-two dollars. I said because of what you said. He then said, 'But you didn't hear it.' I then told him I didn't have to, his first three sentences had convinced me. . . ." Back in Montreal, the Seagram board approved the bid.

"The next big decision was the following Monday," said Bronfman. "By then the worst that could happen was that we'd get 5 percent, and when we started to talk to the arbitragers and others who owned the stock, it became clear that if we didn't drop the net, we couldn't get the stock. But we were convinced that if we did drop the net, we'd get the 20 percent we wanted. We talked to all the experts [the investment bankers] and they came back and said don't drop the net. Well, this was one of the cases where the experts were wrong. And when we did it, that's when Jefferson [DuPont's chief executive] knew he had a problem." How was the decision made to take on DuPont? "It was not a tortuous, climbing-around-the-stairs with strategists. It was just my brother, myself, a few key people, our advisors; we just thought it would be a fantastic coup. So we went ahead, convinced the Seagram board, and did it." The whole process took less than a day.

"We then made the bid anyway and then DuPont came into it. . . . If they hadn't, we probably would have gotten Conoco. I've been wrestling with that as you always do, retrospectively. And I'm not so sure we're not better off with what eventually took place." Ironically, Bronfman later took a look at an Arthur D. Little study of acquisition targets he had commissioned some time before. "They had drawn up a list of fourteen attributes—and anything we invested in should have as many attributes as possible. Well, we looked back at it later, and the DuPont-Conoco combination fulfilled twelve out of the fourteen. But honestly, I'd like to say we studied it, but that's not the way it worked. We knew a little about DuPont, particularly because they were getting into the medical business, which we thought would be important. . . . It was more hunch than brilliant, hard, analytical work. When Charles and I are both in the room and we both say we want to do this, it's a hard fight to change our minds. Obviously, it wasn't crazy or kooky, and all I was really thinking about going from Nice to Montreal was, how will it be to be the largest shareholder in DuPont. I never really doubted we would."

Indeed, when the dust had settled, DuPont had taken the prize, Conoco, but Seagram had ended up as the largest single investor in DuPont, with 22.5 percent (by 1985) of the stock. That gave Seagram a major position in two large, solidly profitable corporations, with a variety of benefits. For one thing, as Bronfman foresaw, Seagram was able to fund continuing operations out of cash flow, and use the DuPont dividends to pay down debt. Moreover, the combination produced a hedging action. For instance, if Bronfman had bought just Conoco, the subsequent decline in oil prices would have battered his investment. But by working through DuPont, the deflationary effects were minimized. "I was talking to Jefferson just last week at a board meeting, and with the price of oil going down, it's actually more benefit to DuPont than it is loss for Conoco. I think 70 percent of their feedstock is petroleum. So, I've come to the conclusion that we've got the best of all possible worlds where we are right now. It would have been kind of exciting to take over one of the larger oil companies. But in the final analysis, if you look at it right now [1984], it looks pretty good the way it is. If Prohibition came back tomorrow," added Bronfman, "DuPont would still be there."

Market Power and Diversification

One of the traditional motivational forces behind mergers and acquisitions is to allow the acquiring firm to gain greater market power. This allows the firm to hold prices above the competitive level and thereby increase profits. There are three types of market power:

- *Vertical market power*, in which one company acquires another that allows it to extend the reach of its business. Vertical integration often allows a firm to demand better profit margins from suppliers and customers.
- *Horizontal market power*, in which one company buys a competitor in the same industry. This allows a firm to reduce or eliminate competition, or to form a tight oligopoly with them.
- *Conglomerate market power*, in which one company buys a number of others in a variety of industries. This offers a company several options. With its greater size and internal financial resources, a conglomerate can pursue strategies of predatory pricing or aggressive advertising which are not available to other, smaller firms in the industry. Some argue that conglomerates that compete in different product markets will be less likely to exploit market power where they are strong, for fear that other organizations will do the same where they are weak. Finally, there are the advantages of reciprocity. In a reciprocity agreement, firm A receives a good purchase price from firm B which, in turn, is a good customer. Some argue that the effect of reciprocity is to place competitors at a disadvantage by blocking their access to suppliers or purchasers.

The drive to gain market power is a subject most CEOs don't care to talk much about. After all, in the past, antitrust regulators often tried to block mergers that they believed would result in greater market power for the acquiring firm, although that era, for the time being at least, has waned. Still, for all the silence—or rather, because of it—gaining market power may be the single most important factor behind most mergers. As Harold Geneen, who drove ITT to absorb some one hundred companies between 1960 and 1970, admitted at a Congressional hearing in 1969, "This subject of 'market concentration' is, in fact, the only real economic issue [in takeovers]."[3]

Indeed, most in-depth research indicates that acquisitions between related companies usually result in increased market concentration for the victor. Furthermore, most studies have shown that some degree of increased market power has usually resulted from the mergers or acquisitions of unrelated conglomerates, although horizontal mergers seem to generate the strongest examples of market power. But again, while strict antitrust enforcement tended to limit horizontal mergers in the past, today, mergers in oil and steel and among financial companies, and joint ventures in the automobile industry, are almost routinely approved by regulators.

But while market concentration remains a forbidden subject, CEOs talk quite a lot about other economic efficiencies that result from diversification via takeovers. After all, smaller companies in need of capital often seek to be acquired by larger firms. And by combining two companies, you can gain economies of scale in areas such as marketing, research, and finance. Not surprisingly, Geneen had a few things to say about the advantages gained by ITT mergers: "With the central management capabilities that ITT has assembled, we can provide receptive and constructive bases for mergers—bases that will pay off in increased efficiency for both parties." This has allowed ITT "to diversify into industries and markets which have good prospects for above-average long-term growth and profitability."

Geneen went on to build a sort of paradigm of the perfectly constructed corporation assembled, of course, through merger or acquisition. The purpose of mergers and acquisitions, he said, were:

- "To diversify into industries and markets which have good prospects for above average long-term growth and profitability.
- To achieve a sound balance between foreign earnings and domestic earnings.
- To achieve a sound balance between high risk, capital-intensive manufacturing operations and less risky service operations.
- To achieve a sound balance between high-risk engineering/labor-intensive electronics manufacturing and less risky commercial and industrial manufacturing.
- To achieve a sound ratio between commercial and industrial products and services, and consumer products and services.
- To achieve a sound ratio between government/defense/space operations, and commercial/industrial/consumer products and services in both foreign and domestic markets.
- To achieve a sound balance between cyclical products and services."[4]

Such a company's diverse parts would function in perfect harmony: manufacturing as a counterweight to service operations; electronics against commercial, government, or defense work, balanced against business in the private sector; domestic earnings set against foreign earnings. And so in theory, everyone wins in such an acquisition. Says Geneen, "We can improve operating efficiencies and profits sufficiently to make the valuation [of the merged companies] worthwhile to both sets of shareholders."

It may be worthwhile to let Geneen himself describe the situation at ITT that led him to embrace this concept of diversification via takeover, because it has proven to be one of the key models for modern American business and it made Geneen a fervid and relentless acquisitor. While many of the chief executives I interviewed admitted to disliking some of Geneen's methods and how far he pushed his strategic plan, few really argued with his basic ideas or the need to hedge risk and reduce cyclicality through assembling a variety of businesses. "When I came in the door at ITT, the first thing was to get a coherent business together," said Geneen. "We had a lot of earnings overseas, and most of the analysts looked on us as a company with about 80 to 90 percent of our earnings overseas. A good share of them came from Latin America, South America, and Cuba, so while 90 percent of our shareholders were American, we were really a foreign company. One of the first strategies we had then was to try to balance these earnings so that we had something more in line with our stockholder group and also to reduce the risk in Latin America. I had been here less than six months when we lost our largest company in the Cuban thing [Fidel Castro's expropriation], so the idea of diversification became important."

Geneen also had other considerations. Acquisitions provided fresh management. More important, they allowed him to reduce ITT's exposure in the telecommunications business, which for the company was predominately European. "It was desirable that we diversify from Europe into the United States and diversify away from our dependence on governments in Europe. I don't have the figures, but I think it was 50 percent of profit [in Europe], and the telecommunications share was about two-thirds. So we diversified in markets and products because telephones are largely a government market, and when they started putting the brakes on telecom expansion in Europe, things got pretty flat. . . . We also wanted to get enough U.S. earnings to pay off all our dividends and have something left over. Today [in 1980], we can." When it came to actually choosing acquisition targets, Geneen was more concerned with stable earnings than with future potential. "It was my general impression," he said, "that good, stable products like pumps and valves and some of these areas, were excellent areas because they represented very stable markets where you were not easily displaced and where the margins were reasonable, as opposed to the semiconductor business where everybody runs in the red to chase each other out of business."

How did Geneen come up with an acquisition strategy? "I took a big sheet of paper," he said, "and sat down and wrote, without reference to what we were in, putting down all the businesses I thought we should, or could, be in. I thought about public utilities, and asked fourteen or fifteen questions about them. They earn five or six percent. Did they have any problem holding their markets? No, they owned it by law. Did they have any trouble raising money? No, they were utilities—bonds and stocks. Was there an unusual strain on management? If there was, I never observed it. I wrote all that up. And I concluded that the risk was practically nothing . . . I went from one to the next. As a result, I found a little small-loan company. They used to be considered robbers in those days, but this one was in St. Louis, and it had been founded by a dentist . . . the man who had it was a very decent guy and I sat down and talked to him about the small-loan business because I really thought it was shylocking, squeezing a lot of poor people. Not at all; he was a sort of poor man's financial counselor. He had that sort of spirit. He wasn't trying to loan to people that didn't deserve a loan."

"I remember I brought this up to the board as a possible acquisition," Geneen continued. "Somebody on the board thought it a degrading business. So at the next board meeting, I went through *Life* magazine and found a big ad for General Motors Acceptance, and another for somebody else's finance company, and another from somebody else who loaned money. So when I got through I had twelve or fifteen of these guys and they were all names like General Electric Corporation (GE), GM, Goodrich Tire Company. . . . So we bought this little loan company. We paid probably $30 or $40 million and it will earn maybe $40 million this year, almost as much as Marine Midland Bank."

Throughout a score of similar acquisitions, Geneen kept in mind the complex interplay of cycles. Take, for instance, his acquisition of Continental Baking. "A consumer-type business has one valuable thing: in lousy economic conditions, people still buy consumer goods such as bread or whatever, while they may stop buying machine tools. You go back to the Great Depression, and I think in one year sales of machine tools were $20 million or something like that. A ridiculous number. They're deferrable-type things. Bread isn't."

The takeover concept as a way of reducing risk can be carried too far, however, as Geneen discovered. His reported attempts in the late 1960s to reduce risk for ITT's Chilean phone company by first trying to prevent the 1970 election of Salvador Allende, then by discussing with the CIA plans for his overthrow, backfired disastrously. Geneen chose not to discuss that incident with me.

Few chief executives take diversification as far as Harold Geneen has. Nonetheless, as I said earlier, most others believe that diversification can provide a hedge against certain risks. Diversifying away from regulated business was also a concern expressed by many other CEOs. But nothing is that simple. Government regulation can also stimulate mergers and acquisitions. Armco Steel, for instance, decided to invest heavily into the government-mandated pollution-control equipment business because, said CEO William Verity, "we spent so much money on pollution control, we think we're experts in that field." Armco was hardly alone. Litton Industries, Grumman Corporation, and General Dynamics Corporation sought take-overs to capitalize on the booming defense business; General Electric and RCA did the same to get government telecommunications contracts; so too did American Hospital Supply Corporation and American Surgical Supply Company in federally reimbursed health care; and Control Data Corporation and General Signal Corporation did the same to win state and federal contracts, respectively, in computers and controls.

As time passed, the limitations on Geneen's grand diversification strategy have become increasingly clear. Geneen's own company, not to mention such high-flying conglomerates as Litton, Gulf & Western Corporation, Bangor Punta, and LTV, all retreated from full-scale conglomeration to a simpler (in the parlance, more "rational") form of organization. While each has suffered its individual woes, all were also undermined in part by the kind of hubris that surrounds most conglomerateurs: a sense that they could manage an infinity of different businesses, and that their whirling creations could remain spinning forever. Alas, gravity is a far more constant factor than managerial genius. Moreover, the truth was that many acquisitors were far better at buying and selling than they were at building good businesses. As we will see in the chapter on financial strategy, David Wallace, the chief executive of Bangor Punta Corporation (like ITT, a company whose diversification strategy arose in reaction to the Castro expropriation in Cuba), argued that despite the best-laid plans of conglomerateurs, all businesses suffer from down cycles. Wallace, who said he still believed in the concept, was quite articulate about the difficulties of managing a conglomerate.

"The real theory of the conglomerate is that you get into businesses that complement each other in their cycles and patterns so that one is helping the other," Wallace said. "That is what we are trying to do. It doesn't always work. . . . We have made no major acquisitions since 1969. That was with Piper [an aircraft company]. You know we had a long, hard siege in getting Piper consolidated. I think things worked out on Piper eventually because we did what conglomerate people in the sixties never seemed to do, and that was to say, 'Here's our plan, and we're going to stick to it. If we can't do that, we're not going to do anything.' In the sixties, you had to always be doing something. You had to be a man in motion. If you do that you are going to make some silly moves. . . . I think what happened to a lot of them [conglomerateurs] was that they just didn't face up to the economic facts of life."

What were those facts? Wallace had his own opinions on that, and on the role of a predominant takeover strategy. "If you look at it, companies are like people," he said. "When you are a child, you need one thing; you have different needs, when you become an adult, a senior citizen, things change. And so with the corporation. . . . For this company, the acquisitions of the sixties that were made were financially opportunistic, and I don't think anything is wrong with opportunism." But Bangor Punta, like ITT, Textron Corporation, and LTV, grew up, and for the most part found it wiser to leave their happy-go-lucky acquisition days behind.

Numbers Can Tell Many Tales

Market share, or market dominance, is of course not the only thing fueling mergers and acquisitions. Since the 1960s, many takeovers have been pursued simply to produce accounting changes that would, on paper, improve a company's valuation. For example, many conglomerates of the 1960s pursued mergers with companies sporting low price earnings in order to get an immediate growth in their own per-share earnings. While the resulting boost often was not much more than a cosmetic improvement, there are a number of circumstances, CEOs argue, that call for a merger or acquisition to spruce up a company's accounting.

For example, consider a firm that has a great amount of tax loss carry-forwards, but has no net income to shelter. The firm is then motivated to acquire a profitable firm against whose income it can apply those carry-forwards. That is exactly what ITT did when it acquired a casualty insurer whose underwriting losses could be applied against ITT's taxable income. Furthermore, its investment income (which in good times can be substantial for insurance companies) would only be taxed at a low intercompany rate of 7 percent, or at nothing if wholly owned. A merger or acquisition can also offer the opportunity to optimize debt capacity, liquidity, or internal financing. Since interest payments are tax deductible, firms may wish to improve their overall performance with a debt-financed acquisition or merger. By the late 1970s and early 1980s, debt had become a major factor in hostile takeovers. Malcolm Salter and Wolf Weinhold pointed out in 1980 that the economic environment of the late 1970s offered opportunities to increase earnings by boosting debt, since the cost of borrowing was negative. This improved returns to investors.[5] However, not much empirical research on negative real interest rates has been carried out as yet.

Economies of scale in cash management could also motivate takeover activity. If firm A has excess liquidity, managers of firm B might well look at it as a potential target because they believe they can use that cash more effectively. Yet excess cash may reflect not only poor management, but also a tax disincentive for a large dividend or a reluctance on the managers' part to repurchase their own stock.

How much should you pay for a company? Sometimes, the price paid is two to three times what the stock market values a company. Are you paying too much then? Not according to one CEO who had just completed a giant takeover. Said he, "Those [the target company's] assets—tankers, trucks, refineries, oil drilling equipment, and land tracts—*are* worth more to my company than they were to [the target company], because I can put them to work immediately generating revenue, whereas they were idle or underused in [the target company]. But in pure accounting terms, it's exactly the same assets on my books that he had on his books. Those assets, they're worth more, maybe double or triple to me, because I can make more with them for me than he could make with them for himself. So I pay more—maybe fifty percent more—for them."

This may be true, but extravagant overpayment by CEOs for target companies is still extremely common—a fact that many CEOs openly admit.

And quite frequently, there is little or no real synergy or economic justification. In such cases, it is fair to examine whether the overvaluation or overpayment stems from misjudgment, the momentum of carrying the deal forward, the herd instinct of the participants, or simply ego—the psychological gratification that many CEOs gain by presiding over a constantly growing company.

The New Stock Market

The stock market, which provides companies with both capital, which chief executives need, and a pool of ownership, which many would rather avoid, has changed over the last few decades. As a result, takeovers are far easier to pull off today than they were, say, in the 1950s. Back then, stock in a company was usually distributed among a large number of relatively small investors, who collected their dividends and stored their certificates in safety deposit boxes, often for decades. Now and again, shareholders might feel they have something to ask "their" company, and so they would submit a question at the annual meeting and listen politely as "their" CEO answered. Those days are gone. Today, most stock is held by a relatively small number of institutions—mutual funds, money markets, brokerage houses, pension funds, insurance companies—in extremely large blocks which are held not for years, but perhaps for a week or a month. These institutions are not willing to sit around and ask polite questions. Instead, they act as a real owner might. "I hate to admit it," said one chief executive, "but my continued career as CEO is somewhat dependent upon those institutional portfolio managers and their decisions to heavily buy or sell our stock."

As a result of this relatively rapid block trading, volatility has increased enormously. Many CEOs find such uncertainty maddening. "Some of these portfolio managers are parasites," one irate CEO exploded in frustration. "They just want instant stock appreciation payoffs. They don't wait for our year-end results to see how we've done. They aren't interested in our long-term strategy or our five-year plan. These bastards could care less, because they aren't investing in us for the long term. No way. It's just in and out, in and out. They're absolute parasites, just living off us. You have no idea how frustrating it is when you're trying to plan your company's long-term strategy, its survival, and these arbitragers [investors who speculate on stock appreciation during takeovers] and institutional investor bastards are pulling your chain and screwing you around."

Takeovers, and the rise of institutional investors, are intimately connected. Because institutions are quick to recognize short-term profit, and because there are so few of them, raiders have found it easier to gain control of major blocks of company stock. As a result, nearly every one of the eighty-nine chief executives interviewed said that in order to ward off hostile raiders, they had personally voted for a variety of so-called "shark repellents," or antitakeover measures: to change their corporate bylaws; their state of incorporation; to reorganize their business; to drastically alter their corporate or stock structure in such a way as to resist advances; to reorganize the structure and bylaws of the board of directors. As hostile takeovers grew in the early 1980s, many chief executives opted for "golden parachute" clauses in their contracts—large severance payments in the event that they should lose their jobs in such a takeover. Many CEOs justify the controversial golden parachutes because they say it insures their objectivity when reviewing a takeover bid.

The rise of institutions and the increase in takeovers have also altered many companies' strategic outlooks. To try to survive in shark-infested waters, many CEOs say they have had to adopt shorter-term strategies, aiming simply at stock appreciation. "They had me in a classic nutcracker," confessed one CEO. "You can't believe the pressure on me from all sides to quit, to sell out, to merge, to somehow change the company's strategy." Just before Revlon was swallowed up in a hostile takeover by Pantry Pride, Michel Bergerac told me, "We all know this threat of a hostile takeover is real, it's out there, and all the CEOs I know are like me in managing their companies somewhat defensively these days."

Prestige, Power, and Job Security

Clearly, not all takeovers are pursued purely for financial ends. Companies, after all, are run by people, whose hearts beat faster at a variety of stimulants. "Let's face it," said one chief executive, "doing acquisitions is very exciting. Your neck is on the line." In fact, he said, it takes an enormous amount of self-control *not* to give in to this excitement of doing mergers and acquisitions and call a halt to one that is in the process of going full steam ahead.

Not all CEOs approve of the idea of takeovers as an indoor sport—or as therapy. In the early 1980s, Nathan R. Owen, the chief executive at General Signal who had done a number of acquisitions of related companies, took a critical view of what he saw as waves of unrelated and nonsensical acquisitions pursued by other CEOs "simply for the sake of their ego gratification or drive for power." A case in point: the acquisition of electric motor company Reliance Electric by Exxon Corporation in the late 1970s. "Taking the specific Exxon-Reliance case," said Owen, "that's nothing but subterfuge. The justification that they've discovered a solid-state way of controlling motor speeds and that the way to get it into the market is to acquire a company that has distribution in motors, is a lot of hooey—and everybody in the motor business knows it." So it turned out. The Reliance acquisition proved to be one of a string of disasters in Exxon's attempt to diversify out of the oil business. Added Owen: "I'm just very surprised that a company of the size and stature of Exxon would be that low-grade and transparent in trying to do an unrelated acquisition. I really am disappointed in Exxon. That was a bad show, and the raid on Babcock & Wilcox by United Technologies . . . was another. The same is true of Carrier Corporation's takeover by United Technologies." Owen finished with a final swipe at unrelated acquisitions: "It's all ego, building up the ego of the CEO and his desire for excitement, power, and prestige."

But again, the world of the CEO is more complex than this would indicate. Although virtually all takeovers aim at providing growth and the capture of an ongoing, profitable business, rationalizations for takeovers have changed over time. In the nineteenth century, giant trusts such as John D. Rockefeller's Standard Oil Company sought absolute dominance through a string of takeovers. But during the conglomerate mergers of the 1960s, takeovers were pursued more for financial reasons—to pump up the stock price, for instance—and to spread out the risk. Despite the fact that the vast majority of takeovers today are justified by CEOs as the purchase of undervalued assets, many admitted to me privately that they knew they had overpaid for their acquisitions—adding, in each case, that it did not really matter. Why? Because mergers and acquisitions offer essentially a means to gain market knowhow and experience, which the acquiring firm lacks. A number of acquisitions made by Exxon, AT & T, Xerox, and General Motors were primarily justified by this key motive.

Consider the complexity of the motives underlying Geneen's acquisition drive. Geneen admitted that ITT was often viewed as incapable of competing in the United States; as a result, he pursued mergers and acquisitions domestically just to prove them wrong. Certainly, ego was involved; but, as we have already seen, Geneen was also able to rationalize the takeovers as a strategy to acquire U.S. managerial experience for a predominately European work force. And he could justify U.S. acquisitions because the bulk of his shareholders were Americans. Finally, and perhaps most important, Geneen argued that he picked up a number of U.S. firms in consumer markets (such as Avis, Incorporated or Continental Baking) to get into businesses with steadier earnings or more stable prospects. Again, Geneen's overarching notion of a company with a host of balanced profit centers comes into play. "I always had a kind of philosophy that it was a good thing for ITT to be in some kind of consumer business," he said. "You get a feeling for the business, you get a feeling of the market—a livelier business in some ways. You can't be stodgy and be successful in a consumer business."

There is also a fascinating psychological dynamic that is put into play during a takeover. Two or more antagonists face each other off, unsure what the other is thinking or planning, unsure, in many cases, of their own motivations. There was no drama quite as exciting in this regard as the Bendix–Martin Marietta war, with the eventual arrival of Allied as white knight. There were, of course, the personalities: Bendix's Bill Agee and Mary Cunningham, and the simmering scandal that followed them about, combative Thomas G. Pownall of Martin Marietta, and cool, calculating Edward Hennessy of Allied. Agee, the eventual loser, clearly saw his original takeover attempt as a simple case of maximizing shareholder values. Of course one man's rationality is another's lunacy. And while Agee focused in on shareholder values, Hennessy and Pownall were undoubtedly justifying their own positions by arguing the long-term benefits of stability.

In fact, takeovers force chief executives to examine exactly what their long-term goals for a company are. Is it a case of maximizing shareholder values? Are there larger social justifications in which the company plays a part? Or should they be responsible to their work force, attempting, for instance, to preserve their jobs? And there are potential conflicts of interest. Should they enrich themselves through a leveraged buyout, even if it is at the shareholders' expense? Should they fight a takeover that would put money in the shareholders' pocket, in order to save their own jobs? Should they demand a golden parachute? Should they engage in "greenmail"?

TAKEOVERS: LIFE IN THE JUNGLE

These are not simple problems, although in a takeover battle, complex motivations are often simplified into black and white. "I felt I was stuck between a rock and a hard place when they demanded greenmail," said one beleaguered chief executive of a company which was forced to pay greenmail not once, but twice, only to lose the company anyway. "I knew it was wrong. I absolutely did not want to pay it. But I haven't spent most of my life building up this company to have some raider take it away." Another CEO, who had founded his company, lost a proxy vote after a long, bitterly contested battle with a raider. He defended his strategies by declaring, "The bastard [the raider] is not interested in the long-term needs of our shareholders. He's just going to bust it up and sell off the pieces. Sure, I'm angry about losing my job because he's taking over; but I tried to protect the future of the company." In fact, the raider did not break up the company; it returned to profitability. Raiders, however, do often focus on the "breakup value" of a company whereas the target companies' CEOs see it quite differently pointing to the value of the current company as a going concern.

Antitrust Regulation

At first glance, it would seem logical that takeover activity would rise and fall as changes are made in antitrust regulations. But while changes in laws have affected the forms and types of takeovers, they were not effective in curbing overall takeover activity. Historically, Samuel Reid[6] notes that a major piece of antitrust regulation was passed prior to each of the merger waves. For example, the Sherman Antitrust Law in 1890 preceded the first wave of horizontal mergers. The Clayton Act and the Federal Trade Commission Act of 1914 came into effect before the second wave, when vertical mergers were commonplace. Finally, the Cellar-Kefauver antimerger amendment of 1950 predates by just a few years the great wave of conglomerate mergers. Reid argues that "a universal lack of concern about the merger problem at high levels of government (with the resultant lack of enforcement of the laws) has also been a contributing factor to this aspect of the environment." Clearly, the current Reagan administration is fostering the deluge of mergers, takeovers, and joint ventures by its increasingly lax enforcement of antitrust laws by the Justice Department and the FTC.

In fact, many corporations use antitrust suits and vigorous lobbying for specific antitrust legislation as a way to reduce competitive uncertainty. Pfeffer and Salancik contrast the number of private antitrust suits brought by competitors in 1960, totaling 255, with that in 1972, which totaled 1,299—or 94 percent of all antitrust suits.[7] Despite the government's lax enforcement, firms continue to attempt to use the government and the laws to control their competitors' behavior. For example, Lee Iacocca, the CEO of Chrysler Corporation, repeatedly complained in his antitrust suits against General Motors and Toyota Motor Corporation that the U.S. government was not enforcing its own antitrust laws.

Despite the current ineffectiveness of antitrust regulation, it has in the past been used to inhibit takeovers. Geneen gave a typical example of how antitrust actions can frustrate the acquiring firm by endless delays, thereby subjecting the participants to continuing uncertainty. In fact, that was exactly what happened when ITT tried to take over the American Broadcasting Company (ABC) in 1968. "The question is, why did we get out [of that takeover attempt]," Geneen mused. "That was harassment. The FTC approved it not only once, but twice, and then the Justice Department got in and finally we got into a lot of acrimony about a free editorial policy. It seemed to us that we were going to be locked in with a big question mark over our heads while we went through with the suit. Our stockholders were wondering whether we had made the acquisition or we hadn't. It wouldn't have made any difference which way it was, as long as we got it over with. Well, it wasn't going to get done very fast, so we decided it was better to drop out."

In contrast to U.S. domestic antitrust policies, we find that many foreign governments provide incentives to mergers, acquisitions, and takeovers by a variety of laws demanding that multinationals seek local partners, co-ownership, or participation. For example, David Rockefeller spoke of the need to carry out acquisitions in order to enter restricted markets. "By the time we [at Chase Manhattan Bank] really started aggressively [to expand abroad] . . . it was not possible to get branches into any of those countries—Brazil, Venezuela, Colombia, Peru, for example. They wouldn't permit this, but we were allowed to acquire an interest in distant local banks. This is what happened, and it finally developed into a 100 percent interest in some cases."

62

TAKEOVERS: LIFE IN THE JUNGLE

Making a Merger Work

In many ways, swallowing a company in a takeover is a far easier task than successfully digesting (integrating and managing) that company later. In an acquisition, both parties must examine in depth several facets of their prospective arrangement in order for their union to occur smoothly. Boucher[8] and Emmett[9] believe that if either party remains unclear concerning the other's objectives, there will be a greater chance of failure during the negotiations. They each say that the acquiring firm should delineate the nature of the business acceptable for acquisition, the preferred rate of return on the investment, the target firm's management capability, and the basis for the exchange.

One good example of a relationship that worked is the Seagram purchase of 20 percent of Conoco, which gave it a chunk of DuPont, as described earlier. The relationship could have been a disaster. The corporate cultures of the two companies were quite different: DuPont was a proud company with, until recently, a history of family control going back far longer than Seagram had even existed, and Seagram's 20-percent stake came out of a bruising takeover battle. Nonetheless, the relationship has been a model. Seagram has five board seats, and Edgar and Charles Bronfman sit on the finance committee. For the most part, however, Seagram allows DuPont to run its own affairs. "The relationship couldn't be closer," said Edgar Bronfman. "Here's an example: our human resources people had to close a plant in Louisville, and didn't have a lot of experience in this. We asked them [DuPont] if we could talk to their people—how they did it, why they did it—they took us through the whole thing. We learned a ton of things. As a result, our plant closing was done as responsibly as possible. We're both very happy."

That relationship may have developed so well because of some longstanding ideas at Seagram. First, Bronfman has always sought to keep his New York headquarters staff as lean as possible. A corollary to that has been his desire not to look for turnaround situations, where his staff would have to provide operational management, but rather to buy companies with strong management. Thus, St. Joe, Conoco, and DuPont. "When you look at a company, you're probably not going to know the management except by reputation. Maybe you've met the chief executive once or twice. Or you can find someone who claims to know them. So what you look at is their track record. How good are they? How imaginative? What's their growth record? Are they sitting around doddering and doing the same things they've been doing for thirty years? What's their new product success?" Once satisfied, Bronfman is more than willing to stay away. "It's their business. They know it, we don't."

There are a number of specific rules for a smooth, successful takeover. Most are commonsensical, though often ignored by hungry would-be takeover artists. For example:

- A nonhostile takeover is likelier when the target company is in an industry the acquirer knows well and when the target company is able to smooth out its own cyclicality or seasonality.
- The acquiring firm should be aware of changes in the target firm's market, including its reputation among customers, suppliers, and competitors.
- The rate of return on investment in a target firm should equal that of the acquiring firm, or at least have the potential to do so in the near future.
- It is important to value the target firm against others in the same industry.

While there are a variety of elaborate computer models today for evaluating these strategic factors for a successful acquisition, it is not clear that any of them have been instrumental in ensuring the success or in shaping the direction, size, or pace of the current takeover deluge. As many critics have noted, the inordinate haste with which many of today's huge takeovers have been consummated demonstrates the scant attention to the factors that lead to a successful acquisition. For example, James M. Mortensen of Young & Rubicam Company spoke with me about the ticklish problems of negotiating the purchase of an advertising firm, a classic example of a business with almost no assets beyond the creative powers of the personnel. "The ownership of an agency of less than $50 million is usually in the hands of maybe six people," said Mortensen. "The only way to approach them is to do it from the top. You focus on the human part of the equation and sort of avoid the subject of money as long as possible, because the key is to get an agreement on a concept. If you can't do that, there's no point in pursuing it. Sometimes you make a mistake. In one case, we knew that the guy didn't really want to be part of it [the acquired company], but we got carried away and wanted to be in that market. We made a bad decision ... we ended up winding the thing down to get rid of him. So you have to focus on the chemistry."

64

TAKEOVERS: LIFE IN THE JUNGLE

The consequences of a hostile takeover—or a takeover that simply does not mesh—can be wide ranging and damaging to both parties. When the takeover has been acrimonious, morale and productivity often plummet. Uncertainty creates anxiety among workers, causing them to grow angry, depressed, resentful, and increasingly critical of the new management. In addition, hostile takeovers can drive out key managers who are needed to ensure the acquisition's success. These personnel problems are particularly troublesome in situations where the target firm has inflamed sentiment against a raider and so allies itself with its unions to try to stop the takeover. That is what Grumman Corporation did in 1981, when it used the cash in its employee pension fund to try to buy back stock, an attempt—which was ultimately successful—to beat back an attack by a subsidiary of LTV.

Once these financial and managerial yardsticks are dealt with, most takeovers come down to the people involved. "The personalities and personal chemistry of the CEOs are the make-it-or-break-it factor as to whether a deal moves forward and is signed or gets stalled," says Dr. Armand Hammer, chairman of Occidental Petroleum Corporation. "But even more important," he emphasized, "the personal chemistry between the two also determines whether the acquisition will succeed in the long run. I've seen plenty of deals fail because the two men find out they simply can't stand each other."

The rules of the phantom club, plus a need to feel each other out, often result in a form of courtesy that is almost mandarin. For example, nearly every CEO I interviewed told me that he always went out of his way to make the first overture to the other company's CEO in the event of a takeover. "It's an expected courtesy between companies," said Roger B. Smith of General Motors, adding that such a courtesy would apply even if GM were taking over a company one-hundredth its size. Such courtesies are the first step toward good relations, particularly if the goal is a friendly takeover. Edward L. Hennessy, Jr., has relayed how natural Allied's merger with Signal Companies was, mostly because of good relations between Signal's Forrest N. Shumway and himself. "The easy informality between the men, born, they say, of business connections that grew into genuine liking, typifies both the way Mr. Hennessy says he prefers to make acquisitions—with a minimum of hostility and tension . . ."[10] In contrast, another CEO told me point-blank: "The personal chemistry between us was just all wrong. . . . So I cut off merger negotiations. It wasn't a question of price, just personality. He's impossible, a total egomaniac. I could see that after one day, and it just raised a red flag in my head. I told my team, let's get out of here."

In his years as head of General Signal, Nathan Owen gained a reputation for friendly acquisitions. Owen, who worked as a venture capitalist for fifteen years before coming to Signal, was spending most of his time on acquisitions when I interviewed him in both 1978 and 1982. With his depth of experience, he rarely relied on outside finders or investment bankers, choosing instead to deal with the top management of target firms personally. His style was low-key, patient, and courteous; he argued that his major concern in any particular deal was the integrity of the target firm's management. As a result, Owen has often been approached as a potential white knight by companies fleeing from raiders. His venture capital background has taught him two key lessons: "One, never to try to outsmart anyone in a deal—that makes for a bad marriage. The other, unless you invest in good people, you're building on sand."

But even if all does go smoothly for the two CEOs, a takeover can go very wrong. And even as careful an acquisitor as Owen can get himself into trouble. "Basically what you're betting on is people," he said. "I don't care whether it's a laser company or a garbage can company, neither one is going to do well without good management. We did make mistakes twice by buying two companies because they were so cheap. It just seemed as if we couldn't lose. You figure that if you only put a million dollars in, that's all you can lose. Well, it doesn't work that way. That's an invitation to walk into a swamp; and once you start, you can never get out for your original investment. We knew in both cases that the management was either weak or nonexistent; it taught me that no acquisition is worth a candle if it doesn't have good management to begin with, or if we don't know precisely the man that we have that we can put into that job. Buying a sick business and then hoping you can put the right people in to turn it around may work for some people, but I think it's better to pay a fair, going price for a business that has good management and good momentum, and just let them pull you on. Our job is to support them."

Conglomerate acquisition is a subject Owen has very strong views on, and one that sets him in opposition not only to acquisitors such as Harold Geneen, but, in part, to his own role at General Signal. "It is the independent entrepreneur who built America," he declares. "I deplore conglomerates. They're bad for the country . . . I am doing something that, in principle, I oppose, so I try to keep these companies the way they are. The only way I can enhance them is by supplying the capital for growth."

TAKEOVERS: LIFE IN THE JUNGLE

Resisting a Hostile Takeover

Although Dr. Hammer also talked of establishing a personal chemistry in a takeover, one fine day in 1978, Occidental Petroleum announced that it was accumulating stock in Mead, a Dayton, Ohio–based maker of paper products that was trying to move into computer databases. Occidental eventually made a billion-dollar tender offer for Mead's shares. The offer came as no real surprise to Mead CEO J. W. McSwiney; the company's stock had been low, and he had heard rumors that someone was buying shares and had quietly formed a defense team to deal with what they considered a hostile takeover. Now it was out in the open. Nonetheless, Mead's defense team kept a public silence even as it labored behind closed doors to formulate a strategy.

By the time Mead did counterattack, it was a well-planned defense made on a number of different fronts. First, Mead's defense lawyers, investment bankers, and public relations staff made themselves available to the press, detailing their objections to Occidental. At the same time, they launched a well-timed flurry of letters to shareholders and ran advertisements in major papers. On the legal front, Mead filed suits against Occidental in state and federal courts for violating securities and antitrust laws. And, perhaps most damning, Mead directly attacked Occidental, demanding that the Los Angeles oil company go public with details about what Mead thought were "doubtful" operations.

Although it was not easy, Mead's strategy worked. Over the years, Mead had had good relations with its employees and shareholders and with Wall Street analysts. And it was a good corporate citizen in Dayton, which was particularly important because it enabled Mead to play on the possibility that Ohio, already suffering from a decline in manufacturing, could lose thousands of more jobs if Occidental succeeded in its takeover attempt. That fear of lost jobs may lie, at least in part, behind Mead's court victories in the U.S. District Court and before the Ohio State Securities Board. Mead was also lucky. A former director of Occidental volunteered that he was required to sign an undated resignation letter as a condition for board membership.[11] Suddenly, with the SEC launching an investigation against it, Occidental was forced to take the defensive. It withdrew its tender offer after much work and court procedures, and Joseph Baird, the then president, resigned soon after that. Occidental continued to smart for some time. One of its operations, by the way, was Hooker Chemical Company, a $1.7 billion subsidiary that was then trying to extricate itself from the chemical wastes problem at Love Canal in upstate New York. Some 1.2 million documents were uncovered during the discovery phase of the Mead suit, some of which were passed on by the SEC to the EPA (Environmental Protection Agency) and a Congressional subcommittee investigating the matter. Occidental was burned badly. As Zoltan Merszei, Baird's replacement, told *Fortune*, "Never try an unfriendly acquisition. Mead was, and is, a pain in the ass."[12]

Because of the continuing lawsuits, McSwiney would not talk to me directly about the Occidental raid. But he did talk about the subject of takeovers. In many ways, McSwiney's and Mead's behavior was that of a typical chief executive at a typical corporation suddenly threatened by a hostile takeover. "We always worried about it [a takeover attempt]," McSwiney admitted, because of the low stock price that stemmed from earnings problems in the early 1970s. "But," he added, "you can't go around in a trauma about it. You just do what you have to do." Some time before the takeover attempt, McSwiney had gone out and hired a takeover defense expert: Joseph Flom, a partner with the New York law firm Skadden, Arps, Meagher & Flom. A large number of the chief executives I spoke with had hired Flom, not only to build a defense but to engineer a takeover or even just to keep him away from the competition.

Said McSwiney, "I felt one simple thing: that if anyone did come in and try to buy us, that we ought to have all the skills at work to be sure that if they were successful, that the shareholders received a fair shake for what was really in the company. Having gone through 1971, when we had earnings problems, we have still not made any bad acquisitions [just to deter a raider]. I had no problem as an individual, a fear of losing my job, or that the board wasn't with me. It seemed to me that in that environment, if you had a sense of fiduciary responsibility, then the worst thing that could happen was to let someone steal the company for less than it was worth."

That fiduciary responsibility weighed heavily on McSwiney: "Our people put a book together on what we should do in the event of a takeover. One of the interesting things is that when it did happen, they brought the book out. I said I had never read a word in it. The reason that I didn't was that when Joe Flom came aboard, he said, 'There is no plan that you can follow. Just look honestly at what's in front of you. If someone comes in and offers you one hundred dollars for something worth seventy-five dollars, you've got to take responsibility if you take it. If they come in and offer twenty-five dollars for something worth seventy-five dollars, you do not have an obligation to take it.' Eventually, people who try to put together books on takeovers find it a waste of time. Every one of them is different, just like children. People would press me and say, 'Didn't you do this because it was in the book?' I told them I'd never read it."

McSwiney did have an idea of what the secret to a good defense was. "What you need in a takeover is the appropriate use of time. If someone walks up with a knife at your throat and says, 'Give me ten dollars,' you don't have time to argue with him. He might not even have a knife that would cut your throat, but how do you know that? If you have time to send his knife to the lab and see if it would cut, you might tell him to go to hell. Time is the most precious thing we have. You have to have enough of it to do anything." Fortunately, Ohio has a law that requires a thirty-day investigation period before a takeover proceeds. That gave time. He also had other advantages. "I had said that I was going to move aside as chief executive as of last April," he said. "So, when something like this came along, it was fortuitous that here was a person who had been with the company since 1934, somewhat skilled in finance, a company with a good, clean track record. This may sound very Sunday-schoolish, but if anyone ever thinks that it doesn't pay to leave a good, clean track record, just let him get involved in something like this. You cannot attack a problem if you're afraid of your background. If your record is clean, you don't have to worry about what someone is going to do to you."

The experience had left McSwiney with his own opinions of takeovers: "My feeling is that unfriendly takeovers seldom make sense. The management is so crucial to the ultimate success of whatever you're doing. If companies join together it should generally be of a voluntary nature. Now, where there are officers doing a poor job and if you [the shareholder] are in the majority, you might like to see another management take it over. It's too general to say that there shouldn't be unfriendly takeovers. Under normal circumstances, where a company is doing a good job of managing its resources, to have someone come in and undo it is probably not in the best interest of society. That's a personal observation. I don't think it runs counter to my fiduciary responsibility."

Mead adopted a variety of common techniques to battle a takeover: public relations, lawsuits, counterattacks. But there are a variety of other, more technical tactics that have become increasingly popular as the wave of hostile takeovers has swelled. Vincent Rennert[13] reviews several of the techniques:

- A firm can change its bylaws to require supermajorities of up to 80 percent of the shareholder vote to complete a merger, sell, lease, or transfer specified assets, or to dissolve the company.
- It can stabilize its board of directors by staggering their elections or by electing them with a majority vote as opposed to an accumulated vote.
- There are stock strategies. It can dole out its shares to "friendly" hands; repurchase its own stock; institute or expand an employee stock plan; acquire a closely held company for stock which would then be safe in the case of a tender offer; issue preferred stock with a right to vote as a class if there were a forced management change; promote the ownership share of long-term investors through an automatic dividend reinvestment plan; or create option plans that allot to management restricted shares with immediate option rights.
- It can seek protection under state takeover statutes. Similarly, if the firm has or can obtain a Canadian subsidiary, it may find protection under Canada's Foreign Investment Review Agency. They may also seek legislation to discourage acquisitions by foreign firms.
- The company's charter can be amended to require the board to consider the social and economic efforts of a tender offer. A long-term effort to build community good will can result in a handsome reward in state security reviews and U.S. District Court opinions.
- Once the threat of a hostile takeover has materialized, the target firm can file antitrust suits and orchestrate its competitors' testimony to support the antitrust allegations. It can bring suppliers and customers to its cause by having them threaten to withdraw from dealings with the firm if it is acquired.
- Its public relations efforts can generate support from shareholders and security analysts while attacking the raider, as Mead did to Occidental, through press releases and stockholder letters. Part of this campaign can involve letters from employees signaling to the raider their intention of leaving should the company be acquired.

There are also some less noteworthy, but increasingly popular, strategies for resisting a takeover. One of them is the payment of "greenmail," so called because of its more than slight resemblance to blackmail. In greenmail, the target company rebuffs a takeover by paying the acquirer an excessive amount of money for the stock it has bought. In fact, these greenmail payments have proven to have almost totally failed to stave off takeover bids. In the cases of the multiple raids on Walt Disney Productions by Saul Steinberg, the Bass brothers, and others, and the successive raids on St.

TAKEOVERS: LIFE IN THE JUNGLE

Regis Paper by Sir James Goldsmith, Loews Corporation, and Rupert Murdoch, the first payment of greenmail simply advertises the target firm's vulnerability. As a result, such a strategy tends to invite other, new takeover bids and leads the management of the threatened firm to act in an even more desperate fashion as the company's cash flow is depleted in successive payoffs.

Another increasingly common method of resisting a takeover—and as poor a strategy as greenmail—is to take the company private, usually by buying back all or most of the stock from public shareholders. The typical variation of this strategy is the so-called "leveraged buyout," in which top management borrows large amounts of capital from banks, using the company's assets and cash flow from operations as collateral for the loan. They then take the company private, all the time hoping to escape that hostile takeover bid. In fact, the opposite often occurs. That is what happened at Norton Simon, a New York conglomerate then run by David Mahoney. No sooner did Mahoney announce a leveraged buyout than a whole group of hostile bids was received from a variety of other companies and investors. Outsiders usually can afford to bid more than internal managers, simply because the outside takeover company can borrow against two sets of assets—its own company's, and the target company's. Within three years— 1983 to 1985—Norton Simon was taken over by Esmark, then Beatrice, and then finally by BCI Holdings Group.

Hostile takeovers may create long-term problems, but that has not stopped them from taking place. And, in fact, unlike the Occidental and Mead imbroglio, most hostile takeovers prevail. In turn, more and more CEOs have implemented extensive levels of defenses, hoping to scare off raiders before they draw too close. And the truth is, many takeovers end up as Pyrrhic victories, winning a smoky, burning shell of a company that is devoid of management. That threat may be the ultimate takeover defense. For example, when I interviewed William C. Norris, the founder and then CEO of Control Data, in 1978, I asked him what he'd do in the event of a hostile takeover, he exploded: "Christ! I'd do everything possible to prevent it, and I can assure you that anybody that tried it has got one hell of a fight and he's going to get stunk up beyond any point that he can imagine. . . . Also, he'd get a company bereft of management. We have something like thirty of our key executives with employment contracts that are automatically abrogated in the event of a hostile takeover. If I had an employee in management who would tolerate working for somebody that took the company over, I wouldn't let him stay more than five minutes. Anybody who doesn't have any more moral fiber than that doesn't belong in a company like Control Data."

Conclusion

The most significant sign that the overall mania for acquisitions since the 1960s has failed to live up to its expectations is the equally powerful trend in divestitures. In practice, most chief executives say, if it doesn't work, unload it on the next sucker. As a result, most CEOs have become increasingly, painfully, aware of the need to adopt an acquisition strategy that realistically anticipates failure. These chief executives were particularly aware of two major problems: first, excessive overpayment for a company so that it can never pay back its cost, a problem fully half of the chief executives I spoke with admitted to succumbing to once or more; and second, a lack of sufficient knowledge about the business being acquired.

Chief executives did have an economic friend in these questionable endeavors: because inflation from 1964 to 1984 was so high, they could bury bad acquisitions; after all, as time flew by and as inflation rose, the cost of past acquisitions diminished in terms of inflationary dollars. Unfortunately, that is no longer the case, and chief executives in a noninflationary, perhaps bordering on deflationary, economy suddenly have to pay the piper and show a little restraint. That is not easy. Chief executives admitted—sometimes sheepishly, sometimes brashly—that they would get caught up in the spell of a takeover struggle and the ego gratification of completing a big deal. It takes discipline to walk away from a big deal, and most of the chief executives simply did not have it in themselves.

Likewise, many of the chief executives knew that they had not managed acquisitions particularly well. Such realizations in individual cases seemed to take about a year to manifest themselves. By then, the incompatibility of work forces, the massive defection of key personnel, and the hidden financial problems all had time to appear. And the optimism of the honeymoon had been replaced by the bickering of a lousy marriage.

Should they not have foreseen these problems? Probably. Amazingly, chief executives often described to me the time spent by planning staffs, investment banking groups, or outside consultants looking at dozens, or even hundreds, of different companies before choosing the right one to buy. This screening process, which was mentioned to me by chief executives such as Edgar Bronfman of Joseph E. Seagram & Sons, was often highly financially oriented. Unfortunately, crunching numbers can tell little about the emotions of the target company's managers, the personality of the chief executive, the compatibility of the two cultures. Sometimes, the attempt can blow up in their faces, as did Agee's attempt to swallow up Martin Marietta—a miscalculation of the largest sort. In other cases, the acquired company proves to be far less than what the financial planners, staring at their numbers, expected.

Successful acquisitions most commonly result from a direct personal contact between two chief executives. If the personal chemistry, trust, and confidence between these two men is good, then the acquisition has a far better chance not only of going through, but of being a success. In the event of hostile takeovers, in which tempers and antagonisms can flare, the odds are far less for a successful marriage.

All of this is common sense. Nonetheless, it is really quite amazing how *little* common sense comes to play in takeovers. For example, many chief executives admitted that they knew of acquisitions which had failed because the CEOs had ignored very obvious warning signs, problems, and incompatibilities. CEOs who had been burned in this way often concluded that acquisitions, if they are to be successful, should take place between companies in similar businesses and industries. They said that, in general, infinitely more time, money, and personnel were required, and more financial risk shouldered, in unrelated acquisitions. They could even take these risks and turn them into numbers: several told me that they had developed a 20 percent discount factor for the assets of an unrelated target. Did that stop such acquisitions from taking place? Usually not. Indeed, in an area where nearly everyone pays too much, a discount factor only serves to reduce the amount of the overexpenditure.

CHAPTER FOUR

TURNAROUND STRATEGIES: LIFE ON THE EDGE

The immediate strategy was to keep the company from going bankrupt. We owed a billion something dollars. The previous year, 1974, we had lost money, although not a great deal. In 1975 we were losing money on a monthly basis. That was one set of conditions. The other set was what the world was like back then. W. T. Grant had just flipped. Morgan was their lead bank, and Morgan was our lead bank. . . . New York City was on the edge of bankruptcy. New York State couldn't float their bonds. The company had to do something dramatic to stop the flow of cash. . . . It was clear to me that what we needed was not a strategy, but a tactic. Stop the company from going bankrupt. Stop the blood from flowing . . .
—JOSEPH B. FLAVIN, chairman and CEO, The Singer Company

I thought we needed some pretty strong medicine and I advocated some pretty severe solutions: firing people who were not good managers, writing off inventories and receivables that weren't any good; getting rid of businesses going nowhere. In many ways, you could say what I was advocating was shrinkage, less profit.
—DAVID W. WALLACE, CEO, Bangor Punta Corporation

The Thrill of the Turnaround

There is nothing more exciting than a turnaround. A company staggering toward oblivion must suddenly adapt drastic measures to save itself: slashing employment, closing down divisions, seeking lines of credit, sometimes even bringing in a whole new management team led by a so-called "turnaround artist." As the crisis deepens, as the press and financial community look on, management labors frantically to keep the corporate body alive.

75

The days fly by; the creditors close in. Can the company be saved? What will it look like when it gets back on its feet? Will the massive surgery save the company, or kill it?

Exciting, yes, and increasingly commonplace. In the past few years, we have seen an escalating number of corporate bankruptcies: more companies went into bankruptcy in 1983 and 1984 than at any time since the Great Depression. Many of these companies have been forced to resort to a variety of complex turnaround strategies both before and after they entered the turbulent world described in the conclusion of this volume. Some have been spectacularly successful, others only partially so, leading on occasion to mergers; some have resulted in dismal failure. No matter the outcome of the turnaround, in almost all cases, the company's profitability is affected by the attempt.

The recent increase in bankruptcies stemmed from a variety of economic and financial factors, particularly the volatility of interest rates. From 1940 to 1970, the business environment in terms of interest rates, foreign competition, and inflation was relatively stable. That environment is no longer as stable. Foreign competition, particularly from Japan, has battered many American companies; inflation (1964–1984) has driven corporate costs through the roof; and interest rates have made expansion, or even basic capital investment, very expensive indeed. And that volatility has paved the way for a new corporate specialist: the turnaround manager, an executive in theory familiar with the most current management techniques, new financing tricks, newfangled marketing approaches, the latest production and distribution methods, and an understanding of the ins and outs of mergers and acquisitions—just in case that alternative should present itself.

Despite the difficulties of the operating environment, there are a number of financing techniques and resources available for a turnaround attempt. Even the managers of critically ill companies have been able to interest new investors who, in the past, would have shunned them. Managers can also rely on an increasingly high level of debt capacity, because lenders are eager to lend even to companies in trouble. One new wrinkle that acts as both debt and equity is a form of convertible security that transforms itself from debt instrument to equity security if and when the turnaround is accomplished.

The federal government has also fostered turnarounds by permitting tax-loss carryforwards, that is, large caches of tax deductions created by massive losses. Such carryforwards give failing companies a bargaining

TURNAROUND STRATEGIES

chip with lenders, investors, or even a potential raider. The federal government has also guaranteed loans to ailing companies: recently Chrysler Corporation and Continental Illinois, but also Penn Central Corporation, Lockheed Corporation, and Grumman Corporation. And various state and local governments have offered corporate tax forgiveness, tax abatements, tax relief, free or low-cost loans, grants, facilities, and direct purchase orders to help failing business remain viable and keep them in the community. Significantly, unions and employees at Chrysler, Eastern Airlines, and many other giant, mid-sized, and small businesses have agreed to wage cuts, pension fund investments, and, in a few cases, have even agreed to take over and manage the companies themselves.

There are as many kind of turnarounds as there are troubled companies. Although many turnarounds involve purely financial strategies, others can emphasize marketing, management, or products. A product turnaround, for example, can involve repositioning an old product such as Johnson & Johnson's baby shampoo for a new audience, in this case, adults. But a typical *new* product turnaround involves introducing a new product into a traditional market. That would be exemplified by Volkswagen's introduction in the United States of the Golf to replace the unsuccessful Rabbit automobiles.

Not all companies are equal in a turnaround situation. Large companies have enormous advantages over their smaller cousins. For example, they take advantage of many more tax laws and financing opportunities than do small companies. Also, a large company has more assets to sell to gain working capital. And the large company is much more likely to attract state and local financial benefits, loans, and tax considerations than is a small business. A medium-sized company, if it is a major employer in a town or region, has some of the same advantages. One example was the massive but foundering steel facility of Republic Steel Corporation, in Weirton, West Virginia, where it is the major employer. If the Weirton facility had closed, the town could well have become a ghost town. Instead, the townspeople and employees rallied to buy the facility and take over the management themselves. So far at least, the turnaround has been a success.

Perhaps the most important element of a successful turnaround is the recognition that the crisis is real and that new top management must be brought in to make the drastic and painful cuts necessary to save the company. Of course, there are rarely enough skilled turnaround managers, so in a crisis, large companies have a far better chance of hiring these managers.

77

After all, many turnaround artists are attracted, like moths to a flame, by the chance to win fame and fortune by turning around a major company, as opposed to an obscure, smaller company.

Assessing the Damage

In a crisis, turnaround artists must immediately try to analyze and understand the company that they have been called in to save. They must determine the company's strengths and weaknesses so that they can deal confidently with directors, managers, unions, stockholders, lenders, suppliers, and customers—and even the state, local, or federal government. They must exploit whatever leverage they can find, exert pressure, and use their personal reputations—or that of the company, if it exists—to wring out concessions.

Although no turnaround takes place in a day, turnaround moves have to be made quickly. Rapidity is everything. Ideally, any mass firings, write-offs, or drastic reorganizations should be carried out all at once, within the first month or so. This minimizes unfavorable reactions within the business and financial communities and hostile, demoralized reactions from employees. The first few days in a turnaround attempt pose the greatest demands on turnaround artists and their staffs, although even later, the pressure rarely subsides. Turnarounds are not for the frail of health. Turnaround artists and their staffs must endure backbreaking 70- to 120-hour weeks for anything from a few weeks to several years. Said William J. Catacosinos, who was then laboring to turn around the critically ill Long Island Lighting Company (Lilco) and who had been hired for his previous turnaround work, "It's a terrible way to live. That's what causes sleepless nights. . . . you're in a one-mistake syndrome—one mistake and you're out. That's like walking the edge of the cliff continuously."[1]

Mastering a complex organization in a short amount of time is not easy. Joseph B. Flavin, an alumnus of IBM and Xerox, described to me how daunting the job of turning around The Singer Company was. "I had been looking at the company for two months because this isn't a job you take on lightly. I did extensive homework. The board supplied me with information, the banks and the auditors gave me their data and opinions. . . .

TURNAROUND STRATEGIES

What I knew was that the business machinery business was in very big trouble. This was true not only in terms of what the financial data showed, but I called customers and found out that some thought we were out of business. . . . Right after I got here, I found a lot more. I started my study on November 11, at home. In fact when I went into the hospital for a hernia operation it was a Monday night; I had the operation Tuesday, and had my first meetings on Wednesday at the hospital. What I started was an analysis of each division with five questions: What is the business? Why are we in it? Should we stay in it? If we get out, what should we do with it? We really didn't see data in any depth until maybe December 9, just before the board meeting on December 11. . . . By December 15, I knew there was no way out of it. We had to get rid of some of these businesses. Naturally, it was very emotional. The banks had to be told we were going to do something."

"We were talking and working and gaining knowledge all the time," said Flavin of his early, frantic days as CEO. "I had a lot to learn. The only business I really understood was computers and, to some degree, sewing, because it was a service problem for them. But all the extra businesses. I'd go out and ask: What's our strategy? We didn't have any. Then: How would you describe us? And that would start off a long series of sentences that had no answer. . . . So it was clear to me I had to understand what we were, if only in pieces." Thus commenced mind-numbing meetings. "We went through this meeting and displayed all this data for nine hours and I learned with the board members by listening, saying nothing. It was incredible." Meetings led to plant inspections. "I went to Utica, New York; San Leandro, California. When I went into the plant in San Leandro, I was shocked. We found huge bays empty. And in talking to the people on the line, we found out that in order to still be working there, you had to be a union member with twenty-two years' seniority. You knew the place was closed, there was just no reason to shut the door yet. The youngest person on the line was in their forties. . . . It was a great shock to me." But, shock or not, Flavin labored on.

If turnaround artists fail to move quickly and decisively, they may wake up one day to find themselves backed into a corner, unable to escape. That is a lesson that Victor H. Palmieri, one of today's most famous turnaround artists, has learned. In 1983, Palmieri was appointed to try to save Baldwin-United Corporation from the complex morass it had rushed into. Baldwin, once strictly a maker of pianos, had been transformed by its management into a rapidly growing (or so it seemed) insurance company specializing in annuities. That complex strategy for growth soon began to topple like a house of cards. As the *New York Times* wrote, "Given Baldwin's 'video game corporate structure,' as Mr. Palmieri put it, and its complicated finances, Mr. Palmieri said there was little he could do to analyze the company before signing on, except review its filings with the Securities and Exchange Commission. . . . 'There were people who had been working for months on this matter who had not cracked the case' [Palmieri said]. . . . he found 'a complete breakdown of internal controls' and noted that forty auditors needed two months . . . to assess the worth of Baldwin-United's assets."[2]

Despite his Herculean efforts, Palmieri failed to save six Baldwin subsidiaries from bankruptcy, because he never had the time to assess realistically the nature of the crisis. Palmieri's lesson is a noteworthy one. When a decision is made to try to rescue a company, the remedial moves must be made very quickly. The chief executive must ask him- or herself: what is this business? Exactly how bad is this crisis? Why are we in it? If we get out of it, what should we do instead? All of this is leading up to the final issue: is the company worth saving, or should it be allowed to slip into bankruptcy?

Finally, one should not think of all turnarounds as disasters. Turnarounds can take place in far quieter ways, and in fairly prosperous companies with executives who recognize problems and move to deal with them. Recognition of problems is the key. In the 1960s, Young & Rubicam had undertaken a massive international expansion effort, which by 1970 was essentially complete. But it was only then that executives of the advertising agency, including James Mortensen, the vice chairman, began to detect problems in the domestic operations. "Because of international," Mortensen said, "the domestic business was being heavily drained in terms of manpower. It was not doing all that well; in fact, the domestic advertising business in general was slipping for the first time since World War II. Market figures were looking soft and the inflation of rising media costs had suddenly ground to a halt. So, over a course of ninety days or so, we decided we had to create a radical change in our domestic product. This was not a small thing. For our first fifty years, we were a consumer agency, serving blue-chip clients, and were arrogant or snobbish enough to believe that that was the total business. It is by no means the total market."

The result was that Young & Rubicam went off in two radically new and quite successful directions: first, into marketing communications, and second, into other areas of the consumer market, such as direct sales and sales promotion. The agency bought some specialized marketers, then expanded geographically, getting away from the Madison Avenue focus, and began to emphasize specialty markets such as oil and banking. Thus, it was just as much a turnaround as any of the more spectacular examples.

Cutting and Slashing

Turnarounds can be a grisly business, requiring managers who, like battlefield surgeons, are not afraid of the sight of blood. Typically, a turnaround is done from within, by new managers. Turnaround artists are often required to make massive reductions in personnel, budget, plants, divisions, operations, and overhead—often in distressed divisions—to allay anxious banks and creditors. This brutal business requires a certain type of person.

Whether heartless or cruel, many business consultants and managers agree that in most cases, the old management has to go. After all, the company's problems often stem directly from the lackluster performance of top managers. Even if it is not directly their fault, their leadership abilities have often been tainted by disaster. That is what happened to several executives at the Crocker National Bank when it found itself awash in red ink. Both David A. Brooks, who headed consumer lending, and J. Hallam Dawson, Crocker's president, hoped to ascend to the post of chief executive. Instead, they were told they were not even being considered, the implication being that they were viewed not as a solution to Crocker's difficulties, but as part of the problem. Small wonder that they decided to go outside the bank for a new CEO. Furthermore, the necessary Draconian steps may be just too difficult and painful for the old management to undertake. It may mean firing old friends, closing down beloved facilities, tearing down what had been so carefully constructed.

Inevitably, new CEOs want people around them who they feel they can trust and respect. Take, for example, Andrew C. Sigler, chief executive of Champion International Corporation, a forest-products company, who brought with him a number of managers from his papermaking division when he was called in 1974 to engineer a turnaround. "Sure, I fired a lot of people and I used people, particularly at the beginning, that I knew," said Sigler. "I'd like to think that the reason the paper people are in most of the jobs is that we had better people—and I think we did. But there's no question that if you don't put in the people that you have confidence in when there's a crisis situation—and [with whom] there's a trust level—you're a goddamn fool. So sure, I got rid of them."

Roy A. Anderson, who was installed at Lockheed when the aeronautics company foundered, argues just the opposite: that a ruthless policy of firing people is impractical, if not impossible to put into effect, in the midst of a financial crisis. When he took over, he said, many expected him to cut a large number of executives. He did remove some, but many remained. These were people who believed that Lockheed was a sound company and, said Anderson, "were willing to fight to save the company." In turn, his top management was careful to keep these executives aware of what was going on, to maintain their morale, and to explain, said Anderson, "where we were going, where we thought we were going, and what our problems were from a total corporate standpoint." His point was that some firings are virtually essential, if only to demonstrate how serious the company's financial crisis is. But massive firings can cause more harm than good and pose a further threat to survival.

Trying to decide between the two poles is difficult, and requires an intuitive grasp of the kind of people working at the company. After all, workers who have been assured of their jobs tend to work harder under a new regime. Others, not so reassured, may react in a negative or nonproductive manner. Said Sigler, when asked about the aftermath of the 1974 firings, "Oh, it scares the hell out of them. That's all they could talk about. . . . It just froze them." So they couldn't work? "Oh, God, no." It paralyzed them? "Oh yeah," said Sigler. While that may seem a bit equivocal, it points up the complexity of the situation. Anderson adds a further twist: sometimes you just cannot go out and find good, new executives. "We couldn't bring in new people," he said, "because not many people wanted to come with Lockheed during the crisis. They didn't know whether we would be there or not."

The Fire Sale

When farmers are hard pressed or face bankruptcy, they often sell off all land that is not productive to raise cash. In the same way, *if* turnaround artists decide that the company they are involved in is worth saving—or, more to the point, that it can be saved—they must determine what foundation to base a recovery on. Then they must make a series of strategic decisions: Should they sell all underutilized assets, stress sales growth, concentrate on cost control, or seek a merger? "The chief executive in a financial crisis must bite the bullet to at least assure the banks and creditors that *something* is going to be done, and the toughest financial decisions and writeoffs have been made," said Flavin. At Singer, this was not easy. All of the months of study were in preparation for this surgery. "There were all kinds of rumors that we were talking about selling. But we didn't even have a booklet together to describe the businesses we wanted to sell. It took us the month of January to work up what we called the White Book for any division we were going to sell," he said. "We had no way to describe it to them [potential buyers]. The accounting records were so bad that it wasn't valid data." Finally, however, a deal was struck—although Singer was forced to take a $400 million writeoff.

Once the situation has been analyzed, one of the first steps in any turnaround is to retire outstanding debt. After all, many of the problems in probability stem from the debt burden. And by slicing off debt, more capital is free for reconstruction. Said Flavin, "The first thing was to pay our debt. Make sure you never have the concern of going bankrupt again. We cannot risk that. That is our primary aim. Run the business to make sure to minimize the debt." One way to get rid of debt is to sell off some subsidiary businesses, even at "fire sale" prices. "The [purpose of] the writeoff," Flavin said, "was to simply stop the blood from flowing. Right off, just do that— obviously, by selling businesses . . . which we eventually did, thank God, or we would have gone bankrupt." This is not an unusual strategy, even in a company that is not threatened immediately by bankruptcy. When Douglas D. Danforth became the chief executive at Westinghouse Electric Corporation, he began a typical series of writeoffs designed not to save the company, but to spruce up profits: he sold pieces of Westinghouse Learning Corporation, a catch-all of educational businesses, and sought buyers for the two remaining pieces, Ideal School Supply Company and Linguaphone Institute Ltd., as well as Longines watches, which was losing money, and an office furniture unit.

Woe to the chief executive who fails to bite the bullet immediately. For example, Frank V. Cahouet, the outsider hired by Midland from Security Pacific Corporation to take over as chairman of the Crocker National Bank of California, was aware of signs of trouble. But instead of cutting the business—and losses—he began making loans to the housing industry to increase the bank's assets. The loans doubled the book value of the bank; but many of these loans, which went to finance expensive condominiums and townhouses in Southern California, were defaulted on. Crocker was forced to repossess many of the units and then offer them for sale through long-term loans. Then, as the red ink rose, the management of Crocker was forced to consider raising more cash by selling its dazzling buildings in Los Angeles and San Francisco. Lacking a clear, decisive turnaround strategy can be slow torture indeed.

A divestiture strategy can be particularly excruciating at a company built through acquisition. That was the case at Bangor Punta, where former real estate man Nicolas Salgo had taken some tax-loss carryforwards from an expropriated Cuban sugar operation and built a conglomerate. However, by the early 1970s, the company was beginning to wobble a bit. That was when David Wallace, a former executive at United Brands Company, began to take control. "At that point," said Wallace, "the company was like a rose that had just bloomed; we had acquired all these things and we could see the petals dropping off here and there." The problem: Salgo remained as chairman, and the company was still smitten by the glory of rapid acquisition. "What I was advocating flew in the face of the policies of the company up to that point," said Wallace. "I was making so much noise about it that the board became concerned. They had not really focused on it and I think the institutional investors were doubtful. You must remember that many of these [conglomerate] promoters, so called, were being enthusiastically supported by leading bankers in the United States in the sixties.

"The trouble with the conglomerates was that they were like the Emperor's new clothes. There were all sorts of basic rules of operation being ignored. People were afraid to say this was wrong. They felt they were quarreling with success and felt that they were nineteenth-century managers, not up to the standards of the modern manager. People were afraid to say something, like 'do you really have enough coverage on your interest?' Because that would elicit the response, 'My God, this guy is living in the age of Gladstone.' "

As we saw in the chapter on takeovers, Wallace did not think the conglomerate strategy was worthless, he just thought it needed tremendous management skills to keep it operating in synch. This was not a dramatic turnaround under crisis conditions, but rather a long, slow slog through a variety of businesses in a variety of industries. Salgo remained on the board, but, said Wallace, "he grew more and more alienated. He thought that his work and policies were being undone by a person he thought of as negative.

TURNAROUND STRATEGIES

It was an honest difference of opinion. The problem was, his philosophy about what was needed for the company was just not going to work." To continue his program, Wallace turned to the board, where the battle over the direction the company would take continued. Finally, in 1973, Wallace decided to quit. Instead, some of the lenders talked Salgo into retiring. "It was really a question of the outside directors standing up and being counted, as far as the philosophy of the corporation was concerned," said Wallace.

Just Give Me Money

"Money," goes the lyric of a popular song, "just give me money." Indeed, that is the cry of the turnaround artist. "To me, management liberation is spelled C-A-S-H," said Robert Wilson, a turnaround artist at both Memorex Corporation and Collins Radio. "In early 1974, Memorex had barely enough cash to keep its doors open. Every aspect of cash management was pursued on an urgent basis, and every employee was encouraged to participate. Programs included such simple items as turning off lights, as well as major efforts on such complex matters as lease-base management."[3]

Although necessary, cash control alone is rarely sufficient to affect a turnaround. Instead, it is the sharp change in management and employee attitudes toward waste and productive growth that is the key. By emphasizing cash control, even by turning off lights, a turnaround artist can begin to alter the corporate culture. That is what Danforth tried to do at Westinghouse. First, he decentralized the control of Westinghouse subsidiaries. Then, he created task-force rescues of ailing divisions. New management was brought in, factories were upgraded, product lines were revamped, and distribution channels were strengthened. "We will aim for a leaner operation," was the way a deputy of Danforth's summarized the turnaround efforts.[4]

All of these decisions are interdependent. Consider some of the strategic steps forced upon Catacosinos, the turnaround artist at Digital Data Systems, a manufacturer of computer terminals, who accepted the chairmanship of Lilco. First, he drastically reduced operating expenses an estimated $734 million in the first year by chopping the company's work force by nearly 20 percent—about a thousand people. Then he moved decisively to gain control of the operating policies of Lilco by dismissing four of the utility's senior executives. "I like to be in control of things," he said. "And I need to know that on important issues I've been involved."[5] He stopped paying dividends on the company's common stock—unprecedented for a utility. He then appealed to the federal government to make his bonds tax exempt, in order to raise the financing for an additional $100 million to keep the company from running out of cash. The pattern should be familiar by now: huge cuts, cash control, and vital personnel decisions are all bundled together in achieving a turnaround. These cannot be single or isolated decisions.

Reconstruction

Once the turnaround manager has generated cash and begun to alter the corporate culture, he has to begin rebuilding the operational foundation of the company. That usually means revitalizing sales. First, and most important, established customers must be reassured—"resold" on the company's products. These customers are going to want assurances that the company will survive, or whether they should seek some other supplier. (Recall what Flavin of Singer had said: "Some [customers] thought we were out of business.")

Lockheed's Roy Anderson agrees. "My God, every airline or every customer in the business would call up and say 'What's going on? You going to make it?' " Anderson responded by compiling a forecast of Lockheed's viability, which he showed to important customers every three months. "It was very precise, and we would take them through it product line by product line. We'd say, 'Okay, three months from now, we'll come back and tell you how we're doing.' " Finally, bolstered by federal loan guarantees, Lockheed won back its credibility with the sale of some Hercules C130 aircraft to the federal government, which in turn led Pan American Airways to agree to order new planes from the company. The Pan Am decision was a signal to the rest of the industry. "When an airline buys an airplane, a new model, they are actually marrying you for fifteen years," said Anderson. "That's how long the airplane is going to last. They have to make sure that the airplane is going to be supported—and we have established enough credibility on the circuit so they believed us." It was a long and exhausting road. "God," said Anderson, "I never want to go through that again."

Sales are not the only yardstick to watch in a turnaround. Inventory turnover must be increased and accounts receivables must be reduced. These two measures indicate that unsold products are not just being stocked in warehouses, and that the company is not shipping goods to customers who are never going to pay. Finally, turnaround artists have to try to dodge the bullet of short-term notes and bank loans by shifting into some form of long-term debt, because short-term debt can bury a company in interest payments. Said Anderson, "Before, we were socking every single bit of cash flow into reducing bank loans." Between 1974 and 1978, Lockheed reduced its obligations to banks from $920 to $300 million. After these drastic reductions, Anderson concluded, "When we started to get out of the hole, and when we could see that we were, then we started to think, okay, now we have set the stage for the long range. We could see that we would have the funds available that we didn't have before."

But most crucial is the difficult process of developing a viable strategy for the future. Again, let us turn to Flavin's description of his turnaround of Singer. Remember, Flavin had studied the situation, sold off some divisions, and stopped the red ink. What should come next? "We started in January to develop a strategy," he said. "We took one of those White Books, which was nothing but a summary of what we owned, and we asked the question: Do we want to be in this business or not? Then we tried to decide what our strengths were. That makes sense because we were an amalgam of things. . . . I had to call it a strategy although it was really a plan—the first step in a strategy. Profits alone aren't the answer.

"Let me give you an example: housing. It was a very profitable business for us. We were the only major industrial company whose housing business was really making money. It's profitable, it's big, and it's about a quarter of a billion dollars in revenue. You say, gee, that's not bad compared to some of the other stuff I've got. But here's a good example of strategizing. As we dug into it, we came to the conclusion that we could not make money long term. So we sold it."

Flavin's logic is illuminating. He discovered that housing was locally based and entrepreneurial. "We had five entities in housing," he said. "One was operated by the Mitchell boys in Alabama. We had bought their business in the early 1970s, when it was a hot thing. But as you looked at it, we really bought a couple of people who knew Mobile and Birmingham well. They knew how to buy land, they knew who was who in each city, what were the likely movements of the city, they knew bankers, they knew everybody. And that's what the housing business is. The building is nothing. It's the purchase of the land at the right time, the right atmosphere, zoning laws. A local decision process."

"Therefore," he continued, "when you looked at our success, we were doing very well because of those people. We had them all under contract through 1977, maybe a few to the spring of 1978. But how do you hold someone under contract? We were going to lose them. They never said that, but you knew it. Why should they stay? They can walk next door and start again. And the day after they left you'd be bankrupt. I don't mean that they would cheat or anything—we'd have the business—but who's going to run it now? I think it was a very smart decision to sell."

After the Shouting

The career of a turnaround artist is a specialized one. Ironically, after all of the necessary measures are taken to save a dying company, the turnaround artist often leaves. One reason for this, says Sigler of Champion International, is that "no one likes to work for a slasher. No one likes to work for somebody who has this macho need to show he is tough, [so] I fired this guy." He added, "Usually, after a turnaround, when it comes to rebuilding a company, you have to find someone else." As a result, the turnaround hero is usually replaced by a person who is less a shock-troop battle commander and more a builder or maintainer. If, like Flavin, Wallace, Sigler, or Anderson, they remain at the helm, the new stage requires new skills. They must now concentrate on continuing to improve productivity, boosting sales, and maintaining a sound financial base, and perhaps look to acquisitions or new ventures. After Douglas D. Danforth reorganized Westinghouse, he launched his own acquisition drive, which included Teleprompter Incorporated, a cable television system, and Unimation Incorporated, a major robot manufacturer. Danforth also tried to build from within by boosting productivity. He improved productivity in the defense group by 10 percent, for example. When Sigler was named chairman at Champion, he concentrated on modernizing its paper business after the turnaround had been negotiated. "We have probably invested more in large, modern pulp and paper mills than anybody. . . . Probably because I came out of the paper business. You play the cards you've got. We had a very strong white paper business, a strong market position. . . . So we threw all the money we had into that."

Anderson's experience at Lockheed offers a good view of the kind of tight strategy required to turn a potential turnaround into a success story. "When we started to get out of the hole and when we could see where we were, we started to think, okay, now we have to set the stage for the long run. We could see what we would have in funds available that we didn't have before when we were socking every bit of cash flow into reducing bank loans. . . . In the fall of 1977 or so, we said, let's look at where we think we'll be in 1985. So we sent each of our operating divisions back to present their own plan—cash flow, balance sheet, everything. . . . Now, during the crisis, a lot of divisions did set their own plans. At the corporate level, it was really never pulled together and analyzed.

"We also said, make the forecast, then add on incrementally what you'd like to do if you had the money. They've done that and it's come back with varying results. Some of the divisions really took the bit between their teeth and ran with it. Others played it safe; they didn't want to extend themselves. But what we've done is put it together on a corporate basis, and that's where the fun starts. We can see now what the divisions think they can do. We can see now from that kind of plan what kind of funds we're going to have. Then we can start to prioritize those added things and see if they make anything worthwhile. But then, more importantly, we'll have a picture of the company as we'll think it'll look in 1985. Then it's up to me and the president and so forth to say, okay, here's the position we want. It's up to us to examine all the strategies."

Finally, one should never confuse the first steps to ensuring survival with an actual turnaround. In May 1984, Continental Illinois National Bank, one of the largest money-center banks in the United States, all but collapsed. Rumors, together with immense losses from disastrous oil and gas drilling loans, spawned a loss of international confidence, the worst of any large bank since the 1930s. A run on bank deposits began. The federal government had to step in to save the day—through a massive loan—in the attempt to prevent a domino effect among other banks, large and small.

On closer look, it turns out that the government was actually rescuing a failing turnaround effort. Continental had lost a billion dollars in the previous year in the collapse of tiny Penn Square Bank in Oklahoma City, forcing the bank to put another $200 million into a loan-loss reserve. Then, in July 1982, more bad news: Nucorp Energy Corporation filed for Chapter 11 bankruptcy. It owed Continental $150 million. Several other customers then took a nose dive, including Braniff Airways Corporation, and like a number of other major banks, Continental Illinois suffered large and continuing losses in overseas loans, particularly in Latin America. At the same time, there was chaos at the bank itself: loan officers fired or resigned, the total mismanagement in the highest executive suites, and hollow-sounding public statements made by the same leadership that had led the bank to disaster in the first place. And there were unanswered questions, particularly concerning the bank's overseas involvement. Of course, the bank put up a brave front, but creditors and depositors, particularly the enormous money market funds, grew nervous. A rumor, to be discounted in an atmosphere of confidence, triggered a run on the bank, draining it of billions of dollars in a matter of days.

Thus, the rescue. By committing billions of dollars, the federal government guaranteed all creditor and depositor obligations. The Federal Reserve agreed to meet "any extraordinary liquidity requirements." Banks, cajoled by the Federal Deposit Insurance Corporation (FDIC), agreed to extend a $4 billion line of credit for thirty days. As the crisis passed, the government could boast that it had saved the bank without resorting to the use of Treasury Department funds. But was this a turnaround? Hardly. The first turnaround attempt, which was internal, had failed. The second, spearheaded by the federal government, was barely a beginning. The short-term problem—survival—was eased, *but for a truly successful turnaround to occur, the company recovery must be self-sustaining.* Since the bailout, a new management team was installed that has been slowly climbing back toward viability.

The Turnaround Artist

Who are these flamboyant figures, turnaround artists? Research indicates that many are extremely hard-driving managers and are often loners who make decisions on their own. No surprise there. As we have seen, the turnaround artist has to fire executives, lay off workers, and sell or close divisions, regardless of the personal grief that results, the careers that are ruined, or the reputations that are swept away. The new executives take control of everything: costs, staffing, sales, cash flow. Like a captain on a sinking ship, they must be ruthless, even dictatorial. Collegiality has almost no role in the turnaround. In the first months of the crisis, they order more and more baggage overboard—cut this, slash that, get rid of the wasteful and the wasting—with no questions, no hesitation. As William S. Anderson, the new chief executive at NCR Corporation, said when he first came aboard, "Until we see a return to profitability, something akin to martial law will be in effect."[6] Said another turnaround artist, "I've been fired a bunch of times and I've fired others a bunch of times. You got to learn to roll with the punches."

Most chief executives involved in a turnaround exert a constant, intense pressure on their employees. "I bust asses," one said to me. "I force the men to sweat blood," said another. Most admit that they use fear to motivate their managers and workers to exceed past performances. They are team builders, and they demand absolute team loyalty. While some turnaround artists say they emphasize the opportunity for improvement, rather than the threat of being summarily fired, all agree that the successful turnaround artists drive no one as hard as they drive themselves. They're tough as nails.

In many ways, the personalities of the raider and the turnaround artist are similar. Take, for instance, Samuel J. Heyman, who wrestled the floundering GAF Corporation from chief executive Jesse Werner, and turned it around before launching an unsuccessful attempt to take over Union Carbide, then reeling from the Bhopal, India, tragedy. In business, Heyman is widely viewed as extraordinarily tough and tenacious. But after talking to friends, enemies, relatives, and colleagues, I discovered that Heyman has been relentless in virtually everything he does, whether tennis, art collecting, investing, his years as an assistant U.S. district attorney (where he claims to have never lost a single jury trial), or as a ferocious litigator for the Justice Department. It even carried over into his romantic life. When he first met his wife-to-be, she was engaged to someone else; the other guy never had a chance. "He kept calling me and kept having friends call me," Ronnie Heyman said. "He left no method of pursuit unturned. That's the way he approaches everything."[7]

How did that drive work at GAF? Well, after seizing control of the company—a war that raged for over a year—he laid off seven hundred people, slashed expenses 23 percent, and moved the headquarters from

Manhattan to less expensive Wayne, New Jersey. Despite having no experience in the building materials or chemical industries, Heyman says that the turnaround came because of his own strategic moves. Others disagree, arguing that Heyman was lucky enough to get in at GAF when the building materials business was taking off. According to ousted chairman Jesse Werner, "The so-called turnaround at GAF was the result of all the work that went into the company over thirty years and because of improvement recently in building materials."[8] No matter; turnaround artists like Heyman would probably agree that it is better to be lucky than good.

Case One: George Romney and American Motors Company

When George Romney was made president of newly created American Motors Company in the late 1950s, the smallest of the major American car companies was perilously close to bankruptcy. To keep the company afloat, Romney initiated "Campaign Survival." For three years, Romney assiduously sold off nonautomotive assets, cut overhead, reduced all executive salaries, shut down plants that were either grossly inefficient or operating below capacity, moved the production of spare parts to other plants, and discontinued almost all low-volume products. Despite these measures, AMC remained in danger and losses mounted. So Romney, good-looking and charismatic (he later became governor of Michigan and a presidential candidate), put himself on the line, launching himself across the country to preach the gospel to trade groups, analysts, and consumers about his new small car, the Rambler, as just what the American public needed in a recession, not the "gas-guzzling dinosaurs of the Big Three automakers."

Romney succeeded in putting AMC on its feet. His strategy was simple: cut, consolidate, and promote. By shutting down plants, discontinuing failing product lines, and slashing costs and salaries, he got the break-even point down low enough so that even modest sales increases could keep the company in business. In essence, he kept the company together long enough so that his personal promotion and marketing effort could be heard.

TURNAROUND STRATEGIES

Case Two: Lee Iacocca and Chrysler Corporation

Romney's turnaround at AMC foreshadows the lineaments of a more current, more famous, turnaround—that of Lee Iacocca and Chrysler Corporation. Romney's strategy of cut, consolidate, and promote is very similar to the strategies that Iacocca installed at Chrysler when he took the helm in 1979. Like AMC, Chrysler was failing badly, battered by recession, imports, and competitive pressures, loaded down with inefficient facilities, and stuck with a reputation for making boring, shoddy cars. No one can tell the tale of Chrysler's turnaround as well as Iacocca, who, like Romney, is a famous and skillful self-promoter. So let us let him describe the turnaround:

"When I came to Chrysler in 1979, the Michigan State Fairgrounds were jammed with thousands of unsold, unwanted, rusting Chryslers, Dodges, and Plymouths. Foreign operations were leaching the lifeblood out of the company. And worst of all, cars were coming off the assembly line with loose doors, chipped paint, and crooked moldings. . . .

"Chrysler was faced with a choice. The company could go under—the suggestion of not a few; or efforts could be made to save the company . . . Chrysler took some basic steps to turn the situation around.

"First, the company reduced salaried expenses dramatically, literally half of the work force from about 160,000 to about 80,000. And those 80,000 are now producing a broader range of cars and trucks than they ever did before. That is the simple definition of productivity—more product, more volume, half the people. Part of the medicine was white-collar. The white-collar work force was cut in half; from 40,000 people to 21,000. Both union and nonunion workers made wage and benefit sacrifices, saving $1.2 billion.

"Second, the company reduced fixed costs by about $2 billion on an annual basis. Chrysler closed or consolidated twenty obsolete and outmoded plants. More important, the company modernized the remaining plants to make them among the most efficient and productive in the industry. This was done well before Ford and GM got rolling. Walk down the aisle of a Chrysler plant today and you will see state-of-the-art robots and welders, computer-controlled engine and power train test stands, just-in-time inventory feeders, hospital-clean uniprime paint shops, and fully manned quality operations—all of which are the equal of anything in the world, including Japan.

"Third, Chrysler simplified operations by reducing the number of different parts in its manufacturing system by one-third—from 75,000 items down to 40,000. And in the process, the company shook $1 billion out of inventory.

"Fourth, Chrysler launched an all-out, deadly serious program to improve the quality of both its finished products and the components that go into them. The company worked meticulously both internally and with its suppliers, using the latest methods of preventive surveillance and statistical controls.

"Fifth, Chrysler restructured its balance sheet. The company retired its U.S. bank debt by converting $1.3 billion into preferred stock and acquired some financial breathing room. The company also changed the preferred into common, which further strengthened Chrysler's capital base."

Iacocca did launch a successful sale of common stock—at the time, the second largest in the history of the New York Stock Exchange—to pay off the obligations to the holders of the preferred stock.

Iacocca continues: "Sixth, and ultimately most important, management insured that Chrysler will be a potent force in the years to come by embarking on a five-year, $6.6 billion product program—the most ambitious in its entire history.

"The results of these striking steps are a matter of public record. Chrysler is now different than it was three years ago: half the size, but twice the company.

"Chrysler cut its break-even point to *half* the level of three years ago. It used to be 2.4 million units, now it's under 1.2 million. (This is the reason for three profitable quarters in 1982, why momentum held despite the costly Canadian strike in the fourth quarter . . .) Management will never allow this company to balloon up again, no matter how much the economy improves, no matter how successful business becomes.

"The company accumulated $1 billion in cash in 1982 in the face of a terrible year in the automotive industry. (This was done by selling off the tank business, tightening bookkeeping, and employing tough management—tough cash controls, tough inventory cuts, tough production coordination. The cash cushion gives the comfort of making normal business decisions in a normal way—especially when the economy still sputters like a wet fuse.)"[9]

Iacocca was tough and direct in his turnaround strategy at Chrysler. But while his six steps were critical, his own charismatic leadership also played an important role. Iacocca inspired both white- and blue-collar employees not only to excel, but to make the kind of superhuman efforts that have gone a long way toward saving the company from bankruptcy.

With that charisma comes a heavy dose of ego. It is very revealing that Iacocca minimizes the importance of perhaps the most important aspect of the Chrysler turnaround—namely, the government bailout, the Congressional guarantee of $3.5 billion in Chrysler loans. In fact, in some speeches and interviews, he has completely ignored the role the guarantees played. Iacocca's unwillingness to acknowledge the role of others is typical of turnaround artists—part and parcel of the tremendous ego that drives the turnaround. But if Iacocca was ruthless with employees, creditors, suppliers, and even Congress, he was also unsparing on himself. That too is typical of his breed.

Case Three: Andrew Sigler and Champion International Corporation

When Andrew Sigler, a self-described "forty-two-year-old squirt," was promoted from the paper products division to the helm of Champion International in 1974, the company was in dire shape. The company was sprawled out over three divisions: paper, building products, and furniture. But it also owned a carpet company and had mountains of building products rotting away in warehouses. And it was losing money fast. "It was a hell of a time to arrive," said Sigler.

Sigler knew he had to move quickly. Fortunately, because he already had been working for Champion, he had some idea of its problems. Still, there was an essential process of assessment taking place prior to moving to freeze wages of salaried employees, cutting the staff through attrition, and reducing costs over the long term. "I think when you're in trouble, you've got to analyze why the hell you're in trouble. If you are noncompetitive in industry, you've got to do some fairly drastic things. So we did the people things. We went from a company that was, say, 11,000 employees, down to X. . . . We cut the dividend. There's something the goddamned analysts and everybody will tell you you can't do. Anybody who, in effect, borrows money to pay a dividend or lays off people or whatever, and then pays a dividend, is a goddamned fool."

95

From there, Sigler moved quickly to restructure the company by getting rid of nonessential businesses. "You rebuild the company by policy," he said. "No more spending, no more this, no more that. We did all those things and pulled the situation down ... and I would say within four or five months we laid out for the board all of the businesses we were going to get out of, and we proceeded within the next year and a half to get out of most of them and eventually all of them." To actually sell the businesses, he hired "a regular businessman" and told him "to sell the businesses when you can sell them and get what you can for them." Said Sigler, "Once we identified the companies to be divested, I gave that to somebody to do. I really had very little involvement, only to the extent of working with him on what the guidelines were and then the deals themselves." Testing the market value of the companies was easy, he said. "All you have to do is make three calls. The next day, you'll have twenty-six people calling you." In the midst of a crisis, all turnaround managers hope to sell the weakest divisions first, holding on to the strongest divisions for as long as possible. Unfortunately, it more often works just the opposite—selling the strong first and abandoning the weak later. In Champion's case, the strong Drexel division had the most appeal and sold first.

Despite that part of his strategy going awry, Sigler adhered to what he called "hardnosed judgments." He said, "When you sell, when you get the paper in return, write it off right then, because eventually, you're going to write it off. You've got to make hardnosed judgments, you really do. . . . The purpose is to get out, to take your writeoffs, put them into discontinued businesses, and get the hell out—and that's what we did." What did Sigler do with the money? First, he decided to modernize the white paper products division. "To be in a basic industry, you've got to be a low-cost producer. . . . In our business, you work off large, modern facilities. So we did that, and held back on the plywood and lumber business." Then, as recovery beckoned, he bought Hoerner Waldorf, not only because it broadened the company's corrugated paperboard product line, but because Hoerner owned three million acres of timber. By the end of the turnaround, Sigler could say "We are not a paper company. We are a forest-products company."

In many ways, Sigler differed from the stereotypical turnaround artist described earlier. First, he was an employee who took the helm, not an outsider. Second, after the turnaround was completed successfully, he remained at Champion. Why? Because, said Sigler, "Boise [Cascade Corporation] and Champion are probably the two best-run companies in the forest-products industry." All of which reveals a final psychological point on which Sigler is similar to nearly every turnaround artist I interviewed: overwhelming self-confidence in his own decision-making ability.

Ten years after Sigler became CEO, Champion acquired St. Regis Corporation. "It put us where we've been trying to get since 1974," said Sigler recently. "We've now got tremendous strength across a spectrum of white paper grades, and through divestitures we've lessened our exposure to the cyclical building products business. We also sold most of our packaging operations to Stone Container. We never did learn to run that business well, but we've kept the timberlands. Now our challenge is to increase profitability. We're out to be the low-cost producer with quality and service second to none."

Case Four: John McKinney, William May, and the Manville Corporation

In 1982, the Manville Corporation (formerly Johns Manville), a manufacturer of asbestos products, was staggering under a firestorm of litigation brought by thousands of people—over sixteen thousand at last count—who, over a period of many years, were injured or had relatives who were killed by inhaling dangerous, fibrous asbestos. Not only were the suits consuming more and more of chief executive John A. McKinney and his staff's time, but the financial toll was threatening to swamp the company. Ironically, Manville was a viable company operationally—the 181st-largest company in America, with assets in excess of $2 billion—although the tidy profit the company was making could be wiped out by the extraordinary costs of settling the $2 billion or so in asbestos suits.

Here was, to say the least, an unusual turnaround situation—and one that raised extraordinary legal and moral questions. After all, evidence had been gathered and presented that executives at Manville had known of the deadly effects of asbestos for over forty years. McKinney, in turn, sent me Manville's statement, published in the *Harvard Business Review*, insisting that Manville not only did *not* cover up the asbestos danger to workers, but the company actually sponsored and assisted in several research studies dating back to the 1920s and 1930s. Said Manville, "Unfortunately, people

97

made mistakes in the past that injured some employees. It appears that some managers at the plant level did not follow all the safety policies that corporate guidelines required. Some workers were not notified about their exposure in a timely manner."[10]

What was more important: the company, or the victims? That is how the public debate was couched, although in actuality it was a far more complex problem than that. "We have a tremendous number of people who have been harmed and who should be compensated, who aren't being compensated," admitted McKinney, a former patent attorney who had served as the company's chief legal officer before taking over as chief executive. "The company had the unhappy situation of directing the strategy in a trial where we beat the widow and five children. She walks out of court with nothing, simply because we couldn't agree that we were at fault. If they were going to say we were at fault, we had to deny that. But if we could participate and contribute to a no-fault scheme to adequately compensate the victims, we'd say, sure, let's do it."

McKinney had the requisite personality for the problem: straightforward, blunt, candid. "The board, when selecting me as president, knew that they would get a straight story, good or bad. They would know the warts, the problems, they would know what was going on. That's the way I'd always been with them. It's not something I try to do, I'm not trying to be candid, it's just my way." It soon became clear that the suits were not a nightmare that would simply go away in the clear light of day. What then? Well, new bankruptcy provisions passed by Congress had made it easier to gain time necessary to reorganize a company—or to go out of business. But that was a radical move that was bound to create intense controversy. Was it right? Was it legal? McKinney put the question to the three outside directors.

William May, then CEO of American Can Company, had been an outside director of Manville since 1963. In the summer of 1982, he was called in to review a series of statistics accumulated by management in order to decide whether to seek bankruptcy. "We hired some excellent epidemiologists who determined what was the future cohort of those suffering from these asbestos diseases," May said. "We took the most optimistic projection, then hired other experts in psychology and human relations to develop data on the propensity to sue." Although the propensity differed depending on the form of disease, the experts did bring back a gloomy picture for Manville: even taking the most optimistic projection, Manville would be beset by a large number of suits right up to the year 2009 or so, when "we felt that most individuals who had been exposed to the asbestos would have had a manifestation." Then they tried to estimate the cost of settlement. Said May, "Under FASB 5 [Federal Accounting Standards Board Rule 5] if you have knowledge of an obligation, you are held by the accounting fraternity to set up reserves to cover it. The exposure was such that it would wipe out the company. Prior to these studies, the company had no way of knowing the degree . . . [or] the extent of this exposure, so they refused to set up a reserve. So for the years 1979, 1980, and 1981, it took a qualified opinion from the auditors with respect to their annual report. Now, with the data in our hand, knowing the *minimum* exposure, we had no real choice but to set up a reserve and essentially wipe out the corporation. We could have toughed it out for a little while, but eventually we would have been wiped out."

The bankruptcy plan was not only controversial, but complex. Manville statutorily had to submit a plan for reorganization—how, in other words, it planned to pay off its creditors, including the claimants—in 120 days, although extensions are often granted and it usually takes two to three years. Said John McKinney, "[It] sounds like a long time, but for a company this complex it's not. Because you have to then sell it to both creditors and equity holders." The court appointed a committee to represent the creditors and, a most unusual move, another committee to represent the asbestos victims. According to William May, "You had a string of people exposed to the asbestos—including maybe one out of twenty wives of workers, who do not get the workers' compensation of their husbands." Generally, downstream victims—those who suffered from asbestos not from the use of the material in a work situation, but later—had a variety of statutory rights that differed from state to state. In Virginia, lawyers for some shipyard workers brought a claim against Manville under admiralty law, where there is no statute of limitations, as opposed to state common law, where there is. "What you're looking at here are injuries that don't show up for twenty or thirty years," May said. Finally, the question was which insurers would be liable for damages: those who covered Manville when the asbestos was sold, or those who were covering Manville when the claims were made. In the meantime, the company was not able to collect on its insurance.

Nonetheless, filing for bankruptcy did freeze this wild multiplicity of claims and bring them all under the purview of one court, the bankruptcy court. "Manville and its attorneys could even argue that those downstream victims, who haven't yet manifested the disease, could be cut out completely if the company didn't take this action," said May. "Manville took the step in part to protect themselves and, in part, to protect the claimants."

That novel turnaround strategy had wide-ranging effects. Over the next few years, other financially troubled firms, from Eastern Airlines to a variety of steel companies, as well as other asbestos and mineral producers, threatened bankruptcy to turn back creditors, unions, bankers, lawsuits, or the federal government. Frank Lorenzo of Texas Air Corporation actually used bankruptcy to fight the unions at Continental Airlines Corporation, in his acquisition, and as a result was able to turn that carrier around and, ironically, swoop in on Eastern in 1986 and take *it* over. Finally, the A. H. Robins Company, collapsing under the weight of suits stemming from its dangerously defective Dalkon Shield Intrauterine Device, also took refuge in Chapter 11. Manville's precedent-shattering turnaround strategy (although escape might be a better description) set the scene for a reevaluation of the bankruptcy laws. In June 1984, for example, the U.S. Supreme Court ruled that corporations could not use bankruptcy as a means to break their existing contracts with unions. That may have been just the beginning.

Case Five: Roy Ash and AM International Inc.

Efforts to save most companies fail. Although I have concentrated on those chief executives who have pulled off successful turnarounds, most executives react too slowly and do too little in the face of a crisis. Some fail to use the five strategies described earlier. Others simply make a bad situation worse.

Let us turn to the fascinating disaster of Roy Ash and AM International. When Roy Ash came to AM (then called Addressograph-Multigraph), he was viewed as a paragon of modern management. A former whiz kid, he had served at Hughes Aircraft Company and Litton under Tex Thornton for many years, before going off to the Nixon cabinet, where he was the first head of the reorganized Office of Management and Budget. When he left OMB, he went looking for other corporate challenges. He found one in Addressograph-Multigraph, a hulking Cleveland-based manufacturer of various electromechanical postal addressers and duplicators which had slowly lost its way. "If we had continued with the strategy in place," said Ash, "it would have been the road to oblivion. It was no longer a competitive one. For the past twenty years, the company had been surviving on momentum. As late as 1962, the official policy of the company was that computers are not here to stay and won't be used by management and out in the marketplace, they won't be competitive with our products. So ignore computers. Nonetheless, the company was working in an area that couldn't ignore computers from either view. In the intervening years, attempts were made to recognize the computer age, but they weren't enough to change the culture, direction, and commitment of the company. It wasn't hard to see that we needed a new strategy that included computers."

And yet the situation looked grim. On Wall Street, the company was dubbed Addressogrief-Multigrief. In a company of twenty thousand employees, only five or so knew anything about computer software. While AM had a visible presence in its markets and a good distribution system, Ash found the marketing strategies similarly antiquated. "We had a culture that was tied to traditional—we used to call them mature—products which weren't tied to new products. We brought in the IBM model; IBM, you'll remember, went from punch cards to electronic data processing by setting up a separate group with its own culture. If you throw new era people in the old culture, they'll get eaten up." Ash began an extensive reorganization of the company, breaking what was one monolithic selling organization into nine divisions, each with its own culture. Symbolically, he changed the name of the company from Addressograph-Multigraph to AM International, and he moved corporate headquarters from Cleveland to Los Angeles, which he considered more conducive to high technology. Like General Motors, or Litton, for that matter, each division was given its own staff, name, and selling organization—"to foster the entrepreneurial spirit," Ash said.

Still, there were problems. "We understood our products," said Ash, "but we didn't understand our markets. If we really want to sell, we have to say to them, 'We understand your business better than you do.' We didn't even know who our customers were. We just offered a product. We even advertised the wrong things. We didn't know why people bought our products. We aimed at the wrong markets, to people who shouldn't be buying our stuff, but should be buying somebody else's. We didn't know any of our markets. We discovered markets under our noses we didn't even know existed. One big market we defaulted to a competitor years ago, and we didn't even remember it. We didn't know who our competition was." Ash admitted he had a tough time convincing the sales staff to change their ways.

While Ash's plans to turn AM from electromechanical duplicators to high-tech office equipment sounded fine, it was a difficult proposition. Despite his talk of generating cash flow from traditional businesses to support new high technology, Ash had to borrow heavily. Debt rose from 34 percent of capital in 1976 to over 55 percent in 1981, and cash plunged from $42 million to $4 million. Much of that capital went toward acquisitions such as Infortext, a maker of terminals for copiers; Jacquard, a maker of word processors; and ECRM, a builder of text-editing machines. Turnover increased, divisions were shut down, losses mounted. Infortext, for example, all but shut down. Perhaps most damaging, Ash alienated people in the company with his exhaustive—and somewhat chilly—analysis of the company's problems. *Fortune* magazine quoted one former AM executive as saying, "Sometimes I wanted to damn near grab Roy by the collar and say, 'There are three alternatives we can take: one, two, or three. Let's do it instead of talking about it.' "[11]

Finally, with the company suffering a $245 million loss in 1981, the AM board met in New York City. Despite a three-hour-long defense of his turnaround at AM, the board reportedly asked Ash to leave. In his place, it appointed Richard Black, who had made a successful turnaround of an auto-parts company called Maremont, to attempt a takeover. But by then, the company had begun a dizzying descent. Black began to unload some of Ash's acquisitions, but then sued AM while still CEO, an almost unheard-of action, in an attempt to get back his investment; he also claimed that the company was in far worse shape than he had been led to believe. Black was replaced by Joe B. Freeman, the chief financial officer, who took it into bankruptcy. Freeman lasted twenty months before he was replaced by Merle H. Banta, another turnaround artist who had saved a far smaller company called the Leisure Group. By the time Banta arrived, the company, now relocated in Chicago, was reeling from the coming and going of executives. Turnover was high, morale disastrously low.

A great deal can be learned from AM International and other unsuccessful turnarounds. For the most part, failed turnarounds result from disastrous strategies, although lack of financial resources and ineffective management can scuttle even the best of turnaround strategies. Giant, stumbling retailers such as W. T. Grant Company or Korvettes Inc. made lots of cuts, shut down lots of stores, and then failed to take the next step: to formulate a clear strategy for future growth. Perhaps the problem in both cases is that neither company had a charismatic chief executive with a ruthless passion for turning the company around. But there is something of a fallacy here:

by definition, an unsuccessful chief executive is one who fails to engineer a turnaround, just as an unsuccessful strategy is one that fails. Hindsight is easy, and if Korvettes had turned itself around, we might be looking at its executives as a good example of turnaround management. In other words, results mean more than style—although there is a general kind of style wielded by successful turnaround artists.

Pessimism is far more pervasive than optimism in any endeavor, and business is no exception. As one chief executive told me, "Nobody believes that it [the turnaround] can be brought about. Each manager writes his resume, makes his head-hunter phone calls, and watches the company bleed to death." Pessimism is easier than optimism—you need not act, after all—and the strategies that flow from such a spirit are often, in retrospect, the easiest, though not the most effective, ways out of difficult situations. It is easy for corporate executives, directors, or owners to see disaster and dissolution as inevitable as death and taxes. A few walk away— from the plant, the office, the corporate suite. Others try to gain more and more tax and credit-line respite; but banks, creditors, and the government are often unwilling to extend the necessary help in the midst of a crisis. Others hunt frantically for merger partners—in effect, trying to get another company to take the mess off their hands.

Mergers sometimes are necessary, but often they come too late in the game. A viable company might be willing to take advantage of the expertise of its employees, and the government often encourages mergers and acquisitions between two failing companies in the same industry to preserve competition, keep employment from dropping, and preserve the tax base of local and state governments. But while a few such forced mergers are spectacularly successful, most are failures. The reasons for those failures are no different than for any other failed turnaround: these companies lack true turnaround strategies, they lack a ruthless turnaround chief executive, and they fail to make the necessarily brutal decisions to slash costs, employees, divisions, product lines, and facilities. As a result, they are unable to save the healthy core of the company. And finally, even if some companies do succeed in the first steps of a turnaround, they often stumble when it comes to formulating a viable rebuilding strategy.

Conclusion

With increasing turbulence in the economy, symptomized by skyrocketing bank failures and company bankruptcies, turnaround strategies have been thrust to center stage. This does not mean, of course, that turnarounds are any more successful today, on average, than they were two decades ago. The failure rate of attempted turnarounds—and the parallel here to the failure rate of new ventures is striking—is fully 90 percent. That said, let me note that tax advantages today provide an incentive for viable companies to take over bankrupt or failing operations in order, among other things, to use their cache of tax-loss carryforwards. This is a real break with the past. Twenty years ago, a turnaround artist was often an operations genius who could disappear into a factory and get it producing efficiently again. Today's takeover artists are financial tinkerers, accountants who work their magic on the balance sheet.

Statistically, all reports indicate that the success rate of operational turnarounds is even worse today than it was a few decades ago. That can be attributed in part to the overall decline in American industry. Nonetheless, those same statistics indicate that financial turnarounds have been improving their success rates over time. I have found these statistical studies a bit misleading because upon closer examination, I discovered that many of these companies have simply written up their assets to inflated heights based on obvious accounting tricks. However, there is some truth there. In the past twenty years or so, there has been an explosion in financial instruments that give turnaround artists a far larger number of arrows in their strategic quiver. The much derided junk bond, for one, has been a highly successful tool with which to reorganize essentially bankrupt companies. Junk bonds enable a turnaround artist to gain some breathing space in order to restructure and recapitalize a company, satisfy its creditors, or search for potential acquirers.

Today, as in the past, successful turnaround strategies focus on installing new management and giving them the freedom to make the painful reductions as quickly as possible. But with the emphasis on financing, much of the human dimension, particularly the necessity to motivate the work force, has been abandoned. Instead, turnaround artists cut and slash personnel, and worry about morale problems later. In an odd twist on corporate mythology, and one that is revealing of our business culture, we now think

TURNAROUND STRATEGIES

of turnaround artists as the same sort of heroes as entrepreneurs and take-over raiders, as sort of latter-day corporate mavericks who can't be contained by the corporate world. On the other hand, we see operations people, line managers, chief executives who can go into a factory and make it tick, as bull-necked conformists in polyester trousers who carry screwdrivers, not pocket computers. That distinction, I think, points as clearly as anything to the decline in American competitiveness and the rise in corporate turn-arounds and failures.

CHAPTER FIVE

FINANCIAL STRATEGIES: THE CEO AS CENTRAL BANKER

The essential ideas in financial plans are really very simple. The problem is in the implementation. —ARJAY MILLER, former president, Ford Motor Company

In 1955, there wasn't a budget [at Chase National Bank]. I really mean that. It was amazing, but I talked to my uncle about it and he said, why did we want a budget. There's no need for it! —DAVID ROCKEFELLER, former CEO, Chase Manhattan Bank

The Yardstick of Success

"I'm the central banker for this company," said one CEO. "I allocate the capital which is *the* scarce resource. And by my decision—good or bad—about which projects to fund and which to kill and how much to give different businesses and different product lines, I determine how well we're going to do overall as a corporation over time. That's the critical role of the chief executive, as I see my job."

Many chief executives I interviewed echoed this statement. Like the fabulously rich man who continues to make money simply as a way of keeping score, so do most corporations find themselves judged strictly by financial yardsticks. Most top managers thus agreed on the critical importance of the corporation's financial strategy and on the role of the chief executive as a central banker of the company. One CEO outlined what he saw as routine financial decisions: "I dole out the cash; I allocate the reserves; I make the investments; I select the level of debt capacity; I plan the corporation's sales of new stock or debt; and I declare the amount of the shareholders' dividend."

These routine financial decisions are not the only ones critical to planning strategy. First, chief executives oversee basic financial portfolio decisions: which businesses should they cultivate; which should they sell off? How much should they invest in research and development? Above all, in this age of merger mania, CEOs have to decide whether to pursue friendly or hostile mergers, what kind of money to spend for target companies, and indeed, what form of financing to use. Likewise, chief executives of companies that had been or were about to be acquired told me that they personally had been the crucial focus of all financial decisions about how much to accept in exchange for being taken over and what form the transaction should take—cash, stock, debt, or other forms of notes, assets, or some mixture of these.

In planning and assessing a company's budget, its financial targets and goals, levels of working capital, level of debt capacity, and timing of its financing, virtually all the chief executives I spoke with stressed how time consuming they found these financial strategy decisions. For many, it was a monthly, weekly, or even daily task. Often, I saw clear evidence of the urgency with which these chief executives viewed their role as financial strategists. For example, during a number of my interviews with these men, we would suddenly be interrupted. A secretary, corporate officer, or assistant would appear and quickly huddle with the CEO, spelling out some financial problem or opportunity, rush in with news about how a takeover or a merger was going, or confer about how well a new stock or debt offering was selling.

Many of the chief executives I interviewed described how an inordinate amount of time each day was spent keeping track of financial conditions, instruments, and markets. Although in theory, many of these tasks were relegated to a chief financial officer, controller, or treasurer, or to a whole cadre of advisors, from underwriters to investment counselors and lenders, many CEOs insisted that they had to keep on top of these concerns personally. "I'm being held accountable financially," said one chief executive. "I'm being measured against a series of financial yardsticks by institutional investors, lenders, and in some cases, by creditors and suppliers and major customers and insurers as never before. With all these financial tests they run on this company and we run on ourselves, it's a wonder we squeeze out enough time to actually make, sell, and deliver our products." For a CEO, the "numbers" are analogous to casualty reports in wartime. They are the CEO's news from the front.

Mixing and Matching Financial Strategies

Marketing experts often speak of assembling a blend of different strategies for different products, a so-called marketing mix. Likewise, effective corporate finance requires a financing mix, an effective blend of financial sources matched to a variety of different uses. To achieve the optimal mix of financing instruments and strategies, a few chief executives I interviewed in financially sophisticated corporations said they had adopted "strategic funds programming," a system of comparing the risks and rewards of various options, using either a computer or a room full of sharp-penciled accountants who map out contingency schedules for employing one financing mix over another, or shifting from one to the other as financial conditions change. Such a program is simply one sign of the times.

A little history is appropriate here. For decades, the vast majority of corporations avoided loading themselves down with debt, strictly limiting their debt capacity—the portion of debt to capital—to one-third or less. Then, in the 1960s, many companies entered a new age, the age of leverage. Corporations piled up the debt, reaching levels of 50 to 70 percent. These were the famous go-go years when the conglomerate first made its appearance on the corporate scene and corporate officers became mesmerized by dramatically increasing their price to earnings multiple, or P/E. (The widely used P/E ratio is simply the relationship between a company's current stock price and its current earnings or profit level.) Hence their value in the red-hot equity markets could increase through a variety of financial strategies.

That age is now dead. Indeed, from 1975 to the early 1980s, many highly leveraged conglomerates suffered from feverishly high interest rates, forcing chief executives to be mindful again of the flaws in a heavily debt-oriented strategy. Across the country, companies simply could not afford the 21 percent prime lending rate and the high cost of bond issues. The result was a wholesale move to reduce debt and interest expenses—cleaning up the balance sheet—by engineering such financial alchemy as debt for equity swaps, in which a company would seek to turn a mountain of debt into stock, often at a price or conversion factor. Unfortunately, that process of slimming down American balance sheets coincided with a general decline in interest rates, creating conditions for a new syndrome: hostile takeovers.

Let us look at one part of this issue: the increasing use of leverage, particularly of junk, or low-grade, bonds, in takeovers. Junk bonds have become very popular: in 1977 only $1 billion were issued as compared to $14 billion in 1984; by 1986 the junk bond market was over $100 billion. Instead of issuing debt so that they can make more products to sell, takeover artists have been peddling debt, usually in the form of these junk bonds, strictly for the purpose of a takeover, or better yet, to extract greenmail payments from their victims. Companies such as T. Boone Pickens's Mesa Petroleum, Irwin L. Jacobs's Minstar, and Saul Steinberg's Reliance Group Holdings, Incorporated made a major part of their earnings from such predatory forays. This is a far different strategy from those of the conglomerates of the 1960s which used debt to buy companies, increasing their P/E ratios, pumping up earnings per share, and keeping the stock aloft. Ironically, many former conglomerates have been restructuring—paring away inefficient units and reducing debt—only to discover that they had become takeover candidates and that, as a defensive measure, they had to gorge themselves on debt once more to keep the wolves away. They are not alone. Even more conservative companies have also been loading up on debt to fight off takeovers. CBS's former chief executive Thomas H. Wyman, for instance, borrowed over $1 billion to buy back 20 percent of CBS stock and hold off Ted Turner.

Such "rationalizations," or "restructurings," also played into the hands of institutional investors who had tended to discount the equity of companies doing business in a variety of industries. "We have all these assets and all these different businesses and products, but the securities analysts on Wall Street won't give us credit for anything other than our one single best-known business," said Joseph Flavin of Singer, a company best known for its sewing machines although it is actually more prominent in aerospace. In fact, in 1986, Flavin spun off the sewing business as a separate company so that it is no longer a part of Singer. "They totally discount the rest of our businesses as if they're worthless—absolute zero," said Flavin. Other chief executives also resented this outside pressure, although many eventually knuckled under and divested themselves of unrecognized or under-performing assets. "I resent it like hell," said one CEO, "that I have to now divest a whole bunch of perfectly good products simply to make this corporation as a whole more understandable to those Wall Street analysts. But I ultimately felt in my last few meetings with the analysts that I had no choice, because institutional investors own 85 percent of our stock. The major buy-and-sell decisions on our stock are based solely on those analysts' narrow-minded perceptions of our assets and earning power as a company. I butted my head up against that wall of analysts for years on that issue before I finally agreed with my board of directors that we had to do something."

It should be clear from these examples that financial strategy is often a delicate balancing act. To put it another way, financial strategies exist in a world of finite capital; they are reactive. Because bonds and stocks—debt and equity—are sold into markets in competition with others, one company has to react to what another is offering, not only to the types of securities offered, but to the total amount of other companies' offerings and timing, and the shifting pattern between different types of securities. Thus, a company has to be concerned not only about its own financial condition and the state of the markets, but about what other companies are offering the community of investors. It is a very complex zero-sum game.

Sudden changes in the environment can offer opportunity as well as risk. A sudden shift in fortunes can open up all sorts of possibilities for financial strategy. When interest rates tumble, as they did in the mid-1980s, chief executive officers suddenly find that they have the flexibility of choosing, say, long-term debt over bank loans or equity. As I said earlier, as a general rule, most chief executives would prefer to finance themselves through bank loans or long-term debt, as opposed to equity sales. The more stock sold and the more the price of the shares is depressed, partic-ularly in a down market, the less money the company can earn on the sale. Even at a high rate of interest, debt over the past few decades has been cheap compared to selling stock. Moreover, chief executives are ex-tremely concerned about their firms' depressed stock prices and the dilution of shareholder values, particularly in an age of takeovers. Raiders find it easy to capitalize on shareholder complaints about depressed stock values. As a result, many chief executives described to me financial strategy that was, in effect, defensive.

There are, as always, reasons for that defensiveness. Shifting financing techniques can be extremely difficult. A company can get locked into certain patterns for years, or even decades—say, through a hammerlock of long-term debt offerings. By the recession of the early 1970s, Lockheed had almost $1 billion in long-term debt, a burden that almost destroyed the company and forced it to seek government loan guarantees. In the atmosphere of tremendous crisis, Lockheed succeeded in whittling down that debt to about $300 million in less than four years, preparing itself for a healthier military contracting market to come. Likewise, AM International saw its debt mushroom when Ash tried to restructure it; that debt load forced Ash out and contributed to large losses and its dizzying decline toward possible bankruptcy.

Why did Lockheed not make changes earlier? Why did Ash let the debt load rise so high? Because after a certain point, they found themselves capable of making only the most marginal of changes; their earlier strategies had increasingly hemmed them in. This may take place even in companies not in a crisis situation. Many chief executives insist on viewing discretionary financial strategy as only the small percentage of financing that is not covered by existing long-term contracts and policies—an obvious case of tunnel vision. They described to me how they were constantly putting projects on the back burner because they did not fit into their financing strategy. As a result, one chief executive said, "When the company hit a bad period, setting priorities among projects really meant eliminating all the low-priority uses of funds. In both the recessions of 1974–77 and 1980–82, my financial strategy was caught in a wringer. In the first recession, we were clogged with inventory. Because we had huge sums of money tied up in inventory we were extremely vulnerable to the continuing downturn in the economy, so we simply could not generate enough cash to regain our financial balance. We learned a painful lesson."

He was not alone. Robert Kinney, the chairman of General Mills Corporation, described how his company was forced to shift its financing strategies during the 1973 and 1974 recession in order to funnel capital to divisions that required it. "Capital is always available," said Kinney. "Back then, we were starting to build a new building; the board had decided we needed more space in our offices in Minneapolis. In April, we voted $10 million, but in June we went back to the board and said cancel the building . . . we need the money for several new lines, for restaurants, for facilities being built for Parker Brothers Company [a subsidiary] in Beverly, [Massachusetts]. In Minneapolis, we were fighting a squeeze, and we canceled and we told other [divisions] to do the same. It worked perfectly. We had all the money we needed to continue to grow, and we went through that time very well. From November to March we got up to $150 million more in working capital."

Other chief executives admitted to me that they did not weather those storms quite as well as General Mills did. Their frustration and confusion led them to view that period as a watershed. Most corporate financial strategies, they say now with hindsight, date from the 1974 Arab oil crisis and the resulting financial constraints put upon the chief executive. "Ever since 1974, we have been forced to have financial contingency plans in place, ready to [be] triggered in case the economy or the industry worsened," said one CEO. "This contingency plan has several important financial strategic components. For example, we now watch their levels of inventories like a hawk, and now most firms in our business operate with a much smaller inventory backup than ever before." Added Peter McColough of Xerox, "Until 1973, very little emphasis was put on the balance sheet. We didn't ignore it, but we only gave it about 5 percent of our attention. We weren't in jeopardy of going bankrupt or anything, but the balance sheet got sloppy. We've had enormous efforts since then on accounts receivables. We realized that while the days outstanding in the United States was pretty good, 35 to 40 days, it was far greater in other countries. An average was 80 days, though it was 180 days in Latin America. So we had a concentrated drive. . . . Europe now has the same as the United States, and that, of course, gives you a lot of cash. Same thing with inventories."

Still, McColough did not believe that a chief executive should get involved in the daily watch over inventories and accounts receivables; even after 1973, he would review, he says, monthly reports. On the other hand, Wallace Rasmussen of Beatrice, a consumer goods company with enormous inventories and receivables, knew to the very dollar the value of cash tied up in inventories and accounts receivables. Rasmussen told me that not only did he check those two figures on a daily basis, he also calculated how much was tied up in nonworking cash. In that way, he claimed to be able to know exactly where to tighten up. "I ask him [Beatrice's credit manager] once a week," said Rasmussen. "You see, one additional day in this company in accounts receivables is $17 million. One additional day in inventory is $15 million. That is $32 million bucks, so you can see why I watch the cash. . . . If the cash is down, compared with last year, I go ask about accounts receivables."

Such a focus on numbers can have a dark side, however, by keeping the chief executive from long-term planning. This is another form of tunnel vision. A glut of short-term data can obscure longer-term trends and convince the chief executive that he or she should be constantly putting out fires in this division or that, instead of stepping back and doing what Roy Ash called "going to the mountain" to get a longer view. Obsessing over operational details is clearly necessary in a turnaround or crisis situation, but in companies with adequate financing and a clean balance sheet, it is a distraction from the CEO's true function. Moreover, it can actually increase costs, because in order to play it safe, many CEOs have turned to keeping a great deal of company cash in short-term instruments, from treasury bills and bankers' acceptances to municipal commercial paper. Short-term instruments give you flexibility, but at a high price.

"Instead of locking in long-term financing when they could best do it, many chief executives have increasingly tied themselves to short-term credit arrangements," said Andrew Sigler of Champion International. "Most CEOs do this simply for the privilege of being able to stay very short term in case of financial crisis or downturn. One key consequence has been that because so many corporations have been shifting their financing to the short term, together, like a herd, they have consistently pushed up the cost of short-term debt, or kept it higher than it otherwise would have been."

We have already stressed how, with equity prices depressed after the go-go years, chief executives were reluctant to sell stock to raise capital and, as a result, tended to load up with debt instead. This seriously eroded the capital base of many companies and shortened maturities. Such a short-term perspective creates its own self-fulfilling crises. Short-term financing fosters an atmosphere of tension—chief executives continually have to make financial decisions about either rolling over their debt or shifting it into a new financial instrument—and drastically narrows the range of options. Said one CEO, "Sometimes, my financial options are simple: do we increase our bank line of credit, increase the letters of credit, or replace them with one short-term note?" Chief executives who have talked themselves into this short-term mentality often suffer from tunnel vision. Instead of taking advantage of the wide and ever-increasing menu of financial options, their choices quickly contract to just a few financing techniques.

The debt crisis for many companies peaked in 1979 and 1980, when the banks' prime interest rates topped 20 percent and forced many companies out of the debt markets. Some went out of business, others were forced to severely tighten their belts. That is a subject that John deButts expanded upon one day in 1978, when he was still chairman of AT & T. Inflation was still running hot, the equity markets were depressed, and AT & T was still a massive, undivested company. He was describing how he maintained

a coordinating role over the Bell System operating companies which, for the most part, managed their own financial strategy and planning, although, he said, he directed the units to raise or lower their goals based on larger macroeconomic targets that he thought appropriate for the company at large. "I'm trying to get the debt ratio down to 40 percent to 45 percent," deButts said. "We were up over 50 percent [debt to equity] and we had to [lower it] because we were in a period when the market was below book and I couldn't go to the equity markets, I had to go to the debt markets." DeButts shook his head. Anyway, he said, he got the debt to equity down again. "We are back to 45 percent this year and we are now generating almost 80 percent of our capital needs internally. In 1970 and 1971, it was about 40 percent. There was one year—1969 I think—when the Bell System raised 25 percent of all capital raised by industry. I never want to get into that position again."

In light of this continuing debt problem, it is significant that the banking industry is also in the throes of great change. Companies have to be aware of both their reliance on bank lending and the precarious nature of the banking system, which has been shaken by bad loans to oil producers, Third World countries, and souring real estate deals, and which, at the same time, is suffering through changes that fit under the rubric of deregulation. In the last few years, we have seen one major money center bank after another battered by massive loan losses: Continental Illinois, Seafirst Corporation of Seattle, Chase Manhattan, First National Bank of Chicago, BankAmerica, and Crocker, with others desperately trying to smother bad loans that were ticking away like bombs in their portfolios. Couple that situation with increased debt dependence by U.S. companies, shorter maturity schedules, declining productive capacity, and the leveraging of firms in takeover attempts or in takeover defenses—and you have a troubling situation.

Sources and Uses of Finance

Financial strategies can be broken up in two ways: by optimizing the choice of sources of funds for a company over time, and by selecting the optimal uses for those funds. Some chief executives see a division between these realms of strategic experience. Some look only at sources of capital or only at the uses for capital, keeping them in isolated boxes. Which role they take depends on a variety of factors. If a company is in seriously bad financial shape, the chief executive will undoubtedly pour much energy into securing capital as cheaply as possible. Alternatively, if a company is throwing off a lot of cash, the chief executive is going to spend time finding ways to invest it.

Ideally, the two halves must fit together into a budget. Every company has a capital budget—right? Wrong. When DeButts took over as chief financial officer of AT & T in the 1960s, there was no capital budget for what was then considered the largest company in the world. DeButts's efforts to construct one and to implement it now seem faintly Chaplinesque. "Until 1970, we didn't have a commitment budget. I tried to put one in in 1967, but [they] wouldn't let me. . . . We had a budget then, but it was abused. In those days, I was responsible for raising money, and I've had all my financing plans made of what the company said they needed, but thirty days later they raised those expenses and all my financial plans would go down the drain and I'd have to start all over again. I'd say the heck with this, we can't operate on this basis, so we established a commitment budget in 1970, the year before I became chairman, so on the first of January we came up with a system that [forecasted] what we expected to earn, what kind of revenues we'll have, and I hold the boys to that. . . . We missed it the first year, but we've beaten it every year but 1974, the year of the recession. Lots of people missed it that year."

Is budgetless AT & T an exception because of its semiregulated status? By no means. David Rockefeller told me that the then Chase National Bank did not have an overall capital budget when he first arrived there in 1955—a sign of how smug and comfortable such institutions could be. "It was amazing," Rockefeller said, "and I talked to my uncle [who ran the bank], and he said why did we want a budget? There's no need for one! This gives you a little idea of the approach to banking in those days. Bear in mind that the Chase National was a highly successful institution, so I'm not trying to belittle the capacities of the people who ran it; they were able as bankers, which meant lending officers."

Traditionally, a company's choice of sources of funds was known as the selection of its capital structure which established the company's percentage of equity versus debt. That structure has grown far more complex over the past decade. For example, companies that want to issue debt have found that in many cases, the only way to sell a bond issue cheaply enough is to attach a variety of sweeteners to it, forming a hybrid security. Thus, a range of convertible securities have been spawned: convertible bonds, convertible preferred stock, stock with various rights or warrants attached that allow investors to buy more stock at a fixed price later. In such an environment, at certain companies plain old vanilla bonds are rarely issued.

But that is only the tip of the financing iceberg. There has been a proliferation of joint-venture financing, project financing, and foreign subsidiary financing, which may or may not be reflected in the reported capital structure of the company. Debt-for-equity swaps, the private placement market, pension funds, and mutual funds have made financing far more complex. Chief executives can now even obtain funds by selling their buildings, real estate, equipment, or other assets to the employees' pension funds or to an insurance company or financial institution and then leasing them back. Such sale–lease-backs have been exploited by companies such as General Motors, American Express, A & P, Lockheed, and Union Carbide—as well as a variety of smaller companies—to obtain cash and capital in difficult times.

Let us look at two instruments that can increase a company's flexibility, but which require enormous financial sophistication to use effectively. First are the so-called shelf registration rules, which allow a company to seek SEC approval on a securities issue of up to $400 million, then to hold onto it until the moment is propitious. In the past, the approval process on a new stock issue would take so long that companies would often miss the window of opportunity. All well and good, but shelf registrations meant that companies had to be sensitive to changing market conditions and to the nuances of securities regulation and the play of the market. "With all these new types of securities," said one CEO, "chief executives are better able to tailor-make the exact financing method and package and mix than they ever were in the past. For example, if I decide to jump into the market this week and issue new securities, and I already have shelf registration filed with the SEC, then I can . . . optimize our financial situation at that current moment."

Second is the leveraged buyout, in which a company, or a division of a company, is taken private by buying back the stock (with loans borrowed against the assets), then paying down the debt through the cash flow of the then-private company. The wave of leveraged buyouts we have seen in the last few years reflects a variety of financial pressures on companies. Chief executives believe that their assets are worth more than the stock exchange is valuing them, sometimes below book value. In addition, they feel pressured by unreasonable demands from institutions to wring out short-term gains. As one chief executive told me, "I feel we've been jerked around by the financial markets and the institutional portfolio managers, the raiders and the whim of bankers. I concluded that if I'm going to be constrained in my financial strategy, and vulnerable to outside takeover because our stock price is so depressed, why don't I take over the company at today's cheap prices? Like all the other leveraged buyers, I'll use the assets and its own earning powers over time to borrow money from the bank or other lenders. I'll pay off the current shareholders and take the company private."

Let us look at another example. For decades, the airline industry was highly regulated, hemmed in by rigid Civil Aeronautics Board constraints on route structure, their service contracts to carry mail for the U.S. Postal Service, landing rights, quality of maintenance, and above all, their regulation of ticket pricing—all exacerbated by the cyclicality of air travel. As a result, financial strategy differed little from one airline to the next. One key financing problem faced by all of the firms was how to finance airplane purchases over a long period of time—what type they should buy, and on what kind of schedule of delivery dates. Huge, long-term debt loads for aircraft characterized most air carriers, and they regularly juggled their debt load, delivery schedules, and cancellation clauses on new orders.

Then came the sudden impact of deregulation. As new carriers rushed into the business, the industry began to shuck off the burden of the old-line union contracts, starting afresh with nonunion labor. The rigid route structure was also done away with, wiping out what had been almost private franchises and allowing the new carriers to compete. And rather than buy new planes, these carriers—from the late Laker Airways Limited to People Express Airlines—started with *used* aircraft, the initial costs of which were far cheaper, though their fuel and maintenance expenses were sometimes higher. This kind of strategy shattered long-held financial dogmas, teaching a lesson to their more established colleagues. Suddenly, major carriers such as Eastern, American Airlines Incorporated, and TWA, suffering from the competition, began to expand their menu of financing alternatives, adopting new ways of raising funds and allocating resources. Instead of buying, they leased. Instead of selling basic bonds, they considered more sophisticated—and cheaper—ways of raising money. And they began reexamining their overall financial strategy.

Financial pressures ultimately forced Trans World Corporation to adopt a drastic financial strategy: namely, the break-up of the company. Stated Trans World to its shareholders in its proxy statement: "On September 6,

FINANCIAL STRATEGIES

1983, the Board of Directors received a report from the investment banking firm of Goldman, Sachs & Co. on structural alternatives available to Trans World. After an extensive review by the Board and its Finance Committee, the Board decided on October 26, 1983 to recommend to the stockholders the separation of TWA from Trans World based upon its determination that this would be in the best interests of Trans World and its stockholders.

"The Board of Directors of Trans World believes that it will be advantageous for Trans World Common stockholders to own separate investments in two trading entities—one engaged in international hotel, food and real estate service operations and the other a major international airline. It is the expectation of the Board and management of Trans World that the market values of the separate stocks of the two trading entities will more accurately reflect the underlying businesses and operations of the respective entities . . ."[1] Within a short time after this spinoff case, Icahn made his hostile raid and took over TWA.

Balancing Risk and Reward

If financial strategy can be active—raising and transforming capital for different purposes—it can also be, in a sense, passive, that is, involved in cost control. In this age of seemingly inexorable foreign competition, cost control remains a potent weapon. That is particularly true in labor-intensive industries. The chief executive in a labor-intensive operation faces a series of choices: move manufacturing overseas to take advantage of low-cost labor, substantial substitution of automation systems to replace workers, piecemeal productivity increases, plant closings, and massive layoffs, or getting out of the business entirely. In short, taking steps to control the largest cost element—labor. Like matter and energy, capital and labor can be transformed one into the other. As a result, financial strategy is inextricably bound up with a company's personnel, technology, and international strategy. A number of chief executives told me that each of their corporate strategies are driven by the exigencies of finances, because, simply put, dollars must yield output. Said Rockefeller, "We're trying to reduce every single, separate component of cost. But so long as a chief executive chooses to keep his corporation in a particular labor-intensive business, he is forced to choose among different labor alternatives or capital investments in high technology to substitute for or replace labor, or make existing labor more productive."

Historically, top management has taken a very long time to chose these alternatives, trying to evaluate each substitution of labor by capital equipment or technology in each separate business they operated, both here and abroad. Said Rockefeller, "If the decision was to go with the capital-intensive technology, to replace labor, then there were different ways that these capital assets could be financed. The financing of capital equipment or new plant during the short term, or transition term, may require increasing the company's line of credit with its existing bank, or seeking out new banks or other lenders." But usually such substantial capital investments required the company's issuance of new debt securities or a new issuance of stock. Accelerated depreciation of those new capital assets, plus the investment tax credit, and the potential for a leasing of those assets or sale–lease-back contracts might all be crucial to such a capital-intensive financing. Market factors might also dictate whether that company financed that capital investment at home or abroad.

"In other cases, the chief executive may simply decide such an enormous capital expenditure is beyond his company's present financial means, and he may opt to do it as a joint venture or a consortium with other corporations or partners, in order to spread the financial cost and reduce the risks. . . . Obviously, the larger the project, the more likely outside partners would be considered, whereas the smaller the project, the less chance that he will choose a joint venture."

What any company has to judge is the critical balance between risk and reward. And that may change as the environment and as the company change. In the early days of biotechnology, most companies—Genentech, Biogen, Cetus—were able to raise cash on the stock markets. As the market turned away from these stocks, however, and as research and development costs mounted, they increasingly turned to different forms of financing. Each of those strategies had an up side and a down side. Some companies began licensing products in development to larger drug firms for cash, and a royalty if the product should get to market. That way, they remained solvent and did not have to finance the care and feeding of a marketing team. The down side? Many mortgaged the future of their companies for a mere 10 percent or so royalty. Then there were limited partnerships, pioneered by Genentech. Here, a small group of partners would ante up the capital to get a specific product to the market, and then license it back to Genentech. The down side here was the possibility of lawsuits if projects fizzled out, and a certain dilution of shareholders' equity. Finally, as the stocks continued to tumble, some companies were forced to go even further, establishing whole sectors of research as joint ventures with larger companies. In such a way, W. R. Grace paid Cetus cash to turn the biotech company's agricultural arm into a joint venture, now called Agracetus.

Nowhere is the risk-reward equation more complex than in the decision to operate abroad. Over the past few decades, more and more companies have found themselves involved in the world economy. Many, of course, have found themselves up against foreign competitors at home. Others have gone abroad not only seeking new markets, but to reduce labor and manufacturing costs or to tap into new pools of capital. That internationalization has made financial strategy far more sophisticated than it was in the days when people would telephone Morgan Stanley to sell some bonds for them. When operating abroad, particularly in a number of different countries, the ability to develop a flexible, alert financial strategy is all important. Consider the basic issue of currency: many companies will borrow funds locally in that country's domestic currency. That may require a defensive strategy—for instance, in cases where (1) the local currency erodes in value because of hyperinflation; (2) a foreign government suddenly prevents the repatriation of earnings from that foreign subsidiary back to the United States or restricts the amount of revenue that can be sent out of the country; (3) a foreign government nationalizes the plant or entire company and takes it over; (4) a foreign government forces the multinational to take on a 51-percent local partner.

For all of these reasons, U.S. companies will frequently choose to adopt a quite different financial strategy in their foreign investments than they do in the United States—or a tailored strategy for each region it operates in. Bangor Punta, for example, was created from a tax-loss carryforward that resulted from the expropriation of an American sugar operation called Punta Allegro in Castro's Cuba. Obviously, if a company has a particularly unhappy experience operating abroad, it would be more anxious, and more aware, of the need for protection—one explanation for Harold Geneen's reported involvement with the CIA and Chile. Operating overseas requires a sort of realism that is not as necessary domestically. Said Peter McColough of Xerox, "I had a very deep feeling that the large American multinational company is not, in the long run, going to be able to hold on to some of the equity in Venezuela or Argentina or various parts of the world. We also think that if you get in with a local partner, you get a lot of advantages.

They know the country, and they can be good in terms of contacts and advice. And also, for example, in Latin America, if you get local partners . . . [at] 25 percent of the equity, and that country decides that it wants 51 percent locally owned, then, because your partner is influential with the government, you might be allowed to remain at 25 percent."

Another, even more typical, financial strategy involves matching liabilities and assets abroad so that one is never exposed beyond a certain point. Or investing abroad only the amount that can be borrowed locally in that local currency so that the foreign subsidiary puts no financial strain on the parent company. Thus, a number of multinationals have developed policies in which operations are financed locally—a segmented strategy. "I have to have a segmented strategy if I'm going to sleep at night," one chief executive commented.

Alternatively, companies may view the world as a single financial marketplace, moving funds between nations and foreign units, divisions, and factories. This enables CEOs to protect foreign earnings in a risky country or to take advantage of currency differentials. By quickly shifting funds from one nation to another whose currency is to be revalued upward, or out of one about to fall—a process made easy through electronics—companies can reap nonoperating gains or at least minimize losses. Many chief executives argue that such shifting of cash has become critical because so much of so many companies' revenues are brought in abroad. At Xerox, currency translations are controlled from headquarters in Stamford, Connecticut. Said McColough, "We have a group of people who are very knowledgeable. When things are hectic they're here at two o'clock in the morning . . . they will instruct our people around the globe and coordinate it from here. It's the central bank." Unlike some banks that have been charged with manipulating currency differences, most chief executives, McColough included, viewed it as a simple means of eliminating downside risk. "We try to stay fairly neutral," he said. "If the French franc is going to appreciate against the dollar or pound, we will pay our bills quickly. If it's the other way, depreciation, we really don't try all that hard."

Like Xerox, many multinationals have begun to engage in an elaborate system of hedging, either by buying forward contracts or by taking options to buy or sell puts and calls on currencies and commodities, all the time hoping to protect against a sudden decline in value. Not all chief executives think that that is a sort of business a company should be in. "We are not gamblers or financial speculators or currency traders," James E. Burke of Johnson & Johnson said. "That's not our business. We don't hedge in foreign currencies because that's simply not our competence to effectively manage currencies on a day-to-day basis." But the inability to hedge has occasionally hurt some companies. Said Burke, "We made a substantial operating profit internationally, but it all got wiped out when we had to translate the losses we suffered on currency declines back into dollars. . . . We simply were not prepared for that. And we're still not quite sure how best to cope with that problem."

Still, chief executives have grown more sophisticated about using foreign sources of capital, particularly since the opening in the 1970s of the Euromoney market, a pool of offshore dollar-denominated capital, at first mostly oil money, centered in London. This enabled a number of U.S. companies to borrow abroad at cheaper rates, and allowed them to become more financially sophisticated. Cheaper rates were not the only reason for diving into the Euromoney market. First, a number of companies discovered that they had used up their borrowing capacity in the United States— but that they could sell a variety of different issues abroad. Second, they could get access to funds abroad with fewer legal restrictions. One example of this is American Medical International, a hospital management company that was built by Royce Diener, a financial man who, previous to coming to AMI, had spent time in the Euromoney markets working with Samuel Warburg, one of the great European financiers. At AMI, Diener launched both an aggressive acquisition program in the United States and a strong foreign expansion effort, building a number of hospitals in Europe. All of that required a lot of capital. The result: AMI sought a listing not only on the New York Stock Exchange, but on the exchanges in London and Zurich as well. And Diener continued to raise investment capital on the Euromoney markets.

The Joy of Tax-Free Bonds and Other Boondoggles

With the passage of cornerstone environmental bills in the 1960s—the Clean Air Act, the Clean Water Act, the Solid Waste Disposal Act—corporations were forced to make a major, historic shift in financial investments and priorities. These pieces of legislation affected industrial corporations with heavy capital needs—mainly paper, steel, aluminum,

123

automobile, and chemical companies—which were forced to shelve their regular investment programs until they had invested in pollution-control equipment such as smokestack scrubbers and filtration equipment on their waste-water systems. The enormous cost of these systems forced some industries, steel being the most publicized, to abandon outmoded operations, some going back to World War II and others as far back as the turn of the century. Youngstown Sheet & Tube Company and a number of other marginal steel operators simply abandoned their older factories and mills rather than attempting to meet the new state, local, and federal regulations.

In one sense, these regulations hastened the natural process of abandoning uneconomic facilities. But they also forced a dramatic shift in financial strategy. Because chief executives could not afford to install pollution controls and build new plants, the federal legislation set an investment agenda for many companies. Long-range strategic plans were delayed, dropped, or drastically scaled back, leading many chief executives to protest that the government was making them less competitive. Said William Verity of Armco Steel, "For this year [1979], we can't afford to invest in anything else if we're to get into compliance. . . . We're trying to delay it through the steel industry [trade association in Washington]. The government has put the industry in a financial straitjacket with all these antipollution laws." Indeed, lobbyists did descend on Congress, and in cases where a plant shutdown would devastate an entire region, delays were approved. But overall, the regulations continued to be enforced. These regulations affected companies differently. Some were forced to the wall, while others were able to make the changes easily. The strong got stronger, the weak weaker. The result: a number of mergers and acquisitions.

The government, however, did not completely ignore these problems. Congress and the IRS approved the use of tax-free municipal bonds to help pay for pollution equipment, because it was deemed a "public purpose." As a result, these companies raised almost $100 billion at a great savings in interest costs. Two important consequences flowed from these bond issues. Many corporations learned the intricacies of tax-exempt financing and became far more adept at getting local government backing for another type of municipal bond known as industrial development bonds, or IDBs. All kinds of corporations, from heavy manufacturers to retailers, attracted by municipal inducements such as tax moratoriums, jumped on the IDB bandwagon. Companies tapping the tax-exempt market were able to reduce their overall cost of capital by as much as one-third.

124

FINANCIAL STRATEGIES

This was a particularly critical strategy for companies building facilities that cost less than $10 million, which were usually the IDB tax-exempt financing limits. Dozens of K Marts, McDonalds, and other franchised operations were built across the country using these IDBs. In 1984, the Congressional Budget Office estimated that about $14 billion in such small-scale IDBs were being floated every year. The gravy train may be ending, however. In 1984, caps were placed on the amount of IDBs that could be floated by individual states. Then, a year or so later, there was widespread discussion in Congress about abuses of IDBs and the "public purpose" doctrine during the tax-reform debates. Finally, in the 1986 tax reform, IDBs were drastically curtailed.

In many companies, and for many chief executives, financial strategy is predominately a manipulation of the balance sheet. Chief executives are under increasing pressure to hit financial benchmarks in order to "look good." This can be achieved either by actually earning a stream of increasing profits, return on equity, assets, or investments, or by manipulating the accounts in such a way that it appears that the corporation is doing better, a practice known euphemistically as "creative accounting," but one that can quickly blend into the more dangerous practice of "cooking the books." Let us take a look at a range of such accounting options.

Consider this illustration offered by William Verity. Like many steel companies, Armco had long ago integrated backward into raw materials such as coal, nickel, and limestone. As Verity said, "There are times, such as 1975, 1976, and 1977, when the only money you'll make will be on raw materials. As a result, we developed a supply of reserves of coal that will last for 100 or 150 years. Then, suddenly, you ask yourself: 'What are things going to be like 100 years from now? Are we really going to be making steel out of coke, or is there going to be some other way of smelting?' You come to the conclusion that you really don't need all those reserves. You can always find more anyway." How could Verity maximize the value of those reserves for current shareholders? Joint ventures. "We have joint ventures we are working with other companies to open up our reserves. . . . Those tons of coal are worth a fortune, but we don't get any credit for it because it's under the ground; the only way to make them worth anything is to put them in some form where they're suddenly on your books and worth something." Thus, Armco could continue to tap its reserves, while putting more of their long-term value on its balance sheets today.

Another way of using the balance sheet involves a simple change in the way one does accounting. Most companies traditionally accounted for inventory and receivables through FIFO—first-in, first-out—which meant that the oldest inventory bought at the cheapest price was sold first. Thus, inventory was valued according to the cost of the first-in or older goods. That was fine, as long as there was no real difference in price between the first-in and the last-in. But in the 1970s, an age of inflation, that difference did develop, and companies, in an attempt to get both a better valuation on inventory and a quick earnings burst, revalued their inventory upward based on the last-in, otherwise known as LIFO (last-in, first-out). Because they would seem to have more assets, they could claim higher costs and lower taxes. This was a one-time change, and well understood by lenders, regulators, and some sophisticated investors—although companies did little to publicize the sudden leap in earnings to less sophisticated investors.

There are a variety of other ways to legally manipulate the balance sheet to inflate earnings. Everyone who has done his or her own taxes knows how they work in theory. Here are a few tricks available to chief executives:

- Tax-free municipal bonds which allow the company to avoid property, improvement, and other taxes—because the securities are officially issued by the locality and thus are not taxable—but which also allow the facilities to be viewed as property of the corporation and therefore depreciable assets that are deductible on federal and state income taxes.
- Various kinds of lease financing: for fleets of aircraft, automobiles, computers, or buildings, plant, and warehouses. Because they are leased from a pension fund or a group of investors, companies can take the liabilities *off* the balance sheet. It is still there, of course; you just cannot see it.
- Joint ventures, partnerships, co-production deals. Again, as in leasing, a deal will be split between a number of partners or investors. The chief executive can then allocate costs, benefits, ownership, and responsibility to the partners, getting it off the balance sheet. For example, one party may get the depreciation and investment tax credit, another the effective ownership of the assets, a third the use of facilities and the right to deduct operating expenses.
- Sale–lease-back agreements. By selling a plant or equipment, then leasing it back, companies can get a sudden infusion of cash. General Motors, for instance, in the midst of the financial slump of 1981, sold its New York City headquarters for $400 million and leased those areas it continued to use.
- Tax-loss carryforwards. A company receives a tax deduction for a loss. Many companies, running large, long-term losses, cannot use the carryforwards, so they sell them to more prosperous firms that can, generating a needed flow of capital.

Such intricacies of finances and the tax system can, like the alchemist, conjure gold from lead. In 1962, Castro expropriated the large sugar com-

126

FINANCIAL STRATEGIES

pany, Punta Allegro. In 1964, Congress decided that it would certify Cuban claims, just in case the Cuban government decided to pay off, which of course it still has not. However, just prior to the expropriation, a clerk in Cuba had wired $4 million to Chase Manhattan in New York. Thus, when the company all but disappeared, shareholders were left with $4 million in the bank and a $21 million tax-loss carryforward. That is when Nicolas Salgo grew interested. A former real estate man, he decided to buy the company and use the tax loss to buy another company, which in turn would finance the purchase out of its tax-sheltered cash flow—a sort of early leveraged buyout (LBO). "He had 100 percent tax free," said David Wallace, a later chief executive at Bangor Punta, "which gave him enough cash to pay off notes that he gave to buy the company."

Here is where it gets fun—and where one can realize the nifty dancing a financial expert can pull off. Said Wallace, "There was this six-hundred-mile potato railroad up in Maine called the Bangor and Aroostock Railroad. It went from nowhere to no place. It barely existed as a railroad. It got its main income not from hauling potatoes, but from leasing out its reaper cars and engines to other railroads during the offseason for potatoes. In other words, they weren't a railroad, they were a leasing company. They knew their future was limited, and they knew they wanted to get out. At the time, it was very popular for railroads to set up subsidiaries or holding companies not under Interstate Commerce Commission jurisdiction, and acquire other companies. They were thinking along those lines, but they didn't have anyone capable of it. Then they saw Punta Allegro doing it out of the tax loss, and they went together on a few acquisitions. They merged in 1964." Presto: Bangor Punta. From nothing to something. The wonders of financing.

Creations like Bangor Punta were all the rage in the 1960s. ITT was the classic example, but all of the conglomerates were, in effect, created out of thin air and financed not all that differently from a pyramid scheme—using the cash flow of new companies to finance future takeovers. The key to the game, as in the pyramid scheme, was to retain the illusion of health through constant quarterly earnings increases. "Financial opportunism was in vogue [in the 1960s]," said Wallace. "The XYZ Company [claims]—this is our fortieth quarter of increased earnings. It's nonsense. No one has increased earnings quarter to quarter unless (a) someone has massaged the earnings or (b) there have been acquisitions that are nondilutable. There is no business yet that does not have a cycle. I just don't believe it."

Inevitably, the drive for continual growth and earnings increases, combined with creative accounting, spawned a series of outright frauds. First, in 1982, there was Saxon Industries, a giant retailer, where a shift from FIFO to LIFO as well as a whole array of inventory distortions helped to cover up a long-ranging decline in operations. Analysts, not to mention ordinary investors and lenders, were fooled for years. When the cosmetics were peeled away, the company was discovered to be all but insolvent; and as a result, chief executive Stanley Lurie later resigned. Not long after, the debacle of Baldwin-United appeared. Baldwin, which started out making pianos, had been turned into a hot-shot peddler of insurance annuities by its chief executive, a former accountant named Morley P. Thompson. It *appeared* as if Baldwin was growing furiously, and the company was the darling of Wall Street. But appearances can be deceiving. In fact, Thompson was building an enormous empire disguised by an unbelievably complex accounting structure. Finally, as a result of a crusade from a lone suspicious Wall Street analyst, Thompson's empire collapsed.

In a litigous society like ours, it is sometimes difficult to separate the legitimate grievances about accounting and stockholder fraud from the spurious. What we do know is that in the past decade, such suits have mushroomed. We also know that these suits, in part, have grown because of an increase in the conscious manipulation of publically disclosed financial information by chief executives and their managers. Corporations, for example, frequently take advantage of the fact that they keep one set of books for themselves (presumably, they do not lie to themselves), one set for shareholders, and one for lenders.

Nonetheless, many of the chief executives I interviewed expressed resentment at SEC reporting requirements because of the time-consuming demands they made on their time. They also claimed that the SEC, FTC, FCC (Federal Communications Commission), Food and Drug Administration (FDA), and just about every other government organization this side of the secret service unfairly conspired to tie them in knots. As a result, several blamed the government for the corporate practice of creative accounting. Said a chief executive who asked to remain anonymous, "I believe we're fully justified in taking every single accounting advantage or marginal legal opinion in our favor, because we're constantly penalized by being forced to meet all government regulations and by not being able to get full credit for lost opportunity costs or our total actual expenses." Verity of Armco Steel agreed in principle, arguing not only that the government penalized Armco by its tax laws, by disallowing a real recognition of costs, but that antitrust policies prohibited joint ventures in new built-from-scratch steelmaking facilities known as "greenfield plants" and that environmental legislation forced it to spend excessive amounts of money on pollution equipment. Finally, Verity condemned the government for inaction against what he called foreign "dumping" of steel. ("Dumping" legally means that a foreign corporation has sold goods in the United States below its own costs of production simply to keep its workers employed or in order to capture U.S. market share.)

It is ironic that while many CEOs bemoan government regulation that hurts, they clamor after regulation that rewards. Armco Steel provides a striking example. Not long after Verity chastised the government for its pollution laws and other sins, he described a venture the company went into in the late 1960s that exists solely because of a twist in tax regulations. "We got into finance leasing in 1968 because of the investment tax credit. We had plenty of extra tax credits, but the airlines, people like that, couldn't take advantage of them. So we'd just buy an airplane and lease it to the airline cheaper than they could buy it because we could use the investment tax credit. It's now [1980] a $300 million business and growing. A lot of the growth is in Australia and Europe because it's a newer game there. Over here, all the banks are into it and it's pretty competitive."

Well, no one ever said that CEOs are a particularly consistent breed. But allow me briefly to point out some important inconsistencies in corporations' government contracts. I will not elaborate on the role and responsibilities of a corporation in a democracy, for they seem to me well known (though not by some CEOs) and fairly obvious. More to the point, accounting, which is really what we are talking about here, is hardly an exact science. Rather, it's an attempt codified in the Financial Accounting Standards Board's (FASB) Generally Accepted Accounting Principles (GAAP) to give the government and the investor a snapshot of the financial condition of a company at a given point in time. Now that is a difficult thing to do, and the FASB is often grappling with issues raised by companies that are attempting to brighten their financial picture a touch. In many cases, complaints about the government are really complaints about GAAP and an attempt to offer investors a somewhat rosy image. Now and again, such complaints are justified, particularly when there are long-term values not reflected on the balance sheet. But overall, by deliberately playing accounting games—onerous regulation or not—companies defraud their ostensible owners, the shareholders.

RUNNING AMERICAN BUSINESS

Dealing with the Government

Doing business with the government is like dealing with no other customer. As companies such as Litton, Lockheed, Allied-Signal, General Dynamics, General Motors, and countless others have discovered, the financing mechanisms used on government contracts tend to be quite different from those for normal commercial projects, and government contract work has proven to be a mixed blessing.

For many CEOs, government contracts provide a bedrock upon which to build their financial strategy. When I spoke with Joseph Flavin of Singer, he described the thought process that went into deciding to make a larger effort in the aerospace business, one heavily dependent on government contracts. "We looked at those businesses," he said, "and our fellows said, 'do you want to be in the aerospace business, can you make money?' And certainly aerospace did not fit the terms of any other of our businesses. What they discovered was that, run well, it's a growth business. (Singer's aerospace electronics businesses have now recorded ten consecutive years of higher revenues.) It's also very predictable. Your contracts are for long periods of time. Take simulation systems . . . we build a system for the F-16. Now the F-16 is the plane of today. And we'll be grinding out those systems for a long time. And it's very predictable. . . . It can die on you, but it'll die over a period of years. If you let it die it's your fault. So it gave us stability, which is what we needed."

That is not to say there are no drawbacks to working for the government; many are self-induced. Again, let us turn to Lockheed, one of the larger military contractors. I spoke with Roy Anderson of Lockheed in the late 1970s just as the company was completing its turnaround. Of particular interest to me was Anderson's descriptions of the hidden pitfalls of government contracting. "We don't record options in the backlog," said Anderson. "They have to be firm and in the government order. For example, when the government contracts to you for the Trident missile, it will be a $2-billion program, but we'll only put in the backlog now the part that has been funded, actually placed on contract in terms of funds. You know they're there. You see, they lay out these funds annually. It has been our experience that the government can stop a program very easily and the way to stop it is usually at the end of the funding year. So, if you include in your backlog what you hope they'll fund, it's going to get you embarrassed."

Anderson also emphasized the financial intricacies of first bidding, then coping with long-term contracts—whether from the government or from civilian markets. "You don't take a fixed-price contract because you get burned every time," said Anderson. "What you do on occasion is take a straight-cost-plus contract, or an incentive contract, where if you do a good job, on schedule, on cost, you get a chance to earn more fee. Some of the incentive contracts we won't touch, because the incentive can go the other way—a penalty clause. When we're pretty sure what we're producing, and we know our design, then we'll look to an incentive contract. When we get a product as far along as the C-130 Hercules airplane, even with modifications, we'll fix price every time. We're modifying a whole fleet of C-141s; it's one of the big cargo planes and there are 270-some airplanes and that's $450 to 500 million in fixed price."

For Lockheed and other contractors, the name of the game is really knowing what a project should cost, and making an accurate bid. "It really comes from developing a whole databank, and you get that after a while," said Anderson. "Even though you're developing a new missile, you go back to developing a missile that you've already worked on and you consider the test problems you ran into, the kinds of materials, technologies. . . . After you've built one, of course, you have the learning curve of experience. Then it becomes fairly routine and there's not much difficulty to it. It's the initial projects that you have to be concerned about."

In essence, successful bidding resembles the same sort of risk and reward analysis of other financial strategies. Not surprisingly, at Lockheed, the analysis of projects for bidding came from the financial side of the company, which would break the projects down into their smallest parts and attempt to estimate costs. Then, as the bidding package is assembled, a risk analyzer is brought in. "We have a guy . . . who can analyze the possibilities of contract losses. Then, in the final review, he's right there to tell us, the president and myself, how much of the company you're betting on this thing." How do projects differ? "It depends on the program," said Anderson. "For example, if it's a completely new missile or space vehicle or whatever— I use them [as an example] because they're the most far out and that's where the risk is usually the greatest—they'll bring up what they think are the greatest risk factors. Have we ever been in this business before? Have we developed one of these things? What has our competition's experience been? They'll sum it all up and say, 'we think this is the extent of the risk.' It may not be a monetary risk at all, but one of reputation."

In the end, of course, those contracts must be integrated into some sort of ongoing picture of the company's financial health. Anderson said that while a military contractor like Lockheed would use the familiar benchmarks—return on investment, assets, and sales—the nature of government contracts makes it more complex. "We're still refining it," he said, "because it's a real problem. When you have a program like the L1011 in the near term you get a terrible return on investment. Your return comes way out, way downstream. So you may have negative returns to begin with. On the other hand, you can have a program like some of our service contracts [for airport maintenance, among others] where you don't have an investment at all. Your customer may have prepaid you. What we try to do is set a target on return on equity, so that we'll make an attractive investment."

The complexities of dealing with the government and with civilian markets at the same time have driven some companies out of the military contracting business. Even CEOs of very profitable government contractors are well aware of these pitfalls. It came as no surprise when Iacocca sold off Chrysler's highly profitable tank division to raise cash and all but bailed out of government contracting. Chief executives of companies that did only a marginal amount of business with the government and for whom government compliance was an onerous departure from normal business practices lamented the government red tape necessary to finance the deals and their long-term payment schedules. In effect, working for the government under the controversial cost-plus contract, in which the government automatically paid for the cost of the project plus a fixed profit, fostered behavior just the opposite of that of most companies: instead of profiting by cutting costs, they profited by inflating them. Waste was not something to be eliminated, but to be accumulated. Many CEOs saw these as bad habits that can seep into an increasingly competitive civilian business.

Conclusion

Since the 1960s, chief executives have been chosen primarily from the ranks of managers with financial experience. And financial strategy was the area above all others that the chief executives I interviewed stressed as their most important function, as well as the area that they thought potential successors should train in. For many chief executives, financial strategy so dominated their concerns and interests that it served as a replacement for an overall, complex, and sophisticated corporate strategy.

The results are obvious. An obsession with finances—with quarterly earnings, the stock price, the opinions of analysts—has created a general neglect for the initiation of more operationally oriented strategies such as technology, marketing, personnel, and new ventures. In some cases, the disproportionate time spent on financial strategies crippled the real strengths of the company. At such firms, I found that marketing had been allowed to atrophy, that risky technological projects were chopped off and discarded at the first sign of strain. And the management of organizational development and the creation of a management team were abandoned for the sheer analysis and manipulation of cash and investments.

The ascendance of financial strategy has been accompanied by the growth of huge, central headquarters organizations that load the company down with excessive red tape and overhead expenses and create all kinds of problems for line managers out in the field. In the late 1960s and 1970s, this trend gathered steam until, battered by the recession in the early 1980s and the incursions by foreign competitors, many companies sliced off layers of management, only to discover how very expensive a large headquarters was. But it was not only the cost of such headquarters that caused difficulties. Once released from the constraints of the financial people back at the headquarters, many production or line managers were released to attempt to creatively produce more and better products cheaper.

Ironically, the sea change of macroeconomic financial conditions following the 1980–81 recession did not drive financial chief executives from office. Instead, they proved as capable as anyone of sniffing out the change in weather, and proved better than most other kinds of managers at ruthlessly slashing away at corporate staffs. The tools of financial analysis, after all, can be used in many ways. Nonetheless, while that cutting and slashing did produce some productivity increases, I have found that, as often as not, the pendulum swings too far in each direction. Both the build-up and the demolition were too extreme. The build-up was called forth by the oppressing need for financial information at headquarters, in order to pull together fast-growing, diversified companies. But as with most bureaucracies, the financial staff grew and grew beyond the needs of simple control. Collection of information became an end in itself, and overheads mushroomed. Likewise, as computers sifted into corporations, far fewer staff was required to gather data, and the information that was assembled could more efficiently be used by managers on the line. Alas, the cutbacks not only eliminated the excessive staff, often they sliced away at essential planning and coordinating functions as well. As a result, companies found themselves turning to the army of outside advisors—lawyers, consultants, accountants, investment bankers, gurus of all sorts—always waiting outside the door.

Throughout all of this, it is quite obvious that financial strategy in these complex times *is* a major requirement for potential chief executives. I described the increasing sophistication of the financial system, both at home and abroad, in the main body of this chapter. But with this sophistication, one can only hope for a little more wisdom, and a more than passing interest in those other strategies for which financing is really nothing more than the fuel that makes them and the company move.

CHAPTER SIX

TECHNOLOGY STRATEGIES: INSIDE THE BLACK BOX

From my perspective, implementation of new technologies can only be achieved with an active support and participation of chief executive officers, with their involvement in it and their understanding of it. Stimulation has to come from the top—a *push* mentality is needed. . . . In every organization that I've known which has successfully introduced these technologies, it has been done in the executive suite. The information technologies are not viewed as an expense item, or as an administrative support tool to control budgets. They are viewed as a profit-making tool—a strategic weapon.
—WILLIAM G. McGOWAN, CEO, MCI Communications Corporation

Coping in a New Age

We live in a technological age. The pace of innovation continues to accelerate, as developments fly from the laboratory to the factory floor to the marketplace in what seems like mere moments. The chief executive who fails to pay attention to new technology faces the prospect of being left in the dust by more aggressive competitors. Increasingly, the price of ignoring technological strategy is corporate oblivion.

There certainly are risks to undertaking technological development. First, it can be very expensive. Investments in new technology require substantial investment and often take a great deal of political clout and financial muscle within the company to bring to fruition. Second, there is the uncertainty of dabbling in science and technology. As the medieval alchemists discovered long ago, no one can be certain that anything at all will result from

135

long-term research and development, or in fact whether the products that may result will ever provide an adequate return on investment. And if they do return a profit, this might not happen in time to be of political use to the managers who started the whole project. Finally, even if profitability is achieved, the question is whether it will be sustained over a long period of time or be stolen, copied, or leapfrogged by competitors.

"Technology" is really a very imprecise word, as it applies to things as basic as the wheel, and as complex as a semiconductor, a laser, or pharmaceuticals. As a result, technology plays different roles in different companies. At some companies, technological development is absolutely essential; at others—say, those companies usually identified as supreme marketers—technology may be but a cosmetic alteration to an already existing product. There are, of course, those famous start-up companies where the founder and chief executive, an engineering Horatio Alger, perfected his or her technology in some obscure and mundane location, usually—at least according to the myth—an attic, a garage, or a basement. In such companies, the chief executive plays an intensely personal role and is involved in everything from the design and manufacture of the product to its marketing, testing, distribution, and further development. From Edwin Land, with his one hundred patents for instant photography, to the youthful Steve Jobs and Steve Wozniak, building their first Apple computer in the heart of Silicon Valley, we have made these engineer entrepreneurs cultural heroes.

Later I will focus on entrepreneurial chief executives and their struggles to move technologies into the marketplace in the form of new products. Here, I will confine myself to chief executives of larger, more complex organizations, where technological development is just one instrument in a symphony of strategic elements—sometimes the most important instrument, sometimes just an accompanist. How can a chief executive successfully bring technology into a large corporation? As we shall see, this question is not amenable to a simple answer. Technology rises less from corporate fiat than from the careful creation of an innovative environment. Technology requires a chief executive who has wide interests and a fine sense of balance, for by definition, innovation works against the rigidity and status quo of the mature corporate organization. And, as we saw earlier, technology alone is only half the battle; once you have a hot product, you must package it, market it, and distribute it.

But before going any further, let us pause for a moment before the all but unfathomable figure who stands at the center of any technological strategy: the inventor. Like the artist, the inventor lives in a world ruled more by inspiration, creativity, and serendipity than most chief executives are comfortable with. *Megatrends* notwithstanding, the advance of technology cannot be predicted; only the conditions that make such advances possible can be fostered. And then you pray. Imagine, if you will, trying to predict the enormous impact of xerography from a man such as Chester Carlson who first patented the technology. "Chester Carlson was a Californian," said Peter McColough, former CEO of Xerox. "Very poor background, graduated Cal Tech in physics in the thirties. He was worse than poor because his father was an invalid and he had to support the family. He couldn't get a job. Finally he got one in New York with the P. R. Mallory Company, battery people, then he went to law school and became a patent attorney."

"His thinking went like this," McColough continued. "He observed that it was very difficult and very expensive to make copies of documents. Usually, in those days, people typed if they needed a copy of something—type this one through and make five copies. Or by that time, the Haloid Company had this great big photostat machine called the Retrograph that could make photographic copies that cost 50 cents apiece, very expensive. ... The thing was, he [Carlson] was probably not going to be much of a manager or a business success. He was a very quiet, unassertive guy. Perhaps he could make an invention, a better way of making copies. ... He went to the New York Public Library at night for years, virtually, and his thinking was that he had to find a new way to make copies. He ignored the photographic process, the chemical process. ... He started looking for phenomena, physical or chemical phenomena that were not part of the photographic process, and he discovered one in reading about the principle of the photoconductor which was well known at that time. A photoconductor is a substance that will hold a charge of electricity in the dark, but not in the light. So he put together—he didn't really invent something in the traditional sense—the idea of using the photoconductor in terms of copying or selectively exposing a charged photoconductor to light to make stains on some areas and no stains on others. Then he put a powder on it that would stick with the charge.

"So he took up the theoretical work from reading the literature in the library and did some experimenting—originally in his kitchen, somewhere over a store on Long Island—and eventually, after five or six years' work, October 22, 1938, he got his first crude image. It was not a machine, just a process. He thought he had a success and tried to sell the idea to American industry. From 1938 to 1944 he went through all kinds of companies—Kodak, IBM, so forth—and nobody had the least interest in the process. Eventually, in 1944 or 1945, he went to Battelle [Laboratory] in Columbus [Ohio]—a not-for-profit institution—and they expressed some interest in developing the process further, because he did not have the resources." The rest, as they say, is history.

Pioneers and Followers

Most executives wrestling with technological strategies can be divided into pioneers and followers. The chief executive who decides that the firm must shoot for technological preeminence is a *pioneer*. This, as a CEO will quickly discover, is a strategy full of risk and uncertainty; yet it is also a strategy that may bring untold riches. Pioneers are often aggressive, confident chief executives who start with the burning conviction that their company must achieve technological preeminence. Listen to how McColough described Joseph Wilson, the founder of Xerox, in the days before xerographic technology had been fully developed as a product: "Mr. Wilson could see that they had to find something, and he was receptive to new technology that would do things better and really compete against Kodak. . . . That day [when McColough spoke with him about a job], he talked about the information explosion he saw coming, and how if someone could do a job of reproduction in government and industry effectively, easily, with high quality—well, there was a great future in it. He really didn't think of it as the copy business. He thought of it in terms of the information business."

The chief executive who is really not interested in high technology or who is repelled by repeated frustrations and failures will usually not be able to sustain the interest and motivation of a large organization over the period of time necessary to forge ahead successfully into high technology. Such chief executives are *followers*. They adopt technology that other firms have pioneered. Roy Ash, former president of Litton, CEO of AM International, and head of the OMB, offered an anecdote that illustrates the differences between the ways technological pioneers and followers think. It was after World War II, and Tex Thornton, the leader of the whiz kids, was approached by the reclusive billionaire, Howard Hughes. Hughes had a problem in the form of a company that had been making airplane armaments during the war; he was not sure of what to do with it. "Noah Dietrich, who was Hughes's man for all kinds of management questions, wanted to close it up," said Ash. "There wasn't much of a market for that sort of thing after the war. But Tex came in and said we can make something of it if we turn around and go in a different direction. Tex had noticed a couple of scientists working on a few things on the side. It was really nothing. But Tex said we can make a business of that and build a big company around that. So Hughes passed over Dietrich, and said to Tex, 'You go make it a big company.'

"When he got there, in 1948, there were seven hundred people. In 1953, there were eighteen thousand." How did Thornton recognize a potentially company-making technology? Well, he was attuned to it; back at Harvard during the war, the whiz kids were one of the first large users of IBM data processing equipment. "We had a confidence not only that we could do things," said Ash, "but that scientists could, and would, do things. We believed in the opportunities. We also, let me say, knew you had to have an organization that could foster these kind of revolutionary, entrepreneurial people that would do it for you. You had to look ahead. Not everybody was."

Technology alone, of course, did not build Hughes. As Ash said, "The scientific guys had a sense of what could be done. In the outside world, the market had a definition of what it wanted. And Tex stood there and brokered this whole thing to build a business, based on his understanding of what the market wanted and the scientists' understanding of what could be done. Intellectual brokerage. Tex was, and is, one of the world's great salesmen. He sold it. He wanted to make a business out of science, which meant connecting it to markets." To complete this tale: while Thornton did build a great business—Hughes Aircraft Corporation—his conflicts with Dietrich simmered. Hughes disappeared into inaccessibility, and Dietrich continued to interfere. In 1953, Dietrich made a move to gain control of the finances of the company—Ash, by the way, was then CFO—and the Thornton team walked out, only to set up another technology company: Litton.

Is it all that important to get into a market first with a technology? Well, there are advantages. First—and we shall pursue this further in the new-venture chapter—there are economic advantages to being first. Through a strategy called "pricing down the experience curve," innovators can seize the advantage and, as they gain more experience manufacturing, say, a semiconductor chip, always stay one step ahead of the competition on price. Second, there is a concept known as the "advantage of the first mover," which, simply put, means that the first company in a market usually gets to make most of the rules. In this case, "rules" can refer to a variety of ground rules, prototypes, models, or specifications for the industry—a computer software operating system, for example, that becomes a standard. The first mover also gets the first shot at a virgin market, which has enormous growth possibilities. At times, the first-mover advantage can be overwhelming. This can happen when a pioneer has quickly established the basic technology for an industry that later developments can only marginally improve upon. Such was the case with Alexander Graham Bell and his telephone, and, to a lesser extent, Thomas Edison and his light bulb.

This early advantage can shape an entire industry, for better or for worse. Consider, for example, the first mover in television technology. The United States, led by RCA, adopted the first rudimentary tube design, which employed very high frequency. Later, when the Europeans developed their own standards, they took as their model a set with a larger number of lines of resolution per square inch, which produced a slightly clearer picture. The point of all of this is not to get bogged down in technical details, but rather to note that by that time, there was no way for the American companies to adjust to the higher standard without cannibalizing the millions of sets already sold. In one sense, the market had crystallized technologically. A similar tale could be told of automobiles. During the early days of cars, there were a variety of technologies—gasoline, diesel, electric—competing for customers. Gasoline won, and as a result, for decades, the competing technologies never received the same level of funding and experimentation, and so they never advanced as far as the internal combustion engine. Technologically, the gas engine retained and built on its advantages.

Followers give up the advantages to being first, in exchange for greater financial security—as long as they can compete on price. Followers often try to undercut pioneers on price, as the Japanese have done, if they can get around patent walls. Usually, followers hope that the pioneers will not be able to successfully restrict patent rights, or will simply light the way into new markets, allowing the followers to use their greater financial resources to rush in afterwards and seize market share. Sony, for example, is famous not for inventing new products, but for capitalizing on its strong marketing organization to fully exploit a market that was pioneered by others. IBM has a similar reputation in the computer business. Alas, the follower strategy really only works in industries such as computers and electronics, where there are many small, inadequately financed pioneers and but a few large, powerful followers.

Today, we can see the effects of first-mover advantages in the computer markets. Because the technology is still in a state of transition, many companies will actually give away software in order to disseminate it as widely as possible, in the hopes that it will become a de facto industry standard. Thus, when IBM moved so quickly into the personal computers, its operating system, called PC-DOS, marketed by a small Washington company called Microsoft, became the industry standard for similarly sized machines. As Apple Computer Corporation discovered, all personal computer companies had to operate in an IBM environment—to be, in other words, compatible with IBM—if they were to prosper in the business user market. The lesson is clear: sometimes, in a fast-changing environment, it is wiser to plunge in with a just adequate technology—and if necessary, give it away—to lock in a wide base of customers for today, and hopefully, a variety of add-ons and services tomorrow.

Technological pioneers are exceedingly vulnerable from a variety of directions. They are like a fat bird out on a long limb—a juicy target for a corporate marksman. The disabling blast can come from two directions: first, from a company with a more advanced technology, the so-called leapfrogging technology; or second, from a company that is a better and stronger marketer. IBM's enormous initial success with its personal computer is a wonderful example of the latter; although the machine was using classic follower technology, IBM's name and marketing expertise all but blew out of the market a host of smaller competitors and forced stronger competitors to give up market share, though not necessarily technological, leadership. IBM's initial coup in personal computers is hardly an unusual case. Size, finances, and entrenched market power can often overwhelm technological advances. As a result, the successes of the first mover are far rarer than conventional wisdom would suggest.

Common-Denominator Technologies

Not all technological advances are alike. Some may be minor indeed— say, an improved jet engine that reduces fuel costs and boosts speed. Some may create new markets, for instance Jobs and Wozniak's first personal computer. And some are what I like to call common-denominator technologies which extend across a range of markets and functions and can propel a company to new heights. Computer technology, lasers, ceramics, and biotechnology are examples of common-denominator technologies.

All of these technologies can be vital to the future prosperity of companies. But for the chief executive of the large company, finding a common-denominator technology may be critical because it provides a foundation upon which to build other technologies and other products. For example, General Signal CEO Nathan Owen argued that "it was essential for this company [General Signal] to keep making acquisitions until we had possession of all the four [energy] control technologies—electrical, hydraulic, magnetic, and fluid. I knew," he said, "that if we got all four, we had succeeded in boxing the compass." How do you break in with those four control technologies? Owen looked for the common denominator, finding it in advanced electronics. Owen saw that electronic controls, based on new microprocessor technology, could be used to master a variety of energy technologies. "No matter what the initial form of energy (coal, oil, gas, nuclear)," said Owen, "it has to be converted into electricity to be usable. That's the way the system works. So we targeted electronic energy controls as our focal point."

Owen's technological strategy involved at least three stages. First was his decision to seek dominance in what he viewed as four key areas, or markets. Second, he appraised the dynamics of a variety of energy industries. Third, he chose a key common-denominator technological solution, in this case, electrical energy, that linked those industries. That was the foundation upon which Owen based all of his other technological development efforts.

William G. McGowan of MCI took a similar approach. He argued that what he called information technology was remaking a variety of companies cutting across a number of industries. Said McGowan, "I believe that the balance of this century will be dominated by the introduction of the information technologies into business—not only here, but throughout the world. While information technologies today account for only five percent of employment, as much as 30 percent of all employees are in positions that can be heavily influenced by them—that is true in the United States as well as Europe. Those who believe that it is imperative to begin to introduce information technologies in our organizations will, I believe, have the advantages in the future." Of course, information technologies depend on communications. And MCI sells communications services. But there is clearly something to McGowan's argument. "Citibank, for example," he commented, "was just a large bank, like any number of large banks, until five years or so ago. Today, it is developing a national banking system. Citibank has put into place the infrastructure of computers and telecommunications that will enable it to grow even faster and introduce new services."

The key here is that companies that adopt common-denominator technologies, such as information technology or electronic controls, can use them to improve their products or services in a variety of areas. McGowan described improvements made at American Hospital Supply when it began using computers: "American Hospital Supply decided it would install terminals in each of its user hospitals so that its salesmen wouldn't have to call on each one, collect an order, and enter it into the database. With that step, the company made itself different from its competitors and found a way to respond to its customers' needs. But that's not all. The company also said to the hospitals, 'Why don't you maintain your own inventory free on the computers, and the orders we can't fill, we'll pass on to the other suppliers.' To the MIS [management information services] executive, this is simply a remote-order entry system, but to executives of American Hospital Supply, it's a strong, competitive, profit-making system."

McGowan offered a final example which shows how a common-denominator strategy can generate new products and profits. McKesson Corporation, a pharmaceutical company, also installed terminals to let its customers input its orders. When McKesson saw how its customers were seeking new items, it broadened its product line. And when it saw how its customers often sought reimbursement for an order from a third party, such as an insurance company, it volunteered to collect them itself. This reduced costs for its drug store customers—and for McKesson, provided a whole new business. Said McGowan, "Information technology provided the strategic opportunity." McKesson acknowledged the importance of the new technology in a recent annual report: "As a result of a $100-million investment in computer technology over the last ten years, our distribution companies have been transformed from high-cost, labor-intensive operations to highly automated, value-added businesses. They represented 13 percent of 1978 profit and 26 percent of 1980 profit, and accounted for 56 percent of our fiscal 1984 profit."

Barriers to Entry

As I will discuss in detail in the next chapter on new-venture strategies, patents are often essential to companies with new products, to provide them a chance to develop and profit from new markets. That, of course, is how Xerox grew to be a major company. But patents are not the only barrier that a company can erect to protect its position in a market. Simple market dominance—IBM is a good example—can keep competitors out of certain markets. Sometimes, as in the case of AT & T, that dominance is legalized, and while competitors are not banned from certain markets, they are certainly not encouraged. Of course, AT & T's traditional role as a legally regulated monopoly in the telephone business ended with deregulation and the opening up of the market to such companies as MCI and GTE Sprint.

McColough first encountered the problem of overwhelming market dominance when he was first considering whether to work at Xerox, then called Haloid. "It was an old photographic company producing photographic papers, mostly for copying, for industry, and business. He [Joseph Wilson] realized that the company could never really [grow] in that particular process of photography, because any improvements that could be made, Kodak would make them. Kodak had such greater resources for making improvements. It [Haloid] was constantly behind Kodak, trying to catch up; as soon as they would get near, Kodak would pull an improved product off the shelf. He [Wilson] had great faith in the future of being able to reproduce documents as a way of supplying information systems, but he had to find a different way, a different technology where we could lead and, perhaps, be unnoticeable for a while, and not have a lot of competition." The rest is history. Wilson found his technology in Chester Carlson's invention, which by then had been refined at Battelle. "We had a research man who read about it [Carlson's technology] in a journal. . . . Mr. Wilson was receptive to the new technology because he knew he needed something to really compete against Kodak in a different way, not directly." In short, xerography created a whole new market that Xerox alone ruled for years. Ironically, its technology created barriers of entry to companies large and small, even Kodak.

One of the most common ways of erecting barriers to entry is by building incompatible technologies. IBM and other computer companies, for instance, often purposely design basic products so that outsiders cannot plug into them and advance their own fortunes. Another strategy has been for large companies to purchase any competing technology and then to lock it away in the vault, therefore ensuring that it does not undercut its own proprietary technology. Major companies such as General Motors, Ford, General Electric, IBM, and AT & T have all been accused of this sort of technological lock-out. While this no doubt happens in certain cases— though probably not as often as it has been charged—it is often more effective as a threat or deterrent to smaller companies. The very fear of retaliation by a giant company has proved daunting to new companies, often leading them to settle prematurely with the large company or to abandon work altogether on the technological breakthrough.

There are other barriers to entry in any given market. Many technologies that may look marvelous in the lab simply are not accepted in the marketplace. The reasons for that rejection vary widely. The product, in rare cases, may simply be too far ahead of its time, providing a product or service for a need that has not yet fully developed. Or it may be too complex or difficult to use. Therefore, while just about everyone knows how to use a telephone, many people continue to express some fear of the complexity of the computer. Finally, many new technologies founder because the old ways are simply extremely effective. In other words, no need exists. Picture telephones never got out of the development stage because most people found the standard telephone an effective and cheap form of communication. Long-life light bulbs at a premium price have so far not been able to dislodge traditional cheap bulbs.

Sometimes, of course, a company has to be patient to allow a very profitable market to develop. That is where the role of the chief executive is crucial, not only in authorizing the original research and development, but in putting adequate resources behind the marketing of the technology to the public. It is foolhardy for a chief executive to go through the difficult slog of waiting for the successful development of a new technology, and then scrimp on resources in telling consumers how to use it. Nevertheless, such failures are widespread. That tends to be a particular problem with entrepreneurs who are also scientists or engineers. These chief executives tend to believe in the obviousness or superiority of their product in a particular market. A classic example is Steve Jobs's belief that Apple's Macintosh computer, which was incompatible with IBM mainframes, the de facto office environment, would succeed in the corporate world simply because of its technological elegance. Jobs, like many entrepreneurs, learned his lesson—but by then it was too late, and Jobs was forced out of his position at Apple.

The government can often raise a final barrier to entry. There really has been only one major new integrated pharmaceutical company to appear on the scene since World War II, Syntex Corporation, which rode the birth-control pill to success. The reason? The cost of regulatory approval on top of the costs of research, marketing, and scale-up is just too heavy for small companies to support. Governmental regulations can also determine the direction technology will take. By controlling Medicare reimbursement rules, the Health Care Finance Administration can also determine which medical technologies will flourish and which will die.

John deButts of AT & T offered a similar example when it came to telecommunications technology. "There are some states that still don't allow us to provide some services that we provide in other states," he said. "We've been trying to offer the American public a mobile telephone system for almost ten years. The technology has all been developed. It wasn't until two years ago that we were allowed to put it into field trial, using our own people. Now they've expanded it and are going to allow us to use some of our customers. But they still haven't authorized a general offering to the public, and the service is just as good as that phone over there, and cheaper than the existing service." Why the problems? "For one thing," deButts answered, "Motorola and other people don't like us. They don't want the competition. They want to compete, but they don't want us to compete. So they fight us." Eventually, of course, cellular telephones were approved—but approval came years after the technology was ready.

Managing Research and Development

In any discussion of the management of research and development, all eyes must turn to the shining example of Bell Laboratories. What Chester Carlson is to the fraternity of lonely, eccentric inventors, so Bell Labs is to the institution of the research laboratory. Consider its achievements. "Long before there was any competition in this business, we invented the computer," said deButts. "We decided we didn't want to get into that business, so we gave it away. We invented the transistor and gave it away. That is

146

what made electronics possible. . . . We converted the whole communications from manual; first step-by-step dialing; then the cross-bar dial; then to a number-five crossbar; and then to electronic switching. We developed the first private branch exchange used in the world—and improved on it many times. All without competition. The telephone has changed twenty times in my career. . . . We invented microwave for transmission because it was cheaper than the tape they were using. Then we used coaxial cable and it was cheaper than microwave; then the labs started making improvements in microwave so they could expand its capacity and it became cheaper than coaxial cable. Then we developed a new coaxial cable and it became cheaper than micro. Now we have developed single sideband to use with microwave and it's cheaper than cable."

To be profitable, a technology must have widespread applicability. That, in turn, will allow it not only to gain market share and make a profit, but also to attract the kind of high-quality managers, engineers, and marketers necessary to drive it on to future successes. It is the bandwagon effect. Moreover, the sophistication of a new technology is not all that important in making a particular technology a success. What is important is applicability; otherwise a company could find itself in a market niche with limited market potential, or without any market at all, save for a handful of experts and dedicated fans who admire it for its complexity or design. That is not to say that some companies have not made money by exploiting such market niches—particularly smaller companies—but simply to stress that it is expensive, difficult, time consuming, and a strain on a variety of resources to develop a new technology, and that to make it worthwhile, it had better be applicable over a variety of markets.

Trying to anticipate such a new, broad-based technology is like trying to capture lightning in a bottle. But once that technology appears, even in an inchoate form, a chief executive can begin to make guesses as to its potential market value. The chief executive should always hammer away at this key point: trying to draw out from engineers, scientists, and developmental personnel a rough feeling for the kind of new products that might come out of that technology. When scientists at Bell Labs stumbled upon the transistor, they did not realize the enormous spectrum of products that it would eventually create, but they did realize that it was an important commercial discovery.

Thus, we see a number of crucial decisions that chief executives are called upon to make over technology. First, should they fund basic research at all? Most companies do not; the vast majority of basic research is still paid for by the government, either directly to the company itself, often in the form of a defense contract, or at universities or independent laboratories. In fact, I have counted only ten American companies that engage in large-scale, high-technological research. The rest pursue what is really development, often just to differentiate products already on the market. When chief executives do decide to fund basic research, they must then try to guess roughly how long it will take to expect a commercial pay-off and how much it will cost. This is crucial; many such research projects have been abandoned when the pay-off receded further and further into the future. Thus, it takes an extremely confident and strong chief executive to stay the course over the long haul that is required to commercialize most new technologies. As the environment changes, so too does the attitude toward research and development. Even the most prestigious companies and the most sympathetic chief executives often take ruthless and short-sighted views of their in-house research efforts. And often they abandon all but the most likely research effort with the shortest possible pay-off time. Thornton Bradshaw, the chief executive of RCA, was a guest speaker in two of my classes at New York University Business School in 1983. He said bluntly at that time that one of the costs he reviewed when that company was floundering so badly was part of its research and development effort, which was then the fourth or fifth largest among U.S. companies. (Bradshaw has since denied making any cuts.) Yet, many experts question how long AT & T will fund Bell Labs, in today's deregulated environment.

At some point, most chief executives of technological companies must face the choice of developing innovation in house, or going out and buying it in the form of a company that has already pioneered it. Mergers and acquisitions are often the cheapest and safest way of breaking into a new technology. That is clearly the object behind the series of acquisitions made by Roger Smith, the chief executive of General Motors: first H. Ross Perot's data-processing giant, Electronic Data Systems, then, for over $5 billion, Hughes Aircraft. The latter was an attempt "to get us into new technologies in the aerospace industry," Smith declared at the time. I will discuss Smith's technological strategy in greater detail later. It is enough here to emphasize that given the risks of technological ventures, it often makes sense to buy an established company with already existing expertise in a particular field. As one chief executive told me, "I know we paid too much for that acquisition, but it was the best way to acquire that new technology—far better than if we'd try to do it ourselves from scratch." Moreover, sometimes, when a technology is protected by patents, the only way to acquire it may be to buy it—and of course pay a premium for it.

Buying technology is not always as simple or as risk free as it seems. Often, technology resides not in a product, but in the minds of a few researchers. Many large companies have been unpleasantly surprised when they have bought up smaller, innovative companies, only to discover that the people with the innovation would rather not work for them. As a result, before moving ahead with a merger or acquisition, many chief executives now investigate whether the key people plan to stay at a company. One chief executive told me in exasperation, "We bought that company for those high-technology people, specifically. But no sooner was the ink dry on the contract, than half those key men either left or were threatening to leave. And that's despite strong personal assurances and written contractual obligations regarding the amount of employee holdover once we acquired them. It's really a souring experience for me."

In fact, the corporate world is littered with the shells of formerly vibrant companies acquired by others for their technologies. Schlumberger had its Fairchild Semiconductor, the first of the great Silicon Valley microchip makers. Exxon bought Zilog, a young chip maker. Xerox picked up Scientific Data Systems, a computer maker, in the 1960s, and Shugart, a disc-drive company, in the 1970s. Johnson & Johnson bought Technicare, a medical imaging company, which it recently sold to General Electric. SmithKline and French Company bought Beckman, a diagnostics company, which has never achieved its former glory. Many have now either been sold off or closed; still, the cycle contines. Biotechnology has now entered the acquisition phase with Eli Lilly picking up Hybritech and Bristol-Myers Company swallowing Genetic Systems. Buying technology is hardly a riskless way to go.

Spy, Counterspy

As we have seen, technology is often an amorphous sort of thing—an idea, a diagram on a scrap of paper, an expertise that resides in a skilled pair of hands or in a brilliant mind. And expensive technology can often go down the elevator and out the front door, never to return. But there are other

149

dangers: there is often ample opportunity for a whole host of individuals who are aware of different stages of technological development to either purposely or inadvertently pass on key strategic information to others either inside or outside the company. And that is not including the number of people who will leave one company, carrying secret charts, models, prototypes, formulas, designs, theories, or computer programs, to set up their own operation. There is nothing new about this kind of phenomenon. What is new is the realization of the importance of new technology, and the sheer amount of sophisticated spying or surveillance techniques.

All of the chief executives I spoke with were acutely aware of how vulnerable their companies were to these sorts of strategic leaks. As a result, many of them have implemented elaborate secret codes, locks, security devices, and at times, lie detector tests for new employees. Moreover, this diffusion of data has meant that many chief executives have chosen *not* to patent their new products or processes for fear that they would divulge too much information to potential competitors when they filed the patent application.

IBM provides a fascinating artifact of this fear of spying in the form of a ringed binder handed out to employees, describing the range of security clearances. The binder could as easily have come from the CIA. From it, employees learn of the four levels of clearance for IBM documents: "IBM internal use only" (blue), "IBM confidential" (green), "IBM confidential-restricted" (yellow), and the highest of all, "registered IBM confidential" (red). How are these documents categorized? It says in the binder that a document should be classified "registered IBM confidential" when it:

- "Provides IBM a very significant competitive edge.
- Means outside disclosure would cause severe damage to IBM.
- Relates to or describes a major and very significant portion of IBM's business.
- Shows strategic and major direction over an extended period of time.
- Is vital to the technical/financial success of a new product."

IBM also details what it calls "control requirements," that is, who gets such documents, how they are passed on, who guards them. For example, internal disclosure documents are for IBM employees with a predetermined need to know and where strict accountability and history of access is required. External disclosure, on the other hand, requires the prior approval of at least a division president or general manager. Employees cannot copy these documents, and they must always be returned—never destroyed—to an employee known as the recorder. Such documents should not be discussed on the telephone or transmitted in any way, unless encrypted. And employees should avoid traveling with them at all costs.

Does it sound faintly Orwellian? Sure, but IBM makes it work—something the government has not been able to do. There is also a flip side, of course. For every chief executive trying to protect trade secrets, there is another trying to ferret them out. This need not be simply spying, and is usually not illegal in any way. Instead, such strategic intelligence-gathering or offensive-scanning techniques allow chief executives to carefully monitor what new technologies are being worked on by the competition, and allow them to estimate how long these technologies will take to reach the marketplace. Many chief executives told me that for the first time they were actively gearing up scanning strategies, concentrating on discovering the competition's basic cost information, differential price/profit data, and other, more esoteric, technological information. Ignoring possible breakthroughs has, said one somewhat shell-shocked chief executive, "blindsided us terribly. We'd be investing heavily in redoing an old plant to increase our production run on some product, when out-of-the-blue some competitor, usually foreign, would launch some slightly better technological product. I've now told my managers I won't tolerate any more of these types of surprises."

Scanning techniques can vary widely in scope, cost, usefulness, and ethics. Michael Porter of Harvard University and other experts have developed elaborate systems that a company can use to systematically create an up-to-date inventory of strategic intelligence. Other experts specialize in monitoring technological developments, often through outside advisors and consultants, or through think tanks or research outfits that can, for a fee, generate market forecasts. Finally, some chief executives depend on hiring away key people from competitors when they think a technology may be reaching commercial viability.

The danger of all of this activity is the likelihood that you can drown in a flood of paper. Too much information pours in, too many details pile up, so that you can't separate the trivial from the essential. One way around this is to assign one person the role of competitor, gathering all information about them and developing a series of scenarios as to what they are likely to do next. This system works best when there is only one major competitor in a given market. Alas, increasingly, a range of external threats make such

151

scanning more and more complex, particularly as industries and markets merge and the pace of innovation and change quickens. The chief executive who has to ask, as one did, "Exactly what strategic arena are we competing in?" has a long and difficult road ahead to gathering effective intelligence.

The Consortium Strategy: The Formation of the Microelectronics and Computer Technology Corporation

Twenty years ago, a joint research consortium of twenty companies or so would have been as illegal as price fixing, a violation of long-established antitrust laws. Consider, for instance, the case of Armco and its chief executive William Verity. For years, Verity said, he had been trying to get permission from the Justice Department to allow a consortium of steel companies—Inland, Jones & Laughlin, and Armco—to jointly build a new, state-of-the-art steel mill. The Justice Department never gave its approval. Meanwhile, Verity said, the U.S. steel industry fell further and further behind steel companies in other countries, not only in terms of profits, but more significantly in the long-run, in its technology. And as the spiral deepened, the window of opportunity for such a new, greenfield plant closed. "Armco has felt that the cost of a new greenfield plant is so high we can't afford to put one in," said Verity. "In my opinion, U.S. Steel doesn't have the clout either. They don't know yet, but they'll find out. . . . It will cost a billion dollars to put in a million tons, so it's just ridiculous." Verity was not far off. I talked with him in the late 1970s. By the early 1980s, the steel industry was flat on its back and indeed, even U.S. Steel, the largest of the integrated steel operators, could not afford such a plant.

Still, the truth is that while the failure to approve a greenfield plant did hurt steel companies like Armco, it really came rather late in the game— a sign of the desperation of the steel industry. In fact, while U.S. companies have been under pressure on price from foreign producers, the decline of the American industry can be viewed as a long-term failure of a technological strategy. While foreign producers were plowing profits back in new technology such as continuous casters and integrated mills, American companies were continuing to use outmoded and relatively inefficient equipment such as open-hearth furnaces. Then, as the market for steel began to shrink, a result of increased uses of plastic and smaller cars, the U.S. companies were caught flat-footed. American producers tried desperately to delay a day of reckoning, by lobbying Congress for a trigger-price mechanism, which meant that foreign steel would come in at higher prices and allow U.S. companies to continue with their outmoded technology—a classic example of long-term health sacrificed on the altar of short-term results. And of course, sought out schemes like the consortium.

Today, the facts have changed, at least for research and development. First, there is a more lenient attitude in Washington under the Reagan administration toward business partnerships, including consortia, takeovers, and joint ventures of all kinds. Second, there exists a clear realization on the part of chief executives of many high-technology companies that their Japanese and European competitors are using such consortia, often with government funding and assistance. Therefore, the logic goes, U.S. corporations also need such partnerships; if they do not form them, they could well find themselves falling behind their overseas competitors as the next generation of technology begins to arrive.

That, in essence, is the genesis of the best known of the recently formed American research consortia, the Microelectronics and Computer Technology Corporation headed up by Bobby R. Inman, the retired admiral and former chief of the National Security Agency. Inman's consortium, known as MCC, represents the most ambitious cooperative research venture in U.S. history. It was founded in 1982 by eleven companies from the computer and semiconductor industries—the number had grown to twenty-one by 1986—to develop the next-generation computer and semiconductor technology. MCC was launched as a response to Japan's so-called fifth-generation computer challenge, an attempt by Japanese companies and Japan's powerful Ministry of International Trade and Industry (MITI) to develop a viable form of computer-based artificial intelligence. Since the consortium was founded, Inman has overseen the construction of a new headquarters and three other buildings in Austin, Texas, and the hiring of more than four hundred employees.

Spearheading the effort to form MCC was William C. Norris, founder and former CEO of Control Data (he retired in January 1986 and became chairman emeritus). Norris has been famous—or infamous, if you talk to his critics—for his insistence that corporations can help both society and themselves by addressing societal needs as profitable business opportunities in cooperation with government and other sectors. As he made clear in a 1978 interview, this approach is profit-oriented, but goes well beyond the

153

conventional wisdom about the role of corporations in American society. "I'm not interested in just making or selling another computer," he told me. "I've done that."

Norris's argument for the creation of MCC was based on the threat that many American companies, including his own, felt from foreign competitors, particularly Japan. In the 1970s, he approached the Western European computer companies several times about forming a similar consortium, but found little interest there. It was only when the threat of Japanese competition loomed large in the early 1980s that he was able to convince American companies of the wisdom—and necessity—of conducting cooperative research and development, which led to the formation of MCC.

But why a consortium, when companies traditionally—and successfully—pursued their own in-house research? Norris and others argued that many chief executives failed to keep the companies at the forefront of technology. This was particularly evident in manufacturing, where many American companies turned to overseas suppliers for crucial components. Whether we look at such items as computer terminals or basic memory chips, we see the same phenomenon: namely, companies are abandoning manufacturing to overseas competitors who, frankly, can make them better at cheaper prices. Thus, from the point of view of some chief executives, it made sense to simply buy all of its components abroad, then assemble the pieces into a finished product.

The result has been the appearance of what *Business Week* has called "the hollow corporation," a company that does very little manufacturing but quite a lot of marketing. The problem, of course, is that overseas suppliers start by building components, but soon move on to packaging the pieces themselves. As a result, American electronics firms have been battered by overseas competitors in markets for VCRs, cameras, radios, and televisions. Is there a lesson here? Chief executives such as Norris believe there is. First, they say, U.S. companies devote their resources to research and develop the component building blocks of products. Then, higher relative costs, particularly in labor, force companies to abandon the component production. And by doing so, those companies relinquish their command of the advancing technology. New components that are pioneered abroad provide the building blocks for new products, which of course would be dominated by overseas companies—thus, the idea of sharing costs in a consortium. "We really had no option but to join," said Thornton Bradshaw of RCA.

154

TECHNOLOGY STRATEGIES

The experience of Texas Instruments is apropos here. As I will discuss in the chapter on marketing, Texas Instruments under chief executive J. Fred Bucy was the key proponent of a marketing strategy called "pricing down the experience curve"—that is, pricing products, such as watches and calculators, with basic semiconductor chips near the break-even point, with the expectation that as volume grew, the cost to make them would fall. While the strategy worked well in the 1960s, it ran into difficulties in the 1970s, as Japanese and other Far Eastern companies learned to master similar technologies and took to riding the same cost curve as that of Texas Instruments. Because of their advantage in cheaper labor costs, a clear strategy of cutting prices to gain export market share, and occasional government subsidies, they were able to quickly undercut Texas Instruments on price. By the 1980s, Bucy had gotten Texas Instruments out of commodity watches and calculators, but was trying to combat overseas competition by pushing forward technologically, into first 16-, then 64- and 256-bit chips. But still, the high cost of innovation took its toll on Texas Instruments and other semiconductor companies. Said one CEO, "I feel I'm fighting with one hand chained behind my back, because the Japanese government gives their corporations the go-ahead, the finance, the technological knowhow. Besides, they have a totally free access to U.S. markets, and we cannot get anything in there."

For all of that, the arguments in favor of a consortium conveniently ignore certain other factors. Members of the technology consortium tend to be so-called BUNCH companies—that is, Burroughs, Univac (a part of Sperry Corporation, both of which have now been acquired by Burroughs), NCR, Control Data, and Honeywell Corporation, which have traditionally sold mainframe computers in the turbulent wake of IBM (which, by the way, has pointedly failed to join Inman's group). So it is not as clear cut as it may seem; these companies are looking for a way to compete cheaply not only against overseas competition, but against a domestic powerhouse, IBM. And by joining together, they protect themselves against any one of their group breaking free from the second tier. Second, failures by these companies in some markets have come as much from poor strategic decisions as they have from overseas competitors. RCA, for instance, bailed out of computers in the 1960s, and in the late 1970s, just prior to Bradshaw taking over, made the disastrous decision to market laser discs instead of videocassettes. As a result, they were blown away by the cheaper and simpler Japanese technology. As for Control Data, it fumbled badly in 1985 and

155

1986, as much a result of its own managerial mistakes as from the bogeyman of overseas competition. As a result, William Norris ultimately had to leave the company he founded.

There is another issue here as well, which no one has yet been able to answer: can consortia such as MCC produce research on demand, or do innovations arise serendipitously? The American experience has always been the latter. Thus, the mythology of the inventor in his garage. For all of the billions spent by the Japanese, the major breakthroughs of the past few decades—particularly computers and biotechnology—have often taken hold in out-of-the-way labs or in the recesses of eccentric minds, in America or Europe. Even at Bell Labs, that exemplar of a research institution, discoveries such as the transistor appeared, as it were, out of nowhere. It may well be that trying to industrialize research is fated to the same sad end as trying to institutionalize marketing or bureaucratize new ventures.

Xerox and AT & T and the Computer Business

Both Xerox and AT & T, two technological powerhouses, have experienced the difficulties of trying to industrialize research and make it pay over the long term. Xerox, of course, sprang from the invention of xerography. But as the original Xerox patents began to expire, the company found itself under competitive pressure, from both American and Japanese companies. At the same time, Xerox made several attempts to get into the computer business, the idea being to build an "office of the future" in which copiers, computers, printers, and other pieces of high-tech hardware are linked in an integrated system.

Alas, success in copiers did not mean success in computers. Xerox's first attempt in the computer business in the 1960s was crushed by IBM. In the 1970s, Xerox made a second attempt, betting on its capacity to innovate. McColough at Xerox described to me how, in a series of key management decisions, Xerox decided to segment off an investigative group doing research and development into an integrated office environment—the genesis of the marketing slogan, "Team Xerox"—consciously placing them not at the company's sleek corporate headquarters in Connecticut, but three thousand miles away at a new facility, the Palo Alto Research Center

TECHNOLOGY STRATEGIES

(PARC), in Silicon Valley. Xerox truly believed that innovation could only be spawned by giving PARC the freedom and funds to go where they had to go, without the stifling effect of the corporate bureaucracy. In effect, Xerox was trying to start a new venture, but a very specialized kind—one designed strictly to create innovative products.

In that, PARC was a raging success. Xerox was able to hire some of the brightest and most imaginative engineers, programmers, and just plain thinkers. As a result, PARC became famous in the computer business for the elegance and brilliance of its designs. Researchers at PARC designed the "mouse," a control device for personal computers; windowing software, which made it easy to manipulate large amounts of information; and icons, the symbolic representation of computer functions; and they contemplated a computer concept called the Dynabook, a notebook-sized computer of the future. Unfortunately, while Xerox managed to take the bureaucracy out of PARC, it could not succeed entirely in taking PARC out of the bureaucracy. Once the innovation left PARC, it was up to the company to package it, manufacture it, and market it. All of that proved far more difficult to Xerox than did innovating. Throughout the 1970s, Xerox's office-of-the-future concept limped along, although today, finally, there are signs that the company has begun to gather momentum in computers.

Ironically, much of the PARC technology did find its way to profitability in the marketplace—but not at Xerox. Steve Jobs at Apple Computer systematically mined the genius of PARC for a variety of products, culminating in Apple's Lisa and Macintosh models, with their easy-to-use windowing software and the "mouse." And Alan Kay, one of the most brilliant of the PARC alumni and one of the major proponents of Dynabook, is now Apple's chief designer. The lesson here—one learned by both Jobs and Xerox—is that it simply is not enough to innovate technologically; the product must be marketed properly as well.

AT & T too saw the necessity of getting into the computer business, but its problems were somewhat different than Xerox's. As former AT & T chief executive John deButts told me, "Although we invented the transistor and let other companies develop computer technology, we gradually began to see that this had to be the wave of the future by combining telecommunications with databanks and computerized processing systems. We realized we would be missing the boat if we just abandoned this work."

AT & T found itself in a most unusual position. As a regulated utility, the company could not begin to compete with IBM and the BUNCH in an area like mainframes. But that didn't mean that AT & T just ignored the technology. Actually, the company was so large that, as deButts said, "we were already the biggest users of computers inside AT & T. So we were already researching, developing, and producing computerized systems of our own make and design, long before we decided to launch the company's sales force into selling these systems." That point came, of course, when AT & T was deregulated.

While the internal market was hardly ideal—it did not provide the sharpening and focusing of competition—it did offer an adequate proving ground for AT & T computers. Slow and clumsy as AT & T's entrance into computers undoubtedly has been, experts long viewed AT & T as a tremendous threat to other computer makers, including mighty IBM, not only because of its financial power, but because of its long record of technological excellence and its secure position in telecommunications, which can provide enormous leverage for selling computer products.

But again, developing technology is one thing, and selling it is another. As I will touch on in the marketing chapter, by mid-1986, three years after Charlie Brown had consented to the unbundling of Bell, and with several years of experience in free markets under its belt, AT & T's Information Services division continued to lose money—$800 million in 1985, with an estimated $100 million directly attributable to computers. In fact, observers could see little improvement: strategic planning was still confused and indecisive, and sometimes contradictory, management turnover was high, and morale was lousy. Again, it was not the technology; AT & T was marketing minicomputers and microcomputers—some bought from outside vendors—that were the equal of IBM's. And AT & T had one edge: years earlier, Bell Labs had developed a highly efficient computer operating system called Unix, that seemed suitable for complex scientific and engineering tasks. But while Unix has been much ballyhooed, AT & T has done a poor job of selling it and its Unix computers. And so far, AT & T has failed to use telecommunications expertise as a way to sell its more traditional computers.

Can AT & T turn itself around? Only time will tell, but the optimism of the year immediately following divestiture is gone, and AT & T is locked into a scrap in one of the fastest changing markets around—a market where technology, while important as a ticket to get in, does not guarantee club membership.

TECHNOLOGY STRATEGIES

Remaking the Corporation

Few executives have as firm a grasp on the new technologies as does William McGowan of MCI. Engaged in a highly technological business and locked in intense competition with AT & T, McGowan is, admittedly, a proselytizer for the new information technology. Still, McGowan offers a longer view on the issue of technology strategies. "The first step, then, has to be to get top management thinking about those technologies not as an expense item, but as a competitive tool," he told me. "That's why I think history will show a watershed was reached when Roger Smith of General Motors decided to merge their MIS department with EDS [a GM acquisition] and thereby transform the entire corporation."

Smith revealed his own thoughts on one of the widest-ranging overhauls of a corporation, focusing on the much ballyhooed Saturn car project: "They [Saturn employees] can start with everything on computers, so you don't start the day with a big bundle of reports on things you didn't really want to know in the first place. . . . It's a clean-sheet approach. We gave them an eight-and-a-half- by eleven-inch sheet of paper, [and] told them to get it all on there and throw out the rest." Smith wanted the project to start not only with state-of-the-art technology, but one linked at all levels by the company's EDS data processing capability—a classic example of a common-denominator technology.

Such an effort was neither inexpensive nor simple to accomplish. But again, the impetus for such a thoroughgoing overhaul—a herculean attempt to drag this huge corporation, often kicking and screaming, into the 1980s— was a reaction to increasingly severe competitive pressures. Top management at the Big Three auto companies, used to all but automatic profits, were jolted by the huge losses suffered in the recession of 1980–81 and by the widening lead that overseas car makers, particularly Japanese, had taken in cost cutting, productivity, and overall quality. Instead of simply diversifying out of cars, as many large companies had in the face of similar crises, Smith and his colleagues at the other two companies—Philip Caldwell at Ford and Lee Iacocca at Chrysler—hunkered down, poured in investment capital, and embraced new technologies. Smith, in particular, chose to diversify into nonautomotive fields that would improve automaking.

159

Smith was aiming at what he called "complementary technologies." For instance, Smith argued that the Hughes Aircraft acquisition would "assist GM in redefining the basic car from a mechanical product, which includes a few electrical subsystems, to one with major electrochemical and electronic elements." That could mean a dramatic leap beyond current electronic dashboards, windows, and fuel injection, into a full-scale attempt to substitute electronic controls for steering, braking, and throttling. Likewise, the EDS acquisition was aimed at not only gaining a profit-making subsidiary, but at providing the data-processing expertise to link together everything from payroll to production, distribution, and sales, and give Smith better strategic control over the sprawling GM empire. The apotheosis of that strategy came with the Saturn project—and the court is still out on the success, or failure, of that ambitious effort.

Conclusion

Technological innovation follows a familiar pattern. Each new technological breakthrough touches off a cycle in which the pathbreaking discovery, invention, or conceptualization disrupts a market and, if it is a basic technology, transforms an industry. Chief executives are crucial in this process, because they are major players in the funding of new technology that begins the cycle. And they are major participants in the range of decisions usually known as development, where the technology is finding itself becoming a part of marketable products. It is the chief executive, for example, who in the last analysis must decide whether to patent, license, develop in house, exploit, or allow the technology to rust on the laboratory shelf. Finally, the chief executive must decide which markets—wide or narrow—to sell into, and how the technology should be presented and packaged.

Making a mistake in any one of these decisions can consign a company to oblivion. Remember Xerox: with copier technology, it was the quintessential growth stock, grasping a technology of the future and, right along the line, moving that technology in just the right directions. But when it came to the computer, the formerly sure-footed Xerox was as clumsy as an elephant on roller skates. For a while, it seemed, Xerox could barely do anything right.

That sort of risk makes most chief executives wary, to say the least, and explains quite a lot about the enthusiasm for risk-sharing consortia. I found that while virtually every chief executive claimed to have a strong belief in the power of technology—is that not one of the reigning beliefs of this age?—in practice, it was not an important priority for most. The research and development budgets of most companies were really very limited and usually only amounted to funding the development of spin-offs of existing products. Thus, in those rare cases where a chief executive had made a major personal commitment to technological research and development—such as Thomas Watson, Jr., at IBM, Edwin Land at Polaroid Corporation, and the long line of Bell CEOs who funded Bell Labs—that corporation often became known for decades as a leader in technology.

The competitive advantage a company derives from technological breakthroughs depends on two key factors: first is the breakthrough fundamental or incremental; second is whether the technology involves an innovation that enhances, or one that substitutes, a product. In both cases, it is a matter of degree. An enhancement innovation—say, a faster semiconductor chip—may mean that you can use existing production machinery through retrofitting and retooling, and that customers will probably be able to easily adjust to the new product. Market leaders are often in the best position to exploit enhancement innovations, which resemble product line extensions, whether they invent them or license them from others. In contrast, a substitution innovation—say, a completely new computer hardware technology, akin to the switch from vacuum tubes to integrated circuits—often renders existing manufacturing facilities obsolete and forces potential customers to reevaluate their needs. As such, a substitution technology can devastate the market position of a market leader. Because these technologies are often spawned in small, obscure companies, they pose an increasingly frequent threat to established firms.

Despite that, chief executives at large companies admitted that they tended to drag their feet when it came to developing substitution technologies on their own. A good example: when the breakthroughs in molecular biology that would lead to biotechnology in the mid-1970s were made, most of the major pharmaceutical firms yawned. Their products were, primarily, chemistry-based, and this new biology seemed far-fetched. Thus, a number of new companies, from Genentech to Biogen and Cetus, stole the march. Now, the pharmaceutical makers are scrambling to catch up, often through acquisition or licensing.

The rise of biotechnology brings up another lesson in the technology game: how long it takes to introduce substitution innovation into the marketplace. While the progress from test tube to market has been rapid compared to the pace of academia, it has been interminable on the time scale of the investment and Wall Street communities. Even today, almost seven years since the first biotech company went public, only a handful of low-selling products have made it through the Food and Drug Administration and into the marketplace. And there is no guarantee that the consumer—in this case, physicians—will go for many of these new products as enthusiastically as biotech proponents insist they will. Similar tales could be told of such breakthroughs as the computer, xerographic copying, or even the automobile. "Although a ball-point pen takes only a minute to use," said Norris of Control Data, "getting the ordinary man in the street to sit down and use a computer has taken years." The nightmare of the inventor—or of the CEO who has funded one—is a breakthrough nobody needs.

For chief executives who fund technology, the ultimate frustration may be that the technology may not reach the development stage when they are still in office. And so the rewards will come to their successors, if in fact there will be any reward at all. And that, as much as any other single factor, lies behind the willingness of chief executives to slash research and development budgets or, in a crisis, to jettison research departments. As Thornton Bradshaw, chief executive at RCA and, prior to that, president of ARCO, said, "The pay-off for major new technological investments we made was often totally problematical." Technological development certainly is important; it is what John A. Young of Hewlett-Packard, a notable technology company, calls "our major national resource." Unfortunately, it is also risky, long term, threatening, and easily expendable.

CHAPTER SEVEN

NEW-VENTURE STRATEGIES: FROM ACORNS TO MIGHTY OAKS

I don't think venture capitalists are classed as entrepreneurs, although I think they have to be a little bit that way, particularly the nutty side of it. Everybody's got to be a little nutty to start a business.　　　　　　　—HERBERT D. DOAN, former CEO, Dow Chemical Company

At Litton, we didn't start out to manage a major company, we were trying to create a major company.　　　　　　　—ROY ASH, former president, Litton Industries Inc.

Nobody Said Giving Birth Would Be Easy

From 1972 to 1982, Exxon, the world's largest company, launched a series of new ventures, none of them connected to its traditional oil business. Over that time, it invested over $4 billion in oil shale production, mining, electric motors, and office equipment. And along with those enormous resources, the company threw the best scientific, engineering, and managerial talent money could buy at the fledgling operations. This was no small effort. In office equipment alone, Exxon spent $500 million for some fifteen companies. Plus it set up three different research facilities in Silicon Valley—Kylex, Epid, and Summit (it was an era of lunacy in naming companies)—and tried to establish a number of new ventures closer to

163

home, including Qwyp, a maker of telephone facsimile equipment, and Qyx, an electronic typewriter maker. Nonetheless, by the end of the decade, Exxon was forced to retreat on each of these ventures, creating significant financial losses and causing considerable corporate embarrassment. Why did Exxon fail? Because it lacked a truly effective new-venture strategy.

New ventures for large corporations usually succeed only when they are truly entrepreneurial—when, in other words, each is allowed to develop and implement its own, individual new-venture strategy. And this is the first problem, for often enough, new ventures are overseen by the same people who have risen in the ranks of the parent corporation, and who intend to manage in the way they always have been told to manage. That just does not work; a new venture is a qualitatively different beast than a big corporation. While this may seem obvious, most large corporations have found it almost impossible *not* to impose their management practices on the delicate, green shoots of the new venture.

Not that starting a new venture is easy for anyone. Fully 80 to 90 percent of all new ventures fail, whether they have been spawned by large companies or by entrepreneurs. One survey of sixty-one new-venture investments by large corporations revealed a median return of *minus* 8 percent. As Herbert D. Doan, a venture capitalist and the former chief executive of Dow Chemical (as had been his father and his grandfather), told me, "I suppose there's two ideas that are funded out of a hundred that come along. I think we see three hundred a year and we do two or three. . . . There are a lot of entrepreneurs out there who don't get funded. This industry gets a bad name from a lot of people that don't choose to put their money in those many, many people. Once you begin to break it down, the venture capital business is, paradoxically, not as risky as you'd think. Once they pick out the two or three, I think the success rate might be 50 percent—and with the good ones [venture capitalists], it might be 80 percent." Doan, of course, was talking about successful in investment terms, not in the growth of the operation into a freestanding company. There are many ventures that return money to their backers but never go much further.

Successful new-venture strategies have changed very little over the years. Today, as yesterday, the key ingredient for success hinges upon the guts and grit, not to say the vision and conviction, of the chief executive who is building the venture. Can larger companies spawn new ventures? IBM has shown that it can. Again, appropriate management, given free reign, was the key. IBM, which for decades has dominated the computer mainframe market, had totally neglected the small but rapidly developing personal computers pioneered by Apple, Coleco Industries, Inc., Atari, and others. To break into the market, IBM made the surprising decision to adapt a strategy that diverged dramatically from the company's traditional practices. First, the personal computer staff was located in Boca Raton, Florida, far from the sometimes stifling presence of headquarters staff in Armonk, New York. Second, it operated under a totally different set of rules and procedures than those of other IBM divisions. Thus, personal computer managers were allowed to purchase components from outside suppliers, in order to get the machine onto the market as soon as possible, while adapting a broad compatibility with software from other personal computers. The manager of the project was Philip D. "Don" Estridge, a long-time IBMer who proved to have enough of the entrepreneurial drive to get the machine out the door and successfully into the marketplace. Estridge described the key to success: "We were allowed to develop like a start-up company. IBM acted as the venture capitalist. It gave us management, guidance, and money, and allowed us to operate on our own."[1] Would that all new ventures resembled the IBM personal computer (PC). Obviously, they do not—not even at IBM. After all, the division that produced the PC also introduced the PC Jr., a smaller, less expensive version, several years later. Poorly designed and poorly positioned in the marketplace against its competitors, the PC Jr. never really took off and production was eventually stopped.

Other large companies, like Exxon, have had less successful ventures. Take CBS's attempt to get into cable television. Here was a corporate venture that was well financed and manned by experienced managers of previously successful enterprises. Unlike many failing new ventures, CBS did not seem to be entering a business that was unrelated to its core business, television. And it is useful to note that during the months when CBS was struggling with its cable venture, Time Incorporated, another media pioneer, was celebrating enormous success with one cable television venture, HBO (Home Box Office), while ignominiously shutting down a second, *TV Cable-Week* magazine. The fact that Time Inc. could fail in this magazine venture and CBS fail in its cable TV venture is evidence, I suppose, that there are no clear-cut formulas when it comes to new ventures.

How could these two giants fail? Hubris perhaps, or simply a blindness and a lethargy that comes with size. Perhaps the two corporations' previous successes in their respective fields played a significant role in the way these ventures were first structured and managed. Because these ventures so closely resembled their core businesses, both companies imposed upon them their traditional management techniques and brought in top corporate managers to run them. But particularly in the case of *TV Cable-Week*, Time Inc. apparently never did the most basic of research—looking to see whether a market existed for the product. As a result, it lost a quick $47 million. Of course, both of these failures are far closer to the usual fate of new ventures than was the rise of CBS from a small band of struggling radio stations.

So we have seen the successful and the unsuccessful, the glories of IBM and the dismal failures of Time Inc. and Exxon. Let us look for a moment at a common phenomenon: a new venture started for all of the right reasons that, alas, teaches a mixed lesson. The company is Armco, a major steel producer led, in the early 1970s, by William Verity. In 1962, when Verity was running Armco's big Kentucky plant, he, among others, spearheaded the start-up of an insurance unit. As Verity said, "In those days, you could do more in Kentucky than you could in Ohio, and it was set up principally to insure Armco facilities that you couldn't get insured by Lloyds of London. It grew because we insured more and more Armco facilities. Then, in 1968, we decided to take a closer look at insurance. We had a lot of capacity so we thought, why don't we expand it?"

Indeed, Belfont Insurance Company—which Armco called it—diversified into direct insurance, re-insurance, and insurance management. And it provided a countercyclical effect to the steel business. "In insurance," said Verity, "you just pile up the money and reinvest it, putting aside reserves to take care of disasters that might befall us. It was a new business for us. Right now, we have $200 million in assets that are being invested. In the steel business, all we did was spend money; we never put any aside. So it's a thrill each month to have a report from the insurance people saying that our assets have grown by $15 million. That's a great business as long as it's well run."

However, by 1986, as Armco's mainline business, steel, continued to suffer, Belfont also sailed into choppy waters along with the rest of the insurance industry. So what had been targeted by Verity as a counter to steel, with different cycles, had become another drain on the parent company.

NEW-VENTURE STRATEGIES

Defining New-Venture Strategies

There are at least seven types of new-venture strategies that well-established firms can adopt:

1. Patent-protection strategies, to safeguard a new product or process from infringement.
2. Strategies to win new market niches, that is, to capture and dominate a narrow, defensible market position for a product or service.
3. Strategies to extend product or service lines into new markets.
4. Lowest-cost production strategies, often through economies of scale, which enable a reduction in prices at a steady rate while steadily reducing costs, or even cutting prices in anticipation of lower production costs.
5. Market-segmentation strategy, entering a new venture in several markets simultaneously.
6. Diversification strategy, forming new ventures unrelated to those of the original company.
7. Merger or acquisition, joint-venture, or consortium strategies for new ventures through a takeover or partnership with another company to share assets, products, customer service base, customers, debt capacity, or technology.

These new strategies are not suited to all companies. Of the seven types of new-venture strategies, some are better suited to large companies, others to small; some to heavy industry, others to light; some to service companies, others to manufacturing. However, no venture strategy is clearly applicable to large and small organizations, *and* to heavy and light manufacturing, *and* to service companies. In short, while there is a wide range of new-venture strategies, it is a rare case when more than one is ideal for any particular company. The rest are inappropriate and frequently lead to failure.

Certain strategies, for example, are well suited only to the largest, best-established companies. General Motors can use its size and brand-name familiarity to implement its market-segmentation strategy—that is, producing many different car models simultaneously, each targeted at a different category of buyer. That type of strategy would hardly be ideal for a small manufacturer, for whom it would be wiser to pursue a small- or medium-sized niche that the major companies ignore. However, there are a number of strategies both share, such as patent protection and diversification. Even the low-cost strategy, which, with its emphasis on economies of scale, would seem to be the province of the giant firm, has broad possibilities. For a number of small corporations have shown the ability to beat out the giant company on cost by focusing all of their efforts on one product. And they do not have the excessive overhead of their larger competitors.

Since we have already taken an extended look at the takeover and diversification strategies, let us turn to the first five new-venture strategies.

The Patent Strategy

Successful new-venture strategies are usually dominated by an overriding concern for survival. For decades, the most easily defensible new-venture strategy to adhere to, in order to take the first step to survival, was filing a patent. Of course, securing a patent depended on having a unique, protectable product or technology, which in turn implies a viable technological strategy. The patent legally grants a monopoly to a company for seventeen years to enter a market—often, in fact, to prevent any competition. Many of the largest companies owe their survival, growth, success, and even their dominance to the vast series of patents they have had, winning for them protection in their years of greatest vulnerability to major competitors.

THE GILLETTE STORY

Patents hold a crucial role in the growth of Gillette Company, the Boston, Massachusetts–based maker of razor blades. The first patent on the disposable razor was filed in 1899 by a bottle-cap salesman named King C. Gillette. The razor needed perfecting, and Gillette was not sure whether he could provide the manufacturing knowhow to mass-produce it and make it a commercial success. Nonetheless, on November 15, 1904, patents 775,134 and 775,135 were granted to Gillette, giving to him the exclusive right for seventeen years to manufacture and sell a product described in the patent application as a "detachable razor blade of such thinness and flexibility as to require no external support to give rigidity to its cutting edge."

168

NEW-VENTURE STRATEGIES

Gillette's fears, thanks to the patents, were unfounded. For the disposable razor blade freed the common man from the expense of a barber, allowing him to shave himself on a regular basis. With no real competition, business boomed. Five years after Gillette's first razors were marketed in 1899, the company reported sales of two million razors, and tens of millions of blades. By World War I, soldiers on both sides of the trenches were using Gillette blades.

Not that Gillette was not threatened by other manufacturers who were trying to get a piece of the lucrative market he had created. Thus began a series of infringement suits against the likes of the Zinn Razor, the Ever Ready Razor, the Gem & Clark Blade & Razor Company, and the Autostrop Razor Company, all accused of borrowing or stealing the Gillette-patented razor and blade technology. The last of these suits lasted over twenty years, and Gillette was forced to buy out Autostrop for fear of losing the suit.

By 1918, Gillette planners began to formulate a strategy to prepare the company for the eventual expiration of the original patent. The company came up with a threefold plan: first, Gillette would announce a new, improved safety razor to retail at the same $5 price as the old razor, while cutting manufacturing costs on the old razor so it could be sold at a cheaper price. Then, a new, cheaper safety razor would be introduced to counter the flood of imitation razors that would enter the market following the expiration of the patent. This amounted to a market-segmentation strategy not much different from that of General Motors. Gillette filed for patents on both the new, higher-priced razor and blade and the new cheaper razor. At the same time, Gillette was forced to mount very expensive marketing and promotional campaigns at hotels, banks, and stores, and it was forced to undersell its rivals by offering huge volume discounts. Finally, over the years, the company discovered it had to compete not only through lower prices, but through diversification; so, it began to offer shaving creams and Toni home permanents, and acquired Paper Mate pens, Right Guard deodorant, and Braun Electric Appliances.

Gillette's experience offers some real lessons about how to use patents in a new-venture strategy—and, just as important, how to adapt to their expiration. First, Gillette protected its position through lawsuits and the timely acquisition of Autostrop. Two, when patents were expiring, the company shifted to mass production and the low-cost product, eventually diversifying into other products.

169

THE XEROX STORY

Xerox provides a more recent example of the use of patents in a new-venture strategy. The product, of course, was the now-ubiquitous photo-copier. Recall what McColough had said about Kodak's enormous dom-inance in the photographic marketplace in the years when Haloid, Xerox's earlier name, was in the document photographing business. Xerox needed a new technology, and one that could be patented and thus protected from Kodak and others. If you will remember, Chester Carlson had taken his invention to Battelle for refinement. In the meantime, he continued to shop it around. "Haloid, at this time," McColough told me, "was making around $12 million a year in revenue [in 1945], and I think their profitability was marginal, a few hundred thousand dollars a year at best. A most unlikely prospect. Mr. Wilson's job was to persuade him [Carlson] to give him limited rights for the development of the process in document copying. His main sales pitch was that if you give it to a big company, it's not going to give it a good look. We're willing to bet our whole company on this, and we don't have anything else, and we'll put our whole life and heart and everything else into this. So he got limited rights and got more rights in 1947."

Those rights would protect Xerox in first the difficult years, then the bountiful years to come. The Xerox case demonstrates not only how a company can gain protection from patents, but "extend" that patent by filing an array of subsidiary patents, component patents, and process pat-ents. More than thirty subsidiary patents were added to the original xerography patent, extending its life well beyond the expiration date of 1958. Not surprisingly, Xerox had to defend its patents from competitors. At first, that raised real fears at the still weak and tiny company. "At the time, there really wasn't any way that people could get around our patents," said McColough. "But if a larger company would have been able to re-produce that machine or its equivalent . . . we would have just been wiped out. In fact, our great fear in those days was that some stronger company— it could have been almost anyone—would invent another process and we would just have no chance."

Early on, the company developed a patent strategy. "Our philosophy of licensing and patenting xerography was that we would not license people for plain-paper copying applications. We wanted to keep that for ourselves. We thought that we had invented many of the process steps—although the initial invention was by Carlson—but we did want to get revenue by licensing other applications. For example, xerography was useful in X rays. For example, equipment utilizing the process for X ray applications. We licensed Bell and Howell, for example, for microphone applications. They never did anything with it." What was behind their decision on licensing? "We needed the revenue," he said flatly. "We also thought that licensing strong companies in other applications would further improve the process, and we had grant backs—exclusive grant backs. So if they made progress in another area that was useful, we could get it back; in fact, we never got too much."

The company's refusal to license out plain-paper copying, however, created difficulties. While some major companies—RCA, IBM, Bell and Howell, General Dynamics—sought licenses, little eventually came of them because everyone was waiting for Kodak to refine its Verifax technology, or 3M its Thermofax copying processes, and no one was willing or able to undertake xerography development themselves. Then, more dangerous yet, the SCM Corporation and the FTC brought antitrust action against Xerox, arguing that it was monopolizing the plain-paper copier market and illegally tying in other products and services to plain-paper copying. In 1970, Xerox was finally forced to share its technology. Since then, its market share has dramatically eroded, particularly in low-priced copiers, although the company has of late fought back hard against first Kodak, on the high end, then Japanese companies such as Ricoh, Mita, and Canon, on the low end. By then, of course, Xerox could hardly be considered a new venture; one sign of that is the shift internally from an emphasis on technology to one on marketing. "You don't count on success just coming from a superior product," says McColough. "You've got to count on it coming from marketing strategy, servicing strategy, and manufacturing efficiency, pricing, and so forth."

Both of the stories of Gillette and Xerox demonstrate how a company starting a new venture must be prepared to face constant patent infringement and lawsuits, and must be ready to battle it out not only for a few years, but for decades. Patents, like everything else, can be bruisingly competitive, and they do not provide a ticket to the Promised Land. While a patent can give a company a theoretically monopolistic position, huge legal expenses can quickly bankrupt a small company with only limited resources. Larger companies can find more comfort in patents, since they have the enormous financial and legal resources needed for a prolonged patent defense.

Recently, many companies—even large ones—have shown an increasing reluctance to patent new products. Why? Because they know how vulnerable or contestable patents can be. And, in making a patent application, a company must describe the product in great detail, explaining the chemistry, for instance, or the electronics. That, in turn, gives the secrets to competitors, allowing them to immediately begin devising ways to sidestep the patent or to contest it.

Seeking Out Market Niches

Traditionally, large companies shied away from market niches, leaving those small and narrow markets to their smaller corporate cousins. And, in fact, while small companies could make a success of those markets, they often found them limiting in terms of customer base, geographic region, or market isolation as they grew larger. The return from a market niche, after all, soon reaches a limit, unless it is a necessary product or service or unless the company retains a monopolistic position in which it can charge almost any price for the product.

For the large company, most market niches seem to offer only a limited market or an insufficient volume to justify start-up costs or a lengthy payback period. Instead, management from the largest companies often try to enter and dominate the far more difficult and expensive national and worldwide markets. As a result, the failure rate for new ventures at large corporations is very high indeed. In some cases, it may have been better if some of these new ventures had aimed to fill niches, rather than going for larger markets.

A number of successful attempts at launching new ventures in market niches were made by General Signal, the Stamford, Connecticut–based manufacturer of a variety of electronic equipment. Signal's chief executive then, Nathan Owen, developed a strategy of pursuing dominance in four different types of control technology. Because Owen had worked for a number of years in venture capital, he had a clear idea of how to plan and implement a market-niche strategy. He explained his thinking: "In most of our businesses—and this isn't 100 percent true, but it is for a very substantial majority—we are the number one company serving that particular market. Most of these are specialist companies. They have carefully defined what their market specialty is, and in that particular market specialty they are number one. . . . My experience, and the experience of others of looking at the profitability of companies, was that the industry leader was usually highly profitable. Profitability tapered down very drastically below number one."

Karl D. Bays, the chief executive of American Hospital Supply (AHS), adopted a similar niche-filling strategy in specialty health-care products which AHS could dominate as a virtual monopolist. Bays was, in effect, adjusting to the nature of the health-care marketplace. "You just can't fathom the size or the scope of the health business," he said. "It is still highly fragmented in many areas. It's an area of technological change, of entrepreneurs—the guy with the better mouse trap (there are a lot of tinkerers out there). With guys like us out there, we get them moving." When I spoke with him, AHS, which has since been swallowed up by Baxter Travenol Corporation, had 120 different market segments, ranging from $100 million in sales to just a few million. "We wanted to have leadership positions in at least a third of these segments," he said, "and we now have at least 40 percent where we're number one." Bays all but mirrored Owen: "We're only interested in being the number one company in each of these narrow market niches. But each one of these products in each one of these niches fits together in our overall hospital supply strategy."

Bays did not limit himself to building new ventures from scratch to fill those niches. "Bootstrapping, joint ventures, research and development, whatever—if you see a market and want to get in it, there are a lot of ways to do it," he said. "Acquisition here tends to come when there's no other way to get in. We are doing fewer acquisitions now than we did. Now, we tend to do more product line extensions. We went through a period, though, say 1972 to 1977, when we were moving into a lot of new stuff. And we've got basic positions there now."

Extending a Product Line

As Bays indicates, the most successful new venture strategy tends to be the extension of an existing product or service line. Usually, in such cases, the company already has a healthy part of the market or at least a base to work from. In such a strategy, management adds only minimal changes to its base products, for example, altering the size, color, or attachments. By extending their product line, companies hope to either wring more out of an existing market or reach totally new markets and customers. Such a strategy has been successfully pursued by a variety of companies: shoe, liquor, furniture, computer software, baking, and even steel companies, which take a basic product, raw steel, and make it into hundreds of different products with different widths, gauges, chemistries, coatings, and strengths. Service companies—banks, insurance companies, consulting firms—can also pursue such a strategy by adding one or two new features to their existing services and making a specialized product for a whole range of specialized customers.

Line extension tends to be a successful strategy because managers are already familiar with the basic business and can use already successful production, distribution, and marketing divisions. There is simply less room for error, whether it comes to gearing up a production method or a delivery system. But that does not mean that line extension is always successful. A poor marketing forecast, a flawed sense of the market, can bring a line-extension strategy grinding to a halt. A warehouse full of green dresses may not sell where dresses of a slightly different color will. No one said it would be easy.

Because line extension seems so simple, managers often make the big mistake of using it when they really need a new-product strategy. The failures of CBS's cable television network and Time Inc.'s cable television magazine can be traced to the alluring sense that these products were not new, but simply extensions of their basic businesses. In fact, they were *not* identical products with only a change in color or size, or with slight adaptations, all managed in the same old way. Instead, both required a new-venture strategy and a new mentality.

Becoming the Low-Cost Producer

The tale of Henry Ford and mass production has been told often enough elsewhere, but it holds classic lessons in the significance of becoming the low-cost producer and bears repeating. Ford, like many entrepreneurs, was not initially a success; twice he tried to produce expensive, custom cars, and failed. When he tried a third time, he had a new strategy: instead of building custom cars, he turned to the manufacture of low-cost, standardized cars which, like Gillette's razors, filled a growing need. In the first fifteen months of operation, Ford sold almost 1,700 cars—astounding for that day. And so was born the Model T and the Ford Motor Company.

Ford's success at cutting costs stemmed from a technological innovation—the development of the automobile assembly line—but it also involved cost cutting in every other aspect of the business, from purchasing to distribution to sales, marketing, and finance. So, while he is justly famous for developing a specialized conveyor belt for the assembly line, interchangeable parts, and coordinated flows of workers and power, it was equally critical that he developed strategies for mass selling, distribution, repair, shipping, even franchising. All of those moves contributed to his ability to sell a lower-cost car than his competitors, and to earn ever-greater profits. "Old Henry was a genius," said Arjay Miller, president of Ford under Henry Ford II. "He had only a few good ideas, but they were of fundamental importance. Mass production was a right idea. Interchangeable parts, a moving assembly line. Those ideas were so basically sound that he could afford to make a great many nonessential mistakes."

Today, the low-cost strategy is as popular and as controversial as it was in Ford's day. Companies in the Far East, for example, often adopt this strategy to compete with higher-cost U.S. firms, in everything from cars to steel and electronics. Traditionally, generating the lowest costs was associated with generating economies of scale. But as Ford proved, a second way to drive costs down is through a dramatic leapfrogging technology. And usually, it is the new venture that comes up with that technology and has the drive to implement it. Consider, for example, the strategy called pricing down the experience curve. To ride this very risky strategy—though it can be quite profitable—requires frequent innovations that will reduce the cost of making a product or improve it in some essential way. Thus, to win increasingly larger market share, the company will pass those cost reductions along to the customers, forcing their competitors to either compete, innovate, or take the loss. It is the ultimate corporate version of hand-to-hand combat.

One of the most successful developers of this strategy was the still young and growing Texas Instruments (TI), under J. Fred Bucy. "Because we knew that dramatic production cost reductions were possible in the 1970s [in computer components, particularly semiconductors], we decided to keep reducing the final retail price of these products. And it was precisely because we forced sharp downward pressure on market prices for over a decade that we achieved ever-increasing market shares in several fields until 1980." Other high-tech executives soon took an interest in TI's use of the experience curve, and began to copy it. By 1980, TI was forced out of markets such as watches and calculators because of foreign competitors which, with cheap labor costs, could use the experience curve against its originator.

Decline in product costs brought about by innovation continues to squeeze many companies, and many chief executives have learned that the experience curve and its resulting price wars, can cut both ways. Not surprisingly, many large, old, rigid companies have never been great fans of the experience curve, because it requires constant innovation and change. On the other hand, small, new ventures know little else but change. They are in a survival mode, and battling it out on price is just another way to survive. While large companies often have the wherewithal to battle on price, they often lack the will, particularly when their stock price begins to sag. Moreover, they have the ability to bail out of markets, which new ventures lack. As Geneen of ITT said, "A bad business is where all the firms keep cutting their prices. You end up giving away the product for free." In many price wars, such as those that have ravaged the computer, consumer electronics, and video game industries, as well as in such basic commodities as oil, steel, grain, milk, coffee, copper, paper, and chemicals, there is no profit left for any of the combatants. Verity, of Armco, which has suffered severely from such price cuts, summed up the danger: "To the extent that price competition is the real basis of a company's marketing strategy, that company is forced more and more into large-volume production facilities that cost a great deal more to build and maintain and supply. You are forced into long-term contracts to ensure supply, forced into a less flexible stance should a newer technology, or a dynamically new or trend-setting product, enter the market."

NEW-VENTURE STRATEGIES

Segmenting the Market

If Henry Ford all but defined the low-cost strategy, another master of the automobile business, Alfred P. Sloan, Jr., embodied the segmentation strategy. In the 1920s, under Will Durant, General Motors was only a loose holding company that, over the years, had acquired a range of miscellaneous businesses, including carriage and truck companies, auto-parts manufacturers, and auto-accessory companies. But GM had no core strategy. In the 1920s, after a series of spectacular failures, Durant was replaced by the aging Pierre S. duPont, who had retired from running the family's booming chemicals business and who stepped in at GM to save the family's 25 percent stake in the car company. Pierre duPont oversaw the rise of Alfred Sloan, a GM executive, who gradually introduced the classic segmentation strategy. Sloan summed it up by saying, "The corporation should produce a line of cars in each price area, from the lowest price up to that of the strictly high-grade production car."[2]

It seems so simple. And it was so successful that it remained intact for the next sixty years—fueling GM's rise to become the largest car company in the world. Even today, GM retains its Sloanian lineup of Chevrolet, Pontiac, Oldsmobile, Buick, and Cadillac. Each sells into a particular price segment of the market. The whole scheme was made possible by that grab bag of subsidiary companies that Durant had reigned over. Those operations made it possible for Sloan to vertically integrate parts manufacturing, car bodies, and accessories, linking them all tightly together into a corporate organization with a coherent strategy to unite them. And it allowed Sloan to use standard parts for more than one line of car, thereby developing a variety of production economies.

Sloan never did follow Ford's strategy of becoming strictly a low-cost producer. Sloan priced each of the five lines at the high end of each bracket, arguing that the GM car in each line *should* cost more because they were of higher quality. While that statement is clearly a bit of clever marketing, the truth is that an emphasis on cost, value, and quality is characteristic of those who decide to apply segmentation strategies.

What is so remarkable about Sloan's strategy is how common it is today. IBM sells a variety of computers segmented according to market and price, from the desktop IBM PC, to the somewhat faster, more powerful IBM AT, and the top-of-the-line Sierra mainframes. Steel companies like Armco traditionally tried to sell into hundreds of market segments, or niches. In the early 1970s, Armco's Verity said, the company hired the Boston Consulting Group to define its segments for it, so that Armco could assign a business manager to each—a sign that Verity recognized that segmentation had taken place; the BCG came up not with 5 or 6 segments, but 150 segments. General Electric sells a product line of washers and driers; Emery Air Freight sells a variety of transport services; even American Express has green, gold, and platinum credit cards. We shall see more of segmentation in the chapter on marketing.

When Emery Air Freight first got off the ground, there was really just one market segment for air freight: large cargo and masses of material such as financial documents. As a result, Emery specialized and dominated that market. Emery was never really threatened until the 1970s, when Federal Express entered the market and began taking over, indeed inventing, the low end—the transportation of single letters and packages. So Emery responded by developing Emery Courier Services, Emery First Flight Service, and by expanding Emery Express and Emery Air Freight. Although Emery was truly segmented after the Federal Express threat, the process had really begun some time earlier. Then, as competition increased, so too did the development of each of these businesses.

Strategy and Structure

Sloan created the classic model of the complex organizational structure that many corporations continue to follow. There are two basic principles to the Sloan organization: One, "the responsibility attached to each chief executive [of the five car companies at GM] shall in no way be limited. Each such organization headed by its chief executive shall be complete in every necessary function and enabled to exercise its full initiation and logical development." And two, "certain central organization functions are absolutely essential to the logical development and proper control of corporate activities."[3]

In other words, Sloan believed in centralizing a few essential functions within a larger context of decentralization. By contrast, Henry Ford concentrated all authority on himself at headquarters, which meant centralized control over all operations. Again, this coupling of a strategy with a specific type of organizational structure is vital to the success of a new venture. New-venture failures, as I said earlier, most frequently stem from mismatches—the wrong strategy imposed on the wrong corporate structure by the wrong type of managers. In fact, when even the largest and most successful companies impose an inappropriate executive structure on a new venture, there is usually no leeway to shift the structure and escape failure.

It is also important to consider the characteristics of the parent company before choosing an appropriate strategy. As mentioned earlier, smaller companies are usually better off choosing a policy based on protecting patents or seeking smaller, niche markets. Large companies can gain a marginal advantage by focusing on strategies that involve high volume and low-cost production runs, by segmenting the market, or through capital-intensive projects requiring complex layers of executive talent and large amounts of money. Thus, there are two contrasting points of view concerning the best new-venture strategy to follow. On one hand, there are those who focus very narrowly on one business, and emphasize low-cost production and delivery and a centralized organization. On the other hand are the creators of complex new ventures who believe in developing a whole range of new businesses, each with its new product in various models to appeal to different price ranges in the marketplace. Both kinds of new ventures are well known. But it is among the second group that are found the chief executives who frequently view new ventures only as a part of overall corporate strategy, not as an independent business operating within a decentralized framework. And it is these ventures that most often fail.

The New-Venture Entrepreneur

For all the talk about the mystique of the entrepreneur—about how he's driven internally to create and innovate—the reality may be far more mundane. The entrepreneur is often simply a refugee from an inhospitable corporate climate. Take William Norris, the founder of Control Data. Was he driven to "create" his company? Well, perhaps. But his motivations were also based on more prosaic problems. "When Sperry acquired

Remington," Norris said, "to form Sperry Rand, I was the manager of the Univac division. Rand had started to go senile. He put [a nut] in charge of the Intellect division and I had always prided myself on being able to work with anyone. I couldn't work for a nut, so I went out and founded a company." He added: "I just wanted to do something important, really, in computer technology. I would have stayed and been very happy."

Strangely, numerous studies indicate that most new-venture managers rarely articulate their ultimate goals, their fundamental policies, or even their strategies for survival and growth. That, I believe, is one major component separating the Wilsons, Fords, and Paleys of business from the legions of unsuccessful new-venture managers. One reason for that non-articulated strategy, I think, is that managers who go into new ventures tend to be experimentalists—trying this, trying that, feeling around in the dark, unsure of what they are looking for, but quite certain they will know it when they find it. For example, it is important to remember that many entrepreneurs (the term is interchangeable with new-venture managers) suffer, like Henry Ford, two or three failures before meeting with success. Those multiple failures build strength and resilience; entrepreneurs seem to have in their personalities a fundamental drive, which is missing in ordinary managers, to turn base failure into golden success. Even if their failure is based on random events, successful entrepreneurs learn from the turn of events, revise their strategy, and move on. Strategies are not immutable.

Entrepreneurs also need to take an almost schizophrenic attitude toward their projects, simultaneously rigid in terms of long-range goals and flexible in the means to achieve them. Sometimes this split forces the adoption of so-called "interim strategies." This is a problem that Peter McColough faced in the early days at Xerox. "We didn't have much money to develop products," he told me, "and they didn't really have mass markets; but we believed that by getting those products on the market, you'd force the technology and you'd make a bit of money you could pour back in the business to develop future products. You're not very happy or very proud [of those products], but they'll make a few million dollars in revenue and significantly force us to develop the technology, more so than if we just sort of sit back and say, 'Here's the ultimate product.' "

McColough pointed out another important lesson when he spoke of the tendency to "sit back and say, 'here's the ultimate product.' " That sort of ossification often stalls a new venture as it's moving from survival to real growth. Henry Ford, for example, is a classic case of a successful entrepreneur who became firmly wedded to his breakthrough product, the Model T, and was unable to accept the fact that a single-product strategy was resulting in a steady decline in sales. Times had changed, and the public was clamoring for the varied offerings of competitors like GM. As Thomas J. McNichols summarized the situation, "There is no doubt that Ford was a major factor in blocking a change in the company's direction. He was enamored of his car—the Model T—and of his product concept which had provided him with industry leadership, fame and fortune. Reluctance to reformulate and discard a tried and true business formula is commonplace in the industrial world. Like Ford, many policymakers become emotionally attached to successful strategies, particularly if they are the ones who conceived them."[4]

Not surprisingly, the psychology of the successful corporate venturer closely resembles the classic entrepreneur. Both tend to be highly independent and used to exercising total authority over their staffs. And unlike conventional managers, both thrive on taking risks and tend to rely as much on their gut instincts as they do on reams of analysis, committees, and meetings. Neither is a traditional organization person. In fact, various studies have shown entrepreneurs to be, in the main, loners and even antisocial, highly egotistical—they are not good at taking orders, for example—and brutally honest. They are often singlemindedly obsessive about their ventures, burning out subordinates in the process. Unlike successful chief executives at long-established companies—who Michael Macoby called "gamesmen" in his famous study[5]—corporate new-venturers tend to be so-called "guerilla fighters" or "craftsmen." They are simply not very good corporate "gamesmen" at all.

Roy Ash provided a fascinating window into the world of the entrepreneurial manager when he discussed the early days at Litton in the mid-1950s. "We had to be in a totally creative mode. It was a different process than to manage, so we needed a creative culture. I guess you could call it entrepreneurial, which required a certain kind of person and a certain setting. We needed to get those two things working. Of the people we did hire I think you'll find a lot of creative people—you can check by finding how many went on to start and build other companies. We had to have a nonbureaucratic, noninstitutional setting, so they would have headroom to do their thing, but not so there'd be anarchy. There had to be a fair amount of interchange." Was this a conscious decision? "We did not write the book ahead of time about what we were going to develop. It happened incrementally. It started with what kind of people we wanted. Then we

181

decided to be quite venturesome. When we purchased our first little company . . . we brought a big stream of before-tax income, which had been all but taxed away, [in the form of] corporate income tax plus an excess-profits tax during the [Korean] war. But if we used it for research and development, it wouldn't have been taxed."

Ash continued: "We took those dollars and spent it on R & D projects that were very entrepreneurial at the time. We spent it to create new businesses. Some succeeded, some failed, but we had a pretty good batting average. Three out of five succeeded: an inertial navigation business, which Henry Singleton got into, big military command and control systems, electronic components, radar equipment. Then we got into the use of radioactive isotopes for X rays. We were pretty brash to think that our job was to spend that money for the right thing. So we got started off with a state of mind that said, 'here we have a meager bank account, but we're going to do five things at once, instead of trying this, then trying that.' "

While Ash and Thornton and the gang were building Litton, entrepreneurs had not quite reached the apotheosis they have today—although clearly start-up managers were recognized as a necessary corporate type. Today, entrepreneurs are in vogue, even lionized, and new ventures are viewed as a way out of whatever quagmire companies are mired in. As a result, hundreds of major corporations have segmented off a portion of their investment funds to be used for new corporate venturing, for venture capital acquisitions of tiny companies, and for partial investments in small start-ups. The differences between these three seemingly similar investment strategies in terms of rates of success are striking. While starting new ventures and acquiring small companies both have a success rate of less than 10 percent, the rate of success from partial investments in start-ups is almost 30 percent. Why the difference? Many chief executives point out that when large companies take positions in start-ups, they provide the capital that a fledgling company needs but do not force it into the corporate bureaucracy. Still, a 70-percent failure rate is substantial.

Why do so many corporate ventures fail? I have asked that question before, and provided some answers. But the issue is a complex one, and the reasons for failure are as varied, it seems, as the weather. Here are some reasons for failure compiled by a well-known venture capitalist, Zenas Block:

· Lack of entrepreneurial manager
· Political problems within the company

182

- No top management corporate sponsor
- Corporate controls that are too tight
- Change in the corporate parent that emphasizes cost cutting
- Venture shifted to operating divisions too soon
- Not enough money allocated
- Too much money allocated
- Too much corporate overhead allocated too soon
- No clear charter or mission for the venture
- Venture management changed too frequently
- Venture management not changed when necessary
- Venture team inexperienced in market served
- Venture managers recruited from too high a level
- Venture managers recruited from too low a level
- Too much corporate red tape
- Insufficient delegation to venture management
- Venture too different from present business
- Venture choice ill advised because of influence of proposer
- Wrong distribution channels used
- Venture too small. Company lost interest
- Failure to read market reaction correctly or report it
- No company support during the early nurturing period
- Change in market and economic conditions
- Venture not in response to market need
- Change in company top management
- Financial controls too general, resulting in throwing in more money and large losses[6]

This list may be daunting, but keep in mind that venture capitalists have a far more concise rule of thumb expressed in the well-known saying, "There are three problems you face in new ventures: management, management, and management." The cash may be inadequate, the capital base poor, the product weak or untried, but all of that can be surmounted if there are competent managers at the top. Those managers must be able to relate not only to the venture's work force and executive staff, but with the corporate parent, banks, suppliers, and customers. And, as I have said before, the CEO must have a management plan and a new-venture strategy. A few other suggestions are noteworthy: a new venture should be located at some distance from corporate headquarters or giant operating units in order to provide its managers autonomy; and top corporate management should be patient, and realize it will take from three to ten years for a new venture to succeed. As one new-venture manager who had just been fired for not bringing his venture into the black in the third year put it, "Impatience is a killer."

Gillette Tries It Again

Gillette has become an enthusiastic advocate of new-venture strategy. Said chairman Colman M. Mockler, Jr., "The bets are initially quite small . . ." These "bets" are a variety of small investments—all under $10 million—in fledgling companies, from dental hygiene, hearing aids, and biotechnology to computer software and accessories. "Our objective, within a five- or ten-year period," [Mockler] says, "is to add two or three core businesses that could grow into $400 million to $500 million worldwide."[7]

This is not the first time that Gillette has tried this strategy. In the 1960s, a diversification move failed badly. Why does Gillette think it can succeed this time around? Mockler thought Gillette could create synergy between existing shaving, hair-care, and deodorant products and newer health-care products, both of which they can sell through the same pipeline to the same national retailers, taking advantage of Gillette's well-known brand name. In fact, Gillette even thought it could sell software that way as well. That proved not to be true.

The tendency to invest only in companies that have some relation to a company's established product line is typical of corporate venturing today, as is the investment and eventual acquisition of start-ups. In our earlier chapter on mergers and acquisitions we looked briefly at small acquisitions of new-venture companies, but one should note that the vast majority of corporate venturing is actually simply acquisitions of other people's new ventures, rather than the establishment from scratch of brand-new companies. Remember the list of companies that Kodak was acquiring in an effort to stimulate a new-venture strategy. That kind of new-venture strategy is very common, and has been pursued by about half of the *Fortune* 500 companies; a healthy $5 billion in such venture capital investments was made in 1983 alone, although 1984–1986 were down years for the high-tech companies that the highly cyclical venture capital industry thrives (or dies) on—and so, investment fell.

NEW-VENTURE STRATEGIES

Tampering with Sloan's General Motors Machine

One of the companies now targeting high-technology new ventures is GM, under its current chief executive, Roger Smith. Smith has acquired a whole range of companies that he hopes will provide strategic growth for the company over the next twenty years and inject a competitive spark into different areas of the GM corporate structure. "You've got to keep leaping," said Smith. "The worst thing you can do is to quit before you get a big breakthrough."

What lessons does the GM case provide? First, notice that, like Gillette, the initiative for new ventures at GM comes straight from the chief executive himself. That makes sense. Changing a company that has coasted along with the originally innovative segmentation strategy developed by Alfred Sloan sixty years ago takes an enormous amount of energy, commitment, and money—and to succeed, it has to come from the top. Second, notice that Smith insists that each venture provide high technology that current GM businesses do not possess: data processing, machine intelligence, electronics, factory process control, computer-aided design. Although GM's joint venture with Toyota to make cars in California has received the most publicity, a more typical example is the joint venture Smith has forged with the Japanese robot maker, Fanuc Ltd. Smith hopes that this venture, a company based in Troy, Michigan, called GMF Robotics, will improve the quality and productivity of the GM assembly lines; he also expects that eventually about half the company's revenues will come from outside of the car business.

In fact, Smith's strategy is looking to break into entirely new industries and escape the cyclical problems of the car business. "There was a desire internally that we would be on the leading edge of the use of computers for office management, communications, data processing," said Smith. The most obvious example of this is the purchase of H. Ross Perot's Electronic Data Systems (EDS). Here, Smith had several goals: not only to form the basis of a GM information processing company, but perhaps more important, to form a core around which GM's enormous data processing needs, from computer-aided design to payroll, pension, and health benefits, could be filled. It is Smith's fundamental belief that only this coordinated computer control of the varied and increasingly complex GM empire can allow it to leapfrog increasingly competitive Japanese and European car makers. I discussed this particular strategy in more detail in the chapter on technology, but here, remember this important lesson: despite the complexity of Smith's strategy, all of these new ventures must be fitted into an overall GM strategy. In Smith's mind, these are not just random ventures.

Of course, there is no guarantee that Smith's grand plan will pan out. Are the GM managers truly entrepreneurial? Will they be hungry enough, or will the huge GM bureaucracy and corporate culture smother these new ventures? Or will they go the way of Exxon, throwing huge amounts of money at new ventures, only to discover their own inadequacies?

Conclusion

The most crucial fact about new ventures is also the most depressing: fully 90 percent of new ventures fail. In light of such statistics, the most important strategic focus in this area probably should be knowing when to bail out, when to cut losses, and look toward something else. One other relevant fact that should be noted is that besides mergers and acquisitions, whose success rate of about 50 percent is nothing to brag about either, launching new ventures is the most important way for corporations to gain substantial growth in new markets and industries. How do we reconcile these two seemingly contradictory trends? The answer may be that chief executives should not simply reject new ventures because they often fail; nor should they restrain them too tightly, strangling them. Rather, all of the evidence suggests that corporations must be prepared to launch a number of start-ups in order to achieve a few major successes. It is like the movies: a single blockbuster can more than make up for a whole season of bombs.

However, the truth is that chief executives often engineer the demise of their own new ventures. Not only do they not screen new ventures well enough, they also do not bite the bullet soon enough. Believing that what works for big companies will work for small, often they will smother the venture in money and management, twist it all out of shape with unrealistic profit goals, or, just as suddenly, stop the money and allow it to starve. As a result, chief executives of major corporations create the conditions for failure, then refuse to believe it is happening to them, eventually souring on the whole idea of start-ups and turning to a new, often more expensive game—acquisitions.

A few new tactics have begun to allow chief executives to limit their down-side risk in new ventures. These are the consortium, often used to pursue expensive high technology; the joint venture, where two or more companies create and share in a third firm; and portfolio investment, in which companies such as Johnson & Johnson take equity stakes in a spectrum of small companies, much as a venture capitalist does. These strategies all share the costs and the benefits with others. The consortium approach is most useful for those extremely risky, expensive ventures, or those with a very long pay-out period. The joint venture is most useful in cases where each partner has something different to bring to the deal: a company entering a foreign country may seek a local partner who knows the market, or a small start-up with a lot of technology but no money may form a venture with a larger, cash-rich partner without the technology. Portfolio investing is useful when a company is unsure of where the breakthrough is coming and when the company has had a bad experience with managing new ventures in the past.

CHAPTER EIGHT

MARKETING STRATEGIES: THAT OLD BLACK MAGIC

The conventional wisdom in this business is that half your advertising dollar is wasted. The problem is to tell which half.   —ALAN HIRSCHFIELD, formerly of Columbia Pictures

Learning to Love the Soapbox

Turn a television on and there they are: Frank Borman of Eastern declaring, "We have to earn our wings every day"; the inimitable Lee Iacocca, who truly popularized the tactic, selling Chrysler automobiles; Frank Perdue peddling chickens; Henry Block urging viewers to have their taxes prepared at H & R Block. Fiddle with the dial, and you might see the earnest chief executives of Greyhound, Remington razor, Avis Rent-A-Car, Golden Nugget casinos. Certainly, there is an element of CEO egotism and a thirst for fame in all of this public display, but such a parade of CEOs also suggests a more important trend: marketing, the simple selling of a product or service, has become an increasingly important part of chief executive strategy. The research backs that up. A recent nationwide survey of thousands of top executives by Yankelovich, Skelly & White and by Coopers & Lybrand, for example, discovered that the foremost priority of American executives for their own firms was to dramatically upgrade their marketing.[1]

Desire, of course, is not the same as results. Despite the widespread desire to improve marketing, many companies have found it extraordinarily

189

difficult to accomplish. Where do they go wrong? Some get into trouble by thinking of marketing strategy as an afterthought once the product has been developed and manufactured, as little more than a sales brochure, a sales staff, or simply advertising. But in fact, marketing strategy should be the first decision, or an integral part of the array of decisions involving which products and services a company should be selling, particularly when a company operates in a variety of markets.

The real problem may be that many chief executives do not care much for either marketing or its executives. For years, marketing managers at all but a few companies were viewed as lightweights, traveling sales people or, because of their higher-than-average turnover, as hucksters, here today, gone tomorrow. In many companies, finance was the quickest route to the executive suite, particularly during the capital crunch of the 1960s, 1970s, and 1980s. Business schools pumped out finance majors by the thousands, and many companies turned to them as a means of navigating through dangerous waters, slashing at marketing departments to save money in hard times. Not surprisingly, marketing, which was unfamiliar, imprecise, and personally distasteful to financial mavens, suffered. When Henry Ford II fired Lee Iacocca, Iacocca remembers Ford saying, "Sometimes you just don't like somebody."[2] This, perhaps, sums up the traditional antagonism between the pin stripes of finance and the loud plaid of marketing. "The marketing people are just very different," another chief executive who ran a major movie studio told me. "It's like a kind of magic when they hit it and it really works. But most times it doesn't work, and some people here regard marketing types as witch doctors or voodoo specialists or rainmakers. I need them, but I never know what's going to work, and so 60 percent of the time we're throwing money into ad campaigns that fizzle, 30 percent of the time it works out as you planned, and 10 percent of the time you hit the jackpot."

That sort of ambivalence is beginning to change, however, as many mature companies struggle to survive in a suddenly treacherous world. For years, older companies chose to defend market share rather than seek new markets. As a result, new companies with new products swept past them like a Corvette passing a Volkswagen Beetle. As we saw in the chapter on turnaround situations, managers are often imprisoned by the rigid structures of the large, complex corporation. That too is changing. Companies such as Procter & Gamble, Colgate, Pepsico, Coca-Cola Company, Philip Morris, and R. J. Reynolds have consciously forced their organizations not only to develop new products, but to market them in new and exciting ways.

MARKETING STRATEGIES

For example, for fifty years the breakfast cereal companies offered the same old fare. Then consumer tastes began to change, and competing products, many from upstart companies, began to appear next to the corn flakes and the Rice Krispies. As a result, in the last decade, the established companies have flooded the market with new brands at the rate of almost one a month. A similar situation exists in banking, insurance, and stock brokerage, where for decades, the concept of marketing was as foreign to them as computers would be to a bushman. In each industry, companies have begun to exploit new marketing techniques, from telemarketing to direct mail, and new channels of distribution. As a result, these firms are spending from three to ten times more money than they used to on marketing.

Marketing can save a mature product from decline. It is then that marketing can become almost magically powerful. In the 1970s, with 90 percent of American households owning at least one set, the television set industry was discovering that sales were declining. Suddenly, the industry found itself replacing broken televisions, not selling to new customers. Then, a blend of new technology and skillful marketing turned it all around. If people had one set in their home, why not two? But was there a need for that second set? It was fortunate for the industry that new uses for the television began to bloom like flowers on a spring day. Video games, home computers, and VCRs appeared on the horizon—all requiring a television screen. At the same time, the industry came up with different kinds of televisions: wide-screen, miniature, automobile, wristwatch, and battery-powered sets. Security monitoring sets appeared in supermarkets, televisions flooded educational institutions, teleconferencing was ushered in. All contributed to the revival of a dying industry, and to the proposition that television is more than just a product for entertainment. That, in essence, is a marketing concept.

Alan Hirschfield, then of Columbia Pictures (and later of 20th Century Fox), provided some examples of the way he tried to wring more efficiency out of the black magic of marketing. He described two techniques that Columbia had used to get more bang for their advertising buck. The first was called "four-walling," which involved hitting smaller markets very hard. Said Hirschfield, "Out of necessity, I guess, and out of the desire to see if it would work, we took certain films we were unwilling to release nationally because of the extraordinary expense, and where we had a low confidence level [in the film], into areas, market by market, and did three to four times the advertising. You know, we'd take a film and play it, then if it was successful, move on to the next market. . . . We found out that

191

for pictures other than major motion pictures that gained national attention with star value you didn't have to take them to New York or Los Angeles, which entailed great expense. You could open them in Texas, Indiana, Oklahoma, and move around the country, getting play dates when they were available. . . . If you're wrong, you just stop."

Hirschfield described two films that benefited from this technique. The first, called *Buster and Billie*, was picked up from an independent producer and cost about $1.4 million, and grossed $4 million, mostly in the South and Southwest. The second, called *Sinbad*, Hirschfield described as "one of the worst movies I ever saw in my life. It was the third in a series on Sinbad which the company had made, and each one had done less. I inherited it when I came to the company and, when it was delivered a year or so later, it cost about $1.2 million, which was a lot of money to use in those days. I didn't want to lose the money, so I asked my distributor what could we do with it. He said it would cost a million-and-a-half dollars to release it nationally, with no guarantee we'd get it back. The last *Sinbad* took in about two-and-a-half million a few years before. But nobody wanted to book this one. I said, 'Why can't we take this thing to a few southern markets, like [we did with] *Buster and Billie*, and really blow it out, spend a few hundred thousand dollars and see if it works. . . .' And he said, 'No, you can't do it with this kind of movie. No one's going to come,' and so on and so on. The meeting adjourned, and about three weeks later I hired a new head of distribution, because I was tired of hearing this sort of thing."

Hirschfield continued, "We decided to try it. We took it down to some southern cities in the Carolinas and we spent an incredible amount of money. We booked it in about three hundred theaters in the area, with TV advertising day and night. We lost about $400,000 having spent $150,000 to $200,000—a huge amount of money [for those markets]. We found out that the movie played every place for about ten days. On the eleventh day, no one would come, even if they opened all the doors for free. We exhausted the marketplace. But then the word began to get around and people began coming to see it again. It finally turned out that for every dollar we spent we grossed two times. The picture ended up grossing $9 million. It was one of the most successful films ever made. So we immediately commissioned a second one, which we released in the exact same pattern—a little more sophisticated in the way we booked it—and it grossed around $13 million at the cost of $2 million. We have a third one out right now. They became what we call program pictures, and they really revolutionized the kind of marketing pattern for these movies."

192

MARKETING STRATEGIES

The second technique involved saturating the market, and depended on what Hirschfield called his supermarket theory. "The classic approach in a supermarket," he said, "is that it costs you just as much to advertise for one store as for thirty. If you went into one market and couldn't find twenty or thirty stores to advertise, then you shouldn't go into the supermarket business. The same thing was true of films." Hirschfield could not understand why major films opened to great expense at a few theaters in New York City and Los Angeles, and played there weeks before opening nationwide. "By the time it really opened, the public could be distracted by some new girl in town," he said. Hirschfield tried to break the pattern with a Charles Bronson film that had cost over $3 million. "His movies had been falling [in popularity], and we took $3 million—which in those days was an unheard-of amount of money—and we released it nationally over the Memorial Day weekend. The picture went out and grossed about $7 million against an estimate of $2 million. Had it been a halfway decent movie, it could've grossed $20 million; anyway, we got our money out of it after two weeks of the run.

"From that, we learned what we could do with a national campaign and a saturation release, so that we were ready for *The Deep* in 1977. Usually, we would have opened in three theaters in New York, one in Los Angeles, one in Chicago, and play for eight weeks before going into a larger pattern of five hundred theaters. Instead, we released *The Deep* to one thousand theaters and grossed $30 million over four weeks—and that is all the picture ever did. Today, the average release is five hundred or six hundred theaters, a complete throwback to the supermarket theory. . . . Even *Close Encounters of the Third Kind*, the crown jewel of our program over the past two years, opened in five hundred theaters. Two years before, it might have opened at 150."

New Tricks for the Old Game

Some companies, such as Xerox and IBM, are well known for being superb marketers. Selling, more than any other corporate activity, seems to be a part of the corporate culture instilled by either a strong chief executive or a long tradition. But for all of the respect afforded to IBM or Xerox, their successes have come as much from a number of other factors—particularly technology—as it has from marketing. On the other hand, there are other companies that, like a stripped-down car built just for speed, are strictly known as marketing companies. Often, they operate in industries where marketing is 90 percent of the game.

There is no company that is as well known for marketing—or that has done it so well for so long—as Procter & Gamble. Based in Cincinnati, the company was all but born as a marketer; its first major product was Ivory soap. That focus has, over the years, been translated into an entire corporate structure devoted to implementing Procter & Gamble's particular marketing style. In 1984, Procter & Gamble spent close to a billion dollars on advertising—more than any other corporation in the world. Procter & Gamble, however, achieved its status as a marketer par excellence not simply because of the huge size of its advertising budget, but because until 1980, it had been the best-known laboratory and proving ground for new marketing techniques. And Procter & Gamble had instituted the world's most famous training program for developing skilled marketers, graduating many top executives who went on to work for Procter & Gamble's competitors.

For twenty-five years, Procter & Gamble had a procedure—some would say an overly rigid procedure—for the development of marketing strategy, new product development, test marketing, product launching, expansion, product-line extensions, and marketing renewal and replacement programs. By going over and over each detail of a marketing program, Procter & Gamble executives were expected to master every aspect of a product's creation, development, and progress over its life span. Executives, for example, were expected to go over memos on each aspect of marketing strategy as many as fifteen times. Not everyone cared for that type of meticulousness. Disgruntled employees often criticized the rigidly controlled and painstaking system. "It keeps the executives in perpetual adolescence," said one top executive who left Procter & Gamble, "forcing them to repeat and repeat their draft memos to higher executives. The Procter & Gamble system never allows anyone to make important marketing decisions entirely on their own, or to make quick decisions, or to act or react suddenly in a fast-changing market. Instead, everything—and I mean everything—has to be done by the Procter & Gamble marketing procedure which requires endless committee meetings all the way up that bureaucratic organization."

More recent events seem evidence of the truth of his criticisms. The Procter & Gamble system worked like a finely tuned machine for decades, as long as the major consumer industries were stable. But as the economy began to move more quickly, Procter & Gamble's machine began to sputter. It was simply not a system that was well adapted to the turbulent, fast-paced, competitive environment of the 1980s. By 1985, a number of Procter & Gamble executives had left to do direct marketing for competitors. Indeed, the alumni of Procter & Gamble proved they could outperform their old school simply because they operated in less rigid environments. As a result, Colgate toothpaste has managed of late to eliminate the two-decade-long dominance of Procter & Gamble's Crest, and Kimberly-Clark's Huggies disposable diapers have swept past Procter & Gamble's Pampers, which pioneered the product. Can Procter & Gamble bounce back? It certainly has the assets, the skills, and the financial power to do it. And the company seems to recognize the danger and has taken steps to loosen the shackles that hold its executives. But a company as old and as successful as Procter & Gamble does not change overnight.

The Advantages of Being on Top

Most research seems to indicate that the degree of market share is directly related to profitability. In many cases, name recognition and instant media identification are important advantages to seizing a dominant market share, then consolidating a leadership position. For with name recognition often comes the hazy but powerful phenomenon known as brand loyalty. "Brand recognition and brand loyalty are our key advantages," said Robert Kinney, the chief executive of General Mills. "Our customers not only keep buying products, sometimes for decades, but those customers tend to proselytize their children, relatives, and friends to use our product. By word of mouth, our customers become our most convincing marketing arm, more so than our sales force, our advertising agency, or our marketing department. These loyal customers are also a key marketing advantage when we introduce a new product."

Many of America's strongest corporations have also learned to use their brand name familiarity when it comes to introducing new products. These include Philip Morris's successful introduction of Marlboro Lights cigarettes, Coca-Cola's Diet Coke cola, Procter & Gamble's Liquid Tide laundry detergent, IBM's IBM PC. Of course, there are down-side risks. "Famous brand name and loyal customer following can be squandered or jeopardized if the company fails to maintain its quality or gouges the customer with unrealistic price increases," Kinney warned.

Usually, however, the process of becoming a market leader generates a bandwagon effect. Advertising agencies will usually devote their best people and their greatest resources to your product, while agencies will be more than happy to develop sample advertising campaigns for you to evaluate— just in case you want to make a change. The large gross sales of market leaders can generate ever-greater dollars poured into new marketing campaigns or defensive marketing strategies in the event of a competitive threat. And the market leader can usually obtain the cheapest rates for television, radio, or print advertising—perhaps 10 percent cheaper than the competition pays. This, in turn, can enable your firm to dictate special terms to advertising agencies in the form of contract concessions or extra services. Shearson American Express, for example, was able to leverage its market leadership and size to wring out unique contracts from its collection of advertising agencies.

Finally, the marketing expertise that one picks up on the way to the top can be applied to new products, such as the ones I mentioned earlier. But sometimes that backfires. The Justice Department refused to allow Procter & Gamble to take over Clorox bleach, because of the tremendous marketing advantages Procter & Gamble already had in the household-cleaning products market. Because of this power, the Justice Department thought that no new companies would dare enter the bleach market if Procter & Gamble were allowed to own Clorox. Clearly, industry leaders can sometimes intimidate potential competitors. Marketing power can intimidate retailers into giving its products extra space, or better terms, or window displays, or other perquisites, simply to keep their brand-name product in the stores. Similarly, market leaders can have enormous leverage with suppliers, as they do with advertising agencies, winning better financing terms, extra terms, and better service, all simply to retain their business. "For a period, some of our suppliers have even worked at a loss for us because we were market leaders," said Reginald Jones, then chief executive at General Electric. "Our suppliers did that in order to win our contract or retain our business, or to show their other clients the quality of their supply work."

There is a legal limit, of course, as to what a market leader can demand. A leader cannot order suppliers, retailers, or distributors to freeze out a competitor. But while the law may be precise, the business world is not. Many of these suppliers and retailers decide independently to handle just the market leader, and so make it more difficult for the competition. Executives of companies trying to sell against a market leader echo the statement of one frustrated chief executive: "We've often experienced supplier resistance, retail store resistance, or other kinds of resistance, which usually requires us to offer extra incentives—bribes—to store owners to sell our directly competitive products. We must really pay to get stores to give us equal shelf space to what [the market leader] secures easily or with little cost. Suppliers have outright refused to deal with us or any other directly competitive products because they are so fearful of losing [the market leader's] business." Even if suppliers do deal with the leader's competition, periods of crisis or scarcity often mean that the leader will get all of the attention.

Finally, there is a ripple effect in becoming a market leader. With such leadership, it becomes much easier to raise financing, to hire the best personnel, or to secure free ideas and advice. Market leaders are swamped by opportunities that are usually brought first to their chief executive or offered on an exclusive basis, at little or no charge, with the right of first refusal. This, of course, lowers the cost of searching for new information and ideas. In other words, marketing power translates directly into other forms of strategic leverage and other types of competitive advantage. The statistics back this up. Booz, Allen & Hamilton Inc., in a 1984 study, found that of the twenty-four major brands existing in 1923, fully nineteen were still the number-one brand in 1983, an incredible sixty years later. Mark Particelli, a vice president of Booz Allen who did the study, concluded that even the other five major brands in 1923 remained in the top five brands in 1983. "So if a company buys a leader, and if they run it correctly, they are buying an annuity, because brand leadership is sustainable," said Particelli.[3]

This and other studies showing the power of brand leadership have served as a key support for a widely used strategy of buying up market leaders. Chief executives have long argued that a takeover would enable their company to secure a strong hold on a particular market by acquiring a market leader, and that they were entitled to pay two or more times the current book value of the lead firm because the strategic value of leadership was defensible over a long period of time. However, as I have shown in the chapter on takeovers, these arguments tend to neglect the fact that most takeovers are *not* managed successfully by the acquirer, and so fail to live up to their projections of earning power. Indeed, the better known the brand name bought, the higher the premium that is paid and, statistically, the poorer the result.

Falling from Grace

Still, being on top is not all wine and roses. Market leadership, like visibility of any sort, makes the company a larger target, and vulnerable in a number of ways. For example:

- Market leaders are more likely to be sued, and because they are leaders, more likely to lose in jury trials. As a result, market leaders pay as much as twenty times more annually in legal fees than do market followers.
- Market leaders tend to be susceptible to whisper campaigns, such as the incredible rumors that Procter & Gamble's corporate symbol—the man in the moon and 13 stars—was that of a Satanic cult. Other wild rumors circulate, such as those that periodically assail chewing gum manufacturers and fast-food franchises concerning contaminated produce. Both are extremely difficult to combat, as Procter & Gamble discovered.
- Market leaders are more vulnerable to federal regulation, particularly to charges of antitrust violations or unfair trade practices. These complaints can be brought by competitors, disgruntled customers, former employees, or the government itself. At times, those pressures can shackle a company, as they did to IBM in the 1970s, as it struggled against an antitrust suit. That ended when the government finally dropped its suit. Often, market leaders also feel they have to meet a higher standard of advertising, employment, lending, or labeling than do smaller competitors. And that means larger overheads, especially in legal and public relations, than the competition has.

Still, for all of the vulnerabilities, the most crucial risk to a market leader is rather easy to understand, and most difficult to battle: complacency—an unwillingness to improve, or an inability to stay alert to competition. Said Peter McColough of Xerox, "Any corporation or its major brand name's division can grow fat and lazy with too much success. It can become overloaded with corporate overhead and excess personnel, instead of being as lean and hungry as its smaller competitors may be." Wallace Rasmussen of Beatrice Foods agreed: "Many market leaders have put their big-name products on automatic pilot. Sometimes I have to force my most successful brands' marketing people to be as lean as my competitors. There's always fat and excess wastage in there, because those Beatrice products like Dannon Yogurt and Tropicana have had a lock on the markets for decades." Arjay Miller agreed: "You have to fight the danger of complacency. You must be alert to danger. You can't simply sit back, because competitors are always trying to move into your markets. So your marketing strategy must anticipate continuing changes in customer demands."

Complacency at advertising agencies who have handled the same products for years can also be a problem. As one CEO told me, "Sometimes that complacency is the ad agencies' fault, sometimes it's the corporation. It can be hard to spot. Sometimes the ad agencies look like they're generating new campaigns, new slogans, and all the rest. And there's no question that their efforts are generating more commissions for the agency. But all their campaigns may not be substantially increasing the sales of our tickets. So when you're looking for signs of complacency in an overall marketing plan, the real test is not, did you change the advertising campaign, but rather, are you getting results?"

Rasmussen put his finger on the danger. "There's the emperor-has-no-clothes problem, that because this product, this brand, has been so very successful for so long, no one dares tell me, the CEO, that it's heading toward a crisis. And maybe I don't bother to ask. . . . Big marketing successes means there are blinders against bad news or against confusing critical pieces of strategic information about competitors that I need—that any CEO needs, early enough to make the tough competitive decisions. This problem is all the worse because a corporation has so much tied up in a product like Tropicana or Dannon, and so may have sunk costs in plant, equipment, land, salaries, marketing, financing arrangements, not to mention personal egos. All that tends to filter out the harsh bad news in time for you to react or take steps to act. If you, or whoever's the CEO, doesn't watch out, those crises tend to be real bad surprises. It's made worse by ignorance at the top. That's why I'm so hard on all these demands of mine for daily and weekly and monthly information. I don't like surprises. I won't tolerate surprises." Rasmussen, a gruff, forceful man, provided an example of how a CEO can force a marketing initiative. "At Dannon Yogurt, we were absolutely floating in whey—wasted whey," he said. "Now I abhor waste in any form whatsoever. I hate to have anything we have go up the smokestack or down the drain or get dumped in the garbage. So I forced those guys to find a market for whey. And you know, they found

199

it. We're now selling whey to hospitals for patients. And does it make money."

One of the key rules of marketing should be: any well-known brand can become as passé as day-old bread. Take the Volkswagen Beetle. Volkswagen used to publish an advertisement showing all of their Beetle models over thirty years or so. All looked almost exactly alike. The point, of course, was that the product was so well made that it could continue to command a market following despite its few outward style changes. But all things pass, and in the 1970s, sales began to slide, forcing Volkswagen to replace the Beetle with a car called the Rabbit which had much the same philosophy behind it as the Beetle. Alas, the Rabbit has also disappeared from the Volkswagen lineup, replaced by the Golf. Something is not right—to say the least—with Volkswagen's marketing strategy.

Jeans maker Levi Strauss & Company also passed through the thresher of a fashion change. For years, Levi Strauss had dominated the blue jeans industry by reducing its prices in real terms, increasing volume worldwide, and making the classic Levi's jeans the industry standard. But by 1978, designer blue jeans appeared. While the cost of making designer jeans was only slightly higher than that of regular blue jeans, they sold at three to ten times the price. Not only was Levi's market share slipping away, but it found its profitability eroding; when it tried to catch up, it failed to succeed in the move into higher-priced clothes. Their traditional customer was simply not willing to pay more for a Levi's designer jean, although he or she would for other companies' designer jeans.

Manipulating Obsolescence

The concept of obsolescence poses a variety of challenges to marketing executives. At one level, the savvy executive can use style shifts, updated models, and other slight changes to convey a feeling that the product is changing. Such a planned obsolescence, as practiced most notably by the car companies, is not usually made for the sake of new technology, although that is often the perception that is conveyed. *True* market obsolescence is quite a different thing—and quite a different problem. Technological obsolescence is one of the most critical problems a chief executive has to cope with. We all know the stories of industries wiped out by a single invention—like the introduction of the steamship eventually making the sailing ship obsolete, or the automobile replacing the horse-drawn carriage as the major means of transport.

If anything, the problem of technological obsolescence has grown more acute as the speed of innovation and development has increased. In the past, major technological changes took decades to be implemented. Today, the obsolescence of products—computers are the clearest example—is startling even to those involved in those markets. Today, chief executives must not only be more attuned to the possibilities of a technology, both to generate new products and to protect themselves from leapfrogging competitors, but they must be concerned with telescoping the pay-back period on the technology. They must carefully calibrate the size of their investment, the number of employees needed, and the marketing plans necessary to cope with technological obsolescence.

Still, a CEO's perceptions can play as much a role in technological obsolescence as it can in superficial styling changes. For example, the formidable IBM, a prime example of a market leader, has long been able to use the "mere" announcement of future introductions to force competitors from the field. Likewise, these announcements of so-called technological innovations often freeze customers from buying existing products. Such a tactic of using announcements to block or confuse competition has been one of the reasons behind the antitrust suits IBM has suffered in the past.

But while IBM worries about lawsuits, marketing strategists can still profit from manipulating the tension between real and perceived obsolescence. William McGowan, the founder and chief executive of MCI, told me, "More and more products are being sold as a total system, or integrated package of different products and services. Customer concerns about technological obsolescence can be triggered by fears about any single element in the package or system, or fears about the technological obsolescence of the whole system over the years. So obsolescence can mean many things, not only the uselessness of the product, but instead, the lack of capacity, lack of access, lack of compatibility, lack of flexibility, as well as a lack of speed and capability. It can also mean a lack of a forward-looking image in customers' minds."

William Norris of Control Data amplified McGowan's views: "These new customer fears about potential obsolescence of your product mean that virtually everyone is hedging their bets. The customer hedges by splitting their order or ordering a small amount or by demanding get-out clauses

201

or tighter delivery schedules or special financing arrangements. The suppliers hedge by trying to wait until they have guaranteed commitments before producing long runs or building new factories to accommodate long runs. And I admit we [as manufacturers] hedge our bets in lots of ways by trying to cover different industries with our marketing and straddle different types of customer needs. We also hedge by trying to build more flexible plants that can be adapted or shifted to something else."

As technology grows more flexible, so too must marketing strategies, to take advantage of short-lived trends or seasonal advantages. As William Verity of Armco said, "Marketing strategy flexibility is required to cope with three things: the increasing perception of global market complexity; threats of potential obsolescence; and perceived lack of long-term stable markets."

Positioning Strategies

Strategic marketing success often depends on a firm's position and performance in specific product markets. Do not confuse this with the strength of a company in any particular industry. General Electric, for instance, operates in hundreds of product markets, but, until 1980 when Jack Welch became CEO, it did not have the number one market leadership in the majority of them. Other, smaller companies that had focused tightly on particular niches often had a larger share of a particular market than GE. Jack Welch has been focusing GE's strategy on this.

GE succeeds because it fine-tunes its position in certain markets to maximize earnings. In some, it may be the low-cost producer with the largest sales volume; in others, the high-quality producer; in yet others, it focuses on a limited market or some narrow segment of a larger market. GE's success teaches an important lesson: chief executives have to be personally involved in the company's positioning of its products. Unfortunately, most companies fail to achieve *any* one of these three basic types of market strategies. Instead, they wind up getting caught in the middle, with only an average quality image, an average sales volume, average costs, and no particular market niche or specialty that can be defended against other competitors. In short, most CEOs are incapable of successfully positioning their companies.

Traditionally, the two first types of positioning strategies have been viewed as opposites. The conflict between them can be summed up in the clash between Henry Ford and his Model T and Alfred Sloan, of GM, and his segmentation strategy. As we saw earlier, the rivalry between these two basic methods of selling cars raged from the early decades of the century to the end of World War II, when Henry Ford II abandoned his grandfather's single-car strategy and followed the path blazed by Sloan. In fact, Arjay Miller, a new executive with Ford in those days, admitted that Ford followed General Motors in adopting a segmentation strategy. But Ford was not alone. Other industries, from cosmetics to fashion, food, and furniture, also followed Sloan. While that does not mean that the low-cost commodity marketing strategy of Henry Ford is dead, it does mean that when it is possible to differentiate a range of products that can be sold to a segmented market, then the chance exists for a range of prices and higher profits.

Segmentation strategy is not as simple as that, of course. Chief executives must make a wide range of decisions before putting into place the correct segmentation strategy for their business. They must first distinguish between specific industries that one's corporation will sell to. Then they must target each product market that lies within each industry, choosing whether to seek consumer, industrial, or institutional customers, and sell through wholesalers, retailers, or distributors. Here, the strategy depends on skill and insight. Depending on the products, they might segment the market into original equipment manufacturers (OEMs) and after-market parts and maintenance. Or they could focus tightly on certain consumer groups, or elect to sell only a tightly focused line of products. They could aim at end users, isolate common buying patterns, market geographically, or just aim at buying groups above a certain size. Finally, they could look to where the potential growth lies, and go after those markets.

Segmentation can even be sought by companies that, at first glance, appear to be commodity producers. While it may seem to be a commodity, steel is actually hundreds of different specialized products, ranging from bars to rods, plates, and rolled sheets, with many different widths, gauges, weights, and coatings. As a result, steel companies have developed highly segmented strategies—a necessary strategy these days because of the continuing steel glut and the increasing complexity and competitiveness not only of the basic steel industry, but of the shipping business and the industries steel serves, such as automobiles. As a result, steel is as deeply segmented as more typically market-driven industries such as cosmetics and clothing. That kind of product segmentation forces steel executives to become intense marketers of their products. "I've been forced to make marketing my turf," says William Verity of Armco. "Today it is my primary concern, because this company's survival depends upon my decisions about which specific submarkets in steel we stay in and fight it out, and which ones we decide to fold up our cards and abandon. So I'm involved in every basic marketing decision, every basic pricing decision on our price lists. And increasingly, I've had to get involved in all decisions about when we discount to hold business and remain competitive."

The Ups and Downs of Product Extensions

New products are the lifeblood of most companies, particularly those selling into predominately consumer markets. As in the obsolescence issue, there are new products, and then there are *new* products. For example, a company such as Procter & Gamble has traditionally been very successful in introducing line extensions—that is, an addition to a product line of a new size or color, although the product itself remains unchanged. Line extensions are usually very safe and cheap marketing strategies.

But do not let the usual situation fool you. As we have seen, line extensions that seem simple often can be treacherous. That is a lesson Procter & Gamble learned not long ago when it introduced an extension on the Tide detergent product line—Liquid Tide—which was really an entirely new formulation. Procter & Gamble promoted Liquid Tide with tremendous advertising support, trying to compete with Liquid Wisk detergent, a Lever Brothers (which is a division of Unilever) product. Less than a year later, Liquid Tide was doing quite well, but, alas, at the expense of Procter & Gamble's powdered detergents.

What went wrong? Research showed that many consumers wanted to remain faithful to their traditional product, Tide, while checking out the liquid detergent. Many of these buyers had used Tide for years, as had their mothers. Now that they had switched to Liquid Tide, they weakened

204

their loyalty to the old product—and so the next switch, to a non–Procter & Gamble product, became easier. At the same time, Liquid Tide failed to make much of an inroad among loyal Liquid Wisk users. In short, Liquid Tide was cannibalizing other Procter & Gamble products. Still, a Procter & Gamble executive defended the strategy: "We had no choice but to launch a liquid detergent to compete with Liquid Wisk, and Liquid Tide was the strongest option we had. In the initial period of a new product introduction, you have to expect a good deal of cannibalization."

Is there a way to avoid cannibalization? Well, one should note that when Coca-Cola launched new brands such as Fresca, Rambl'n Rootbeer, Sprite, and its line of mixers, it did not use the Coke name at all. In fact, when some Coke bottlers began selling mixers, they used Seagram's name instead, while selling them through their own marketing and distribution network. Edgar Bronfman of Seagram summed it up: "It's fascinating because we were not then in the soft drink business. We just got the royalty; the original licensing arrangement was done with Coke of New York [a major Coke bottler]. We approve the formula and advertising. For us to go into the soft drink business at that time—well, I never really thought about it. They did the studies and came up with the idea that it would really work." In fact, the project was something of a major success, surprising even Coca-Cola, a part owner of the bottler, which had originally not looked with favor on the project.

Product-line extensions, which are really a marketing phenomenon, can go wrong for a variety of operational reasons. For example, listen to Andrall E. Pearson of Pepsico describe the attempt by the Pizza Hut subsidiary to establish pan pizza, an extension of its traditional pizza line: "When you're not executing well you can come up with the greatest idea and screw it up very easily. Currently we're launching a five-minute pan pizza at Pizza Hut. We launched that same product three years ago and it failed. Now it's one of the great successes in the restaurant business. That product has converted Pizza Hut from not much lunch business to a lot of lunch business virtually overnight. Three years ago, our execution capability was very poor—we didn't have the ovens, we didn't have the pans, the service, the mentality to get the product to the consumer in five minutes. And we didn't have the nerve to make the claim that if we don't get it to you in five minutes, the next one's free. We had to get our execution up to speed so that we could capitalize on a good strategic idea. This may not sound like a breathtaking idea, but the results were breathtaking. We raised our lunch business from 10 percent or so of sales to 26 percent." The lesson here: the best marketing idea in the world won't go anywhere unless you can actually produce and distribute the product you promise the customer.

Finally, new markets can mean new profits. After product-line extensions, the most popular type of marketing strategy is to transfer already existing products or services to new markets. Computer services companies, for instance, have become very adept at repackaging their services for a variety of industries that need data processing, inventory control, or even computerized graphics.

Take the case of the sale of movies directly to consumers for use in home VCRs. This was not a product-line extension, but rather an entirely new market. As Alan Hirschfield told me, "Even when the ultimate viewer of the film is exactly the same person in the theater or in front of a television, that video cassette of the film you are selling or renting is a new product. So my marketing strategy has to be different. The advertising medium must be different. The sales people required will be different. Production facilities and distribution network will be different. Any chief executive must be fully prepared to launch an entirely different marketing strategy for their new cassette sale."

Again, the problem of cannibalization looms. "Video cassettes," said Hirschfield, "can pose a threat to my current films' gross rental revenue in theater chains, and a danger to the value of my existing film library or for television network rentals. Sure, you can say movie studio executives had already coped with cannibalization when they sold movies to television. But the video cassette revolution poses new and more difficult marketing dilemmas, such as how to prevent the enormous amount of video piracy that takes place when a film goes into mass circulation."

Chief executives have to take each of these issues into account when they hammer together pricing structures, distribution systems, sales versus rental agreements, budgets for legal expenses. For example, a movie company must decide how much video piracy they can live with and still make a reasonable profit. That gains in urgency because of the changing nature of the movie business. Movie companies now say that only one in ten films makes money at the box office. Only by selling to television, to cable, and in the form of video cassettes can these companies make money— which makes marketing all that more important.

MARKETING STRATEGIES

New Technology, New Techniques

Technology has altered not only the environment that companies operate in, but marketing itself. For example, direct-mail marketing and telemarketing have allowed all kinds of corporations to market directly to consumers in their homes, rather than waiting for them to come into a store. Consumer marketing studies have shown that potential buyers are far more likely to buy once they have had a conversation about a product. Telemarketing uses the telephone to get into the home, while direct mail, usually not as effective as telemarketing, enables the company to build lists of potential customers in larger geographic areas, without establishing stores or hiring sales people there. As small a response rate as 1 percent in a direct mail campaign, for example, can mean a successful campaign. The building, buying, and renting of lists for direct mail and telemarketing has become an industry all its own. The important lesson here is that such new techniques have radically affected a number of industries, such as insurance, brokerage, retailing, publishing, and banking, because they have essentially homogenized the ways that companies can reach their customers.

A second trend also attempts to go after customers before they can take the initiative. Marketers have begun to prepackage materials to make it easier for the consumers to buy products or services they did not actively seek out in the first place. Such techniques are becoming more invasive and aggressive—and more successful—in industries as diverse as banking, insurance, securities, furniture, automobiles, and computers. Edwin L. Smart, the chief executive of Trans World, which owned Century 21, said, "Century 21 offers not only tours of different houses for the buyer to select one, but offers to help arrange mortgage financing, your swing loan, the sale of your old house or rental of it until it can be sold." And, said Smart, airlines are now offering everything from the plane ticket to rental cars, hotel rooms, secretarial assistance, limousines, and conference rooms in varying packages. Computer companies sell packages that include hardware, software, courses of instruction, maintenance contracts, and upgrading capabilities, plus financing. And furniture companies will sell you a whole room, or a whole house, of furniture arrangements, throw in the use of an interior decorator, and offer free financing for six months, to boot."

207

International Marketing

For the past eighty years or so, international marketing was all but non-existent in most American companies. Only a few U.S. corporations developed overseas markets before 1950, and then only on an ad hoc or piecemeal basis. But as we have seen, the world has changed of late, and American companies have found that if they do not market overseas, overseas companies will certainly market, ruthlessly and effectively, here. Certainly, foreign companies have cheaper labor costs and a longer-term outlook that allows them to sell at a loss to gain market share; but that just increases the pressure on American companies to whip their marketing divisions into shape.

When in 1982 I interviewed the chief executives of Interpublic, which was at the time the world's largest advertising agency, and Young & Rubicam, the second-largest, both firms stressed that they had been driven overseas not by their own initiative, but at the demands of their corporate clients. Said James Mortensen, vice chairman of Young & Rubicam, "In the 1950s, the chief executives of Procter & Gamble and one or two other companies, who were already our clients, came to Y & R and said, 'We want to start marketing in such and such country; will you open a foreign office there?' Naturally, we complied."

The fact that companies such as Ford, Coca-Cola, and Philip Morris relied for decades on foreign sales to maintain their profit levels meant that overseas marketing got considerable attention. Such companies were exceptions, however. Competitors such as General Motors, 7-Up Company, and the American Tobacco Company were never dependent on foreign sales. That, of course, was before foreign competition began hammering on their doors. Today, talk of "global marketing" has become a very hot topic at such companies, and corporate marketing departments are racing to assemble global marketing strategies before their competitors do. Said Wallace Rasmussen, of Beatrice, in 1979, "I've ordered my marketing department point-blank to get some clear rational streamlined plan into effect that would produce steadier and more reliable forecasts and results for worldwide marketing."

MARKETING STRATEGIES

Classic Chief Executive Marketers

There have been many legendary chief executive marketers beyond Alfred Sloan and Henry Ford. Many of them all but define their own particular industry: Ray Kroc at McDonalds Corporation, the pioneer of fast food; Walter Wriston at Citibank, the pioneer of financial services; Charles Revson at Revlon; Steven Jobs at Apple. While not all of these won out in the end, all were marketing pioneers, because they saw a new product and service and then sold that concept assiduously.

THOMAS WATSON, JR., AND IBM

No company has a higher reputation for marketing than IBM. The father of that reputation is undoubtedly Thomas Watson, Jr., the son of Thomas Watson, Sr., who had turned IBM from a small regional company to a national power. Watson, Jr., however, set IBM on the road to computers; and it is that fine intuition for new products that separates Watson, Jr., from the run-of-the-mill chief executive. "I was wandering around the building with my father," he told Harry Levinson and Stuart Rosenthal in their book *CEO*. "He used to sort of go into the corners of 590 Madison Avenue in New York City, and we came upon a keypunch, and the keypunch was hooked to a box with black covers. I said, 'What's this?' and the man said, 'Well, we're using radio tubes to add, subtract, and multiply. And it does it very fast.' He said, 'It takes one-tenth of the card cycle to do this, and nine-tenths of the card cycle is waiting for the mechanical operation of the keypunch to punch the answer, to go to the next card.' They were doing payroll. . . . That impressed me as though somebody had hit me on the head with a hammer, because it was a relatively simple device. And I said, 'Dad, let's put that thing on the market, and let's call it the first electronic multiplier.' I don't think people were using the word computer in those days. And he said, 'Why not?' and within a year we announced it. And, you know, we thought we might sell a couple or three to justify the ad, because we took a full-page ad in the *New York Times*. But we sold . . . twenty or thirty, and everybody who bought them said, 'Well, if you could just make it do the following we would order a lot more.' And we did . . . and then we sold literally hundreds."[4]

209

The electronic multiplier became IBM's first great product, the 604 calculator. "Though the young Watson hadn't seen 'the great future of the computer business,' " wrote Levinson and Rosenthal, "he already had the ability to see the marketing possibilities for a new invention."[5]

PETER McCOLOUGH AND XEROX CORPORATION

It is not only at IBM that we find an executive with a particular flair for marketing molding the character of an entire organization—or industry. Consider, for example, the story of Xerox, where one executive's personal focus on marketing might well have meant the difference between failure and success. "My first job at the Haloid Company, the predecessor to Xerox, was to form a committee that would provide some marketing input on what we called the first xerographic equipment," Peter McColough told me. "We'd done market surveys, and from our sales force and calling on customers, we knew that for a high-quality copier, there was potentially a large market. People already had copiers that were not very good. 3M had the Thermofax process started about 1955. They were doing very well, but their copy image disappeared when exposed to sunlight. Kodak had a process called Verifax, which was a dye transfer thing, very manual, not very good. There was a photographic process originating in Germany called a diffusion transfer that was also not very good. So we saw potentially a large market.

"In the late 1950s, we had two copiers. Around 1955, IBM came to us and said they 'might be interested in getting into the copier business by taking on the job of manufacturing and distributing those two copiers— would we be interested?' We said, 'we'll listen to you and consider that,' because we had no manufacturing capability and very limited marketing capability. We shared all information with them, they saw the machines; and to make a long story short, they hired Arthur D. Little to do a market survey on those two machines. After about a year of work, IBM came back and said, on the basis of the Arthur D. Little work, both those Xerox machines had no future and they were not interested in taking them on. To have the largest office-equipment company in the world say these two machines were unmarketable and are going to be absolute failures and they didn't want to touch them, was a jolt. These were absolute turkeys as far as IBM was concerned.

"So I copied traditional IBM pricing. . . . We had a selling price for the machine that was $75,000. Expensive. So instead, I copied IBM and charged for that first machine $1,250 a month for the first shift. What I found out was that nobody was paying us for a second shift and the machines were being used around the clock. The customers weren't cheating us, because they said this wasn't a regularly scheduled shift; the machine just happened to be used every night. So after about two or three years of this (about 1957), I said *this is for the birds.* These machines are being used heavily and we're only being paid for one shift. We're going to a different kind of pricing. Put a meter on the machine and charge so much per foot. The heck with how much a month, we had a minimum on that. . . . That's where Xerox marketing strategy came from. It wasn't exactly someone sitting around in an office and having a brilliant idea. It came from hard experience, trying it, and having it work. IBM didn't know that. People said it wouldn't work. They'll be cheating on you. But it does work. It's very easy to have someone read a meter at the end of the month.

"That pricing strategy—that way of marketing—took Xerox from very small revenues to very large revenues very quickly. Our pricing philosophy, that marketing plan, was just as important to the success of those machines as the technology."

Marketing Crises

Clearly, for chief executives with a yen for marketing, a variety of strategies exist to help them toward their goals. And even for chief executives who do not have a feel for the marketing game, there is usually time to put a task force together, hire some top-flight marketing whizzes, or contract out with any of a small army of consultants prepared to assemble and package a strategy. Sometimes, however, such time does not exist. For many companies, marketing resembles the mythical football lineman who is never noticed until something goes wrong. How do top-flight companies and their chief executives react to a marketing crisis? That is what we shall examine next. There are three basic types of marketing crises which I shall look at in detail: a threat to the survival of the company that only a marketing strategy can cure, or a sudden, forced shift from almost no marketing to dependence on marketing; a problem with a product, such as a series of deaths, that forces a marketing response; and a marketing strategy that blunders or backfires.

CHARLIE BROWN AND THE TRANSFORMATION OF AT & T

"When I became chief executive of AT & T in 1979," said Charlie Brown, "I immediately set my principal objective to finding a way out of the legal and regulatory quagmire." And so it came to pass: AT & T was unbundled from its operating companies, freed from the shackles of government regulation, and thrust into a new life as a market-competitive company. AT & T continued as a powerful force, of course, with Bell Labs, Western Electric—now called AT & T Technologies—and Long Lines, under its corporate umbrella. But it also faced new, aggressive competitors: MCI, GTE Sprint, Northern Telecom, Rolm, and ITT, with mighty IBM waiting in the wings. Could AT & T transform itself culturally from a safe, conservative operation to a freewheeling competitor?

That was a question that both Brown and his predecessor, John deButts, agonized over. Said deButts, just before the break-up, "In many ways, AT & T has been learning to compete in a number of narrow markets for years. This company has a running jump into a marketing strategy environment." DeButts may well have overestimated that ability, for during his tenure, no AT & T unit was totally dependent on its competitive skills and marketing expertise. DeButts partially acknowledged that. "The new competitive marketing strategy has got to permeate the entire company," he said. "Most of the old employees are going to make it, but others simply will not be able to." DeButts was convinced that AT & T's technological leadership would be the central focus of the marketing strategy. By the time of the break-up, however, it was clear to Brown that a technological reputation was not enough. Somehow, some way, various divisions had to be taught to sell, how to think and plan for themselves, how to act not like bureaucrats, but like entrepreneurs. It was not easy. Batteries of consultants were brought in to help plan marketing strategies—and to hold hands. Decentralization was the catch word, for in the past, each division and department had existed within the cocoon of the parent company, responding to artificial corporate protocols, not market pressures.

Brown faced other difficult tasks as well. "Over the years," he said, "we educated consumers to undervalue basic telephone service because—and for good reason at the time—we made it artificially cheap. And, we were able to do it in a regulated monopoly environment. Ultimately, the American public will have to come to understand that a regulated monopoly has its costs and benefits. Competition has its costs and benefits. There is no way to get the benefits of both."

Can AT & T make it? Some experts cite a long list of problems hobbling AT & T still, particularly drawbacks in its marketing strategy. AT & T has managed to send a jumble of different computers into the marketplace, but, by mid-1986, it had not begun to develop a coordinated strategy to sell them. One microcomputer competes with the next; networking systems are talked about, but not integrated with other products; the edge from a software product developed at Bell Labs, called Unix, is allowed to slip away; selling groups are fragmented and uncommunicative. Meanwhile, the market continues to change rapidly, and the players—facing a computer glut—compete ever more fiercely. So far, at least, Charlie Brown's plan to make AT & T a fierce marketing machine has yet to develop.

THE TYLENOL CRISIS: MAKING THE BEST OF A BAD SITUATION

No chief executive knows the true test of leadership until he or she has survived a full-fledged crisis. Imagine this scenario: your largest selling product has just killed three people in a forty-eight-hour period. No one knows exactly how it happened, or if more deaths will follow. Do you yank the product off the shelves, stop manufacturing, or hope the crisis will pass? How do you placate an increasingly edgy public which, despite your company's apparent innocence, still associates your product with death? How do you deal with Wall Street, which is dumping your stock; the media, which gathers with cameras at your doorstep; and your employees, who are all but paralyzed?

That, approximately, was the situation faced—not once, but twice—by James Burke, the chief executive of Johnson & Johnson. In both cases, someone tampered with Tylenol capsules, injecting cyanide into them, first in 1984, then again in early 1986. Each time, it resulted in death. The first crisis, in particular, posed excruciatingly complex problems under extremely high pressures. When news of the deaths arrived, Burke and his executives immediately went into round-the-clock sessions to assess the situation. The problem was this: despite the continuing bad publicity, the police wanted Johnson & Johnson to continue selling Tylenol capsules so

213

they could catch the killers. But Burke concluded differently: he decided to yank the product off the shelves, halt production, and launch a massive ad campaign to urge people *not* to use Tylenol capsules.

In 1984, Burke described to a class of mine at the New York University Business School how Johnson & Johnson's decision making was conducted during the crisis: "Despite the fact that the Tylenol recall cost us over $100 million, everyone inside the company was behind the decision. The reason they were able to make the decision so quickly and unanimously was that the company had operated almost from its founding under a credo, or corporate philosophy, of General Johnson [a son of the founder] that puts customer needs first. Each year some of our managers meet to personally and individually challenge the Johnson credo, to decide if it's outmoded or should be replaced. Those years of credo challenge sessions were critically important."

How to remarket a product as tainted as Tylenol? Johnson & Johnson executives, Burke said, briefly considered changing the name, or abandoning the market altogether. "In the end," he said, "we decided we had to go all out to recapture the Tylenol market and rebuild that strong product image and consumer confidence—not only to protect our earnings and sales of Tylenol, but because of the irreparable damage that could be caused to all of Johnson & Johnson if our reputation for safety and absolute quality was smeared with the cyanide brush." Burke kicked off the remarketing campaign by, first, going on television to explain the company's position— an unusual move by normally media-shy Johnson & Johnson executives— and of course he approved responses to the media and those ads warning people not to take Tylenol capsules. Then, as the crisis passed, new ads urged consumers to consider Tylenol again. More important, Johnson & Johnson tried to regain consumer trust by redesigning the Tylenol package so it was tamper-resistant. "Our entire packing and production department went on a crash schedule to develop a tamper-resistant bottle with three seals . . . within a year, Johnson & Johnson had recaptured 95 percent of our previous Tylenol market," Burke said.

The sheer complexity of the effort was staggering. "Our marketing strategy," said Burke, "had to coordinate many different departments within the corporation involving many different functional specialties. Also, we had to protect our reputation with hospital purchasing departments, with doctors, with pharmacists, with patients, not to mention explaining ourselves to current and potential stockholders. Finally, we had to answer the concerns of the banks and bondholders, government regulators, and respond to media investigations, and the concerns of the public at large." Burke described this period as "one of the most important in the company's history, and the most demanding task I ever faced as a chief executive."

Perhaps. But Burke was in for even greater shocks: a second Tylenol cyanide tampering, another death, in 1986. If anything, this posed even greater problems. Not only was Burke forced to pull capsules off the market, he was forced to admit that the capsule form of the drug was not as tamper-resistant as he had once thought. "We see no way to assure the public that capsules are tamper-proof," Burke said. "No way. That's why we've recalled all the capsules and why we will now cease to sell any of our over-the-counter drugs in capsule form. None. We took over a $150-million loss on this decision. But it was necessary."

COCA-COLA: TURNING DISASTER INTO PROFITS

Few industries are as intensely marketing-driven as the $23-billion soft drink business. And few companies are as skillful as Coca-Cola in putting together the intensive promotions, advertising, and cooperative agreements with retail outlets and fast-food chains necessary to sell a carbonated sweet drink. It came as some surprise, then, to see Coca-Cola make an important switch in marketing strategy—sweetening the ninety-nine-year-old formula and introducing "a new taste of Coke"—without, it seems, realizing the full scope of the decision.

Coca-Cola, of course, was hit by a storm of protests from loyal Coke drinkers. "Our initial roll-out marketing campaign for New Coke in 1985 was successful," insisted chief executive Roberto C. Goizueta. However, "week by week, the general public was becoming less and less favorable towards it, and there were more and more demands for the return of old Coke. Groups were formed to protest the killing of old Coke. Our problem appeared to grow in magnitude and press attention each week."

The crisis at Coca-Cola had been building for some time. Coke steadily had been losing market share in certain key submarkets to Pepsi Cola's aggressive marketing. Particularly damaging had been an advertising campaign called "The Pepsi Challenge," which featured a direct taste test targeted at younger drinkers, the "Pepsi Generation." Younger consumers drink more soft drinks than do older consumers—the latter being Coke's core group—and Coca-Cola began to fear that its century-long dominance in soft drinks would fade as its core audience passed away. Pepsico also

215

put Coca-Cola on the defensive with aggressive supermarket deals, featuring a tie-in between Pepsi and its Frito-Lay corn chips subsidiary. As Cuban-born Goizueta told *Business Week*, "We tried everything—more marketing, more spending. The only thing we had not tried was claiming product superiority."[6] Andrall Pearson, Pepsico's president, independently affirmed that the number two soft drink company was making a move. "My preeminent business strategy was to steadily and incrementally improve the performance of every aspect of Pepsico, starting with supermarket sales and marketing. We succeeded in doing that with Frito-Lay and Pepsi Cola."

Despite the defensiveness, Coca-Cola and Goizueta were riding high on new introductions. In the past few years, the company had successfully introduced both Diet Coke and Cherry Coke. Goizueta was particularly proud of launching Diet Coke, which became the third-largest-selling soft drink in America in only three years, despite the fact that the company also sold another diet drink, Tab. Goizueta had also personally negotiated the purchase of Columbia Pictures, which was widely viewed as a triumph for the company. The scene was thus set; Coca-Cola was burdened with a sense of its own skills, almost a hubris, undercut by a quickening sense of urgency about Pepsi. New Coke was thus tossed into the marketplace, and the consumer revolt, slow to begin but quick to gather momentum, took hold. What went wrong? Coke's experience reveals the limitations of marketing. As Goizueta told *Business Week*, "We knew some people were going to be unhappy, but we could never have predicted the depth of their unhappiness. Just as I could not have predicted the emotional disruption that resulted from my leaving Cuba [which he left in the wake of the Castro revolution]—you cannot quantify emotion."[7]

The result, of course, is as well known as the original New Coke introduction: Coca-Cola's famous strategic retreat and the resurrection of old Coke, rechristened Coca-Cola Classic. From the jaws of defeat, the company had snatched a mighty marketing victory. Media coverage, if anything, was more extensive than it had been for the introduction of New Coke. "To all of you who wrote and phoned us to ask us to bring back the original Coke, we hear you," said a series of new advertisements. Goizueta allocated $100 million more to promote the two new colas, and encouraged local bottlers to slash prices and seize market share not only from archrival Pepsi Cola, but from weaker competitors such as Royal Crown Cola, Dr Pepper, and 7-Up. "Coke has the most developed distribution system [in the industry]," Seven-Up's Edward W. Frantel told *Business Week*, "and they're using all the tools at hand to dominate, or almost monopolize, the business."

216

MARKETING STRATEGIES

Not that Coca-Cola did not face serious constraints with the bold move, and intense competition. Would it dilute its image with too many different varieties? Were there limits to supermarket shelf space, too few soft drink nozzles at fast-food chains or slots in vending machines? Pepsico, with a simpler product image, struck back, launching a campaign that made fun of Coca-Cola's confusion, and boasting again of its successes in consumer taste tests. It was a battle that brought marketing issues into most American homes, and provided fodder for cocktail party chatter and street corner punditry. All of American business was suddenly discussing the ins and outs of marketing.

In the short term, however, Goizueta emerged the winner. While Pepsi became the single largest brand of cola sold in the United States, the two Cokes, New and Classic, actually did better nationwide than the original Coke a year before. And Goizueta is confident that he can increase his 18 percent market share to 26 percent or so over the longer term. "Time will tell," he said, "but I'm willing to take bets on this one. . . . Having known in April what I know today, I definitely would have introduced the new Coke." He laughed. "Then I could have said I planned the whole thing."[8] Not all of the experts agree. Many still believe that eventually, Pepsi will steal the march on Coke. But for now, Goizueta can bask in the glow of a new triumph that could have been a classic failure.

Conclusion

For all of the talk of chief executives making aggressive moves, seizing a challenge and running with it, and wading in and solving problems, they are really a very risk-averse group. Marketing is a perfect example. In the world of financially oriented chief executives, where reality can often be broken into sheets of orderly numbers streaming down a page, the ineffable quality of the born sales person—an H. Ross Perot, say, who once sold his quota of IBM computers in the first week of the year—is eccentric at best, disorderly and disturbing at worst.

As a result, marketing strategy is only now beginning to gain the respect, if not the love, of most chief executives. Although marketing strategy was always taken very seriously indeed by a few of the corporate elite, such as

IBM and Procter & Gamble (where, no coincidence, both are known for their exceedingly button-down, corporate culture; their strategists might be sales people, but they do not wear loud suits and drink in seedy hotel bars), it has been a stepchild, particularly among the old-line manufacturing operations known as Smokestack America. Instead of being one of the first considerations in the construction of a strategic plan, many chief executives would turn to marketing only after crucial production and financing decisions were made. Then, the "sales boys" were ordered to somehow sell the product.

A wonderful example of this attitude is Roy Ash's description of the state of marketing at AM International when he walked in the door. Scores of products were sold through one monolithic marketing department. No one knew who was buying what, or why. Some markets seemed to have been forgotten about and had disappeared, while others had been emphasized, despite their lack of a need for the product. Ash described AM International as twenty or so years out of date; sadly, its marketing may not be as out of date, compared to the average company, as one would like to think.

According to those chief executives who do show an interest in the esoteric art of marketing, the essential starting point for a good marketing strategy is to focus on the narrowest target market. First, they say, break down each separate industry to which your company sells into the smallest component area where competition takes place. Second, realistically evaluate your own competitive strengths and weaknesses, as well as those of your primary competitors, based on your ability to either dominate or hold share in a market. Third, stress product improvements, whether they are incremental or fundamental. Small companies can move in and take over market niches with a new technology or a new approach. Thus, the only way to preserve share is to steadily move forward, putting constant pressure on tiny competitors to keep up—a particular burden for smaller, cash-tight companies. And of course, market continually. It may not get respect, it may seem like hocus-pocus, it may be all but impossible to pin down. But without it, the machine grinds to a halt.

CHAPTER NINE

MANPOWER STRATEGIES: MAKING THE WHEELS TURN

When you come in as CEO, you inherit an ongoing work force. You fire, you reposition people, you hire new guys, but ultimately you must manage via the brains and efforts of those managers you decide to keep.　　　—JOHN DEBUTTS, former CEO, AT & T Company

The chief executive is the guy who has to really set the tone, and he's the guy who has to spur the people on to do the planning. It's the easiest thing for operating divisions to just sit in their sphere. . . . Now, you're just not going to have an aggressive company if you simply sit there and add up the total of all the operating divisions and say, this is it.
　　　　　　　　—ROY A. ANDERSON, CEO, Lockheed Corporation

A corporation's managers have to discipline themselves if they are to continue as a decentralized company. It's up to them as individuals. . . . If they exercise discipline in their own operations, there's no need for centralization. It's the same as in any democratic society. Every individual has to discipline himself to live within the system.
　　　　　　　　—WALLACE N. RASMUSSEN, former CEO, Beatrice Foods Co.

How Strategy Is Made: Top Down, Bottom Up

Corporations are complex organizations made up of thousands of individuals. How those pieces coordinate into a smoothly running organization is something I have chosen to call *manpower strategy*. In general, manpower strategy is the way a chief executive creates a good working environment, and resembles what Thomas Peters and Robert Waterman, in *In Search of Excellence*, call "corporate culture."[1] However, unlike Peters and Waterman, I do not believe that a splendid corporate culture alone is enough to ensure excellence. Instead, long-term success is created by linking corporate culture to a rational and orderly process of strategic planning. Call it tying the brains to the emotions. To use another metaphor, manpower strategy is the fertilized field waiting for the seeds of strategy, whether it is technology, new ventures, or marketing. Feeling good about working for a Kodak or a Caterpillar Corporation, as Peters and Waterman suggest, is not enough to achieve success; the failures of some of their corporate paragons of late, I think, points out the weakness of their argument. After all, a fertilized field is no good if no one is planting seeds.

For all the plethora of studies about business strategies, few deal with the role of chief executives in formulating and implementing a strategic plan, or with their chosen instruments of action—their top managers. And yet, this is the crucial arena of action in all corporations. The classical model posits a situation where the chief executive of a large, diversified operation plans strategy from the top down, and implies that only the chief executive has the wisdom, experience, and perspective necessary for the job of long-range planning. By the 1960s, however, the top-down model began to be supplanted by the increasing popularity of what might be called the bottom-up approach, in which the chief executive delegates many of the planning functions to strategic planning departments, which then recommend action. This approach carries with it the implication that planning is too large and important a role to leave to just one executive—even the chief executive—and that it belongs within the realm of those trained to do it.

In my research into this problem, I found that the situation was far more complex than these simple models would suggest. Somewhat to my surprise, I discovered, first of all, that far fewer executives than I had expected embraced the top-down approach. Moreover, a fairly large percentage could not be placed into either camp; rather, they used a combination of the top-down and bottom-up approaches. In fact, overall, chief executives tended to view their choice of strategic decision-making behavior not as an either/ or selection, but rather as a suit of clothes or a hat one would put on to fit the situation. This was mentioned many times by individual CEOs. As such, this item gives some indication of the complexity of the choice of strategic decision-making behavior by a CEO.

220

MANPOWER STRATEGIES

I also found that preferences for a certain kind of decision-making structure differed with the type of company. For example, capital-intensive firms such as AT & T and General Electric, at least for a major period in their pasts, tended to adopt a predominately bottom-up planning structure. Whether this is due strictly to the capital intensiveness of the firm or to some other variable such as the degree of vertical integration is hard to say, although these firms did tend to be heavily broken up into divisions and extensively decentralized. The markets these firms operated in were stable and evolving slowly. These CEOs indicated that they primarily delegated routine decisions, and only handled matters on an "exception" basis. Yet other technically oriented conglomerates, from ITT to Bangor Punta, were almost always controlled strategically from the top. Later in this chapter, I will describe the tight central control exercised by Harold Geneen of ITT as one example of the characteristic planning structure of the conglomerate, or multiindustry firm. As we will see, the existence of a bottom-up planning apparatus within ITT did not appear to mitigate the need for a CEO in a central coordinating and synthesizing role. This need for control, for day-to-day involvement, was mentioned by chief executives as the key to combating the rapid evolution of markets, products, and technologies, although the chief executive in such a situation normally obtained information from the lower ranks before making a decision. Let us now look more closely at three major companies and their chief executives.

WILLIAM NORRIS AND CONTROL DATA

One of the clearest examples of a strong top-down approach to management came from William Norris, the founder—and until 1986 chairman and CEO—of Control Data, the Minneapolis-based computer and computer services company which had 1985 revenues of $3.67 billion. What makes the Norris case particularly interesting was that he saw his company not only as a tool for producing profit, but as a vehicle for social change as well. While a number of chief executives I talked to boasted of their firms' social responsibility, none went quite as far as Norris. Notice the paradox here: Norris, who sees the potential for corporations to take the initiative in cooperation with government and other sectors to bring about social change as part of their normal business operations, is also one of the more autocratic of executives.

Norris's theory of manpower strategy is grounded on what he views as an essential difference between "leaders" and "managers." Leaders oversee companies that are making what he calls "revolutionary" changes, while managers are suited for companies—he uses the automobile industry as an example—that are engaged in "microevolution," that is, making incremental alterations on a fundamental strategy laid down in the distant past. Major deviations from strategy at such a firm can only be made by chief executives themselves.

Norris, of course, saw himself as leading the American business community in a new direction that would enable the private sector to help find solutions to the deep-rooted and heretofore insoluble social problems that have defied government paternalism and private philanthropy. Under his leadership, Control Data adopted a long-term strategy of addressing the major unmet needs of society as profitable business opportunities in cooperation with government and other sectors. This strategy led the company into such areas as computer-based education, health care, revitalizing rural America, and providing jobs in the inner city.

"What I'm talking about is entering into really new things, like putting a new plant in a blighted city," he said. "That has to come from the top. I believe the chief executive has to do it because that's where the risk is. That's where the big commitment for change is. We have a great many people at Control Data that are efficient managers. That's different from leadership. Where you have an established product, any manager who's really adequate for the job ought to be able to identify and make solutions, and implement them. On the other hand, something like computer education, that's different, and I want to work with them closely on that. You need a leader. Leadership and management are not necessarily the same thing. The people that run companies most successfully are leaders, and there are not too many of them around. . . . You can outline a new concept to some people and they can't see it for anything. They can't see the merits in it. A leader thinks how great it would be to do this. I'm sure there will be some problems . . . managers are the ones that will solve the problems."

When I first interviewed Norris in 1978, he and Control Data were riding high. Unfortunately, Control Data slid into a bath of red ink in 1985 after it ran into some unprecedented problems in its peripheral business, due primarily to rapidly changing competitive conditions, which were exacerbated by the slump in the computer industry. In January 1986, Norris, then 74, announced his retirement in accordance with a succession plan put in place five years earlier.

MANPOWER STRATEGIES

REGINALD JONES AND GENERAL ELECTRIC

General Electric under Reginald Jones represented one of the starkest examples of a company run primarily by a bottom-up strategy, just the opposite of Control Data. GE, which dates back to Thomas Edison and the development of the incandescent light bulb, went through a reorganization under Jones, who retired in 1981. GE had been organized into five business sectors, each of which centered on different industries. Each sector worked as both a management and planning organization, and consisted of a number of strategic business units, or SBUs, which ranged in size from a department to a division and which reported to a senior executive. Thus, planning was both broad and deep at GE.

Jones's planning system was installed in 1970, as a response to growing sales but declining earnings and return on investment at GE. It seemed as if GE had lost its energy. Restructuring began with Jones trimming operating units from two hundred to forty-three, each of which was called an SBU. Linked by shared market characteristics, the SBU system lent itself to a common planning strategy. Next, the business was divided into five sectors: consumer products and services; industrial products and components; power systems; technical systems and materials; international. Jones freed up his office by installing a new layer of executives, the sector executive, in the hope that he and his assistants could move freely throughout the intricate structure and promote synergistic relationships between normally separate groups.

That novel SBU system, which achieved a degree of corporate fame, arose because of flaws in GE's previous organization, a sort of decentralized structure with a strategic-planning system superimposed. "We had one fatal flaw," said William Rothschild, one of GE's top strategic planners, "and that was the assumption that a manager can't manage anything over $100 million, or some magic sales figure. Every time we got to that figure, we reorganized. And that's when we wound up with 117 product departments. That lost the impact of having a strategy that was closely coupled to the overall business environment; each business became so internalized that we couldn't manage them. All we did with the SBU system was to put the pieces back together. What strategic planning really did was to put the individual businesses back into some kind of composite to help them relate better."

If imitation is the sincerest form of flattery, then General Electric has been praised to the skies. A great number of CEOs I interviewed mentioned GE's planning process as a model for their own companies. At GE, according to Jones, "Planning began in January when the SBUs drew up their preliminary plans based on the economic and social factors they saw as critical to their units' success. Plans were then sent to the sector executive, whose job was to integrate all of the disparate plans into a master plan for the sector. The policy review board and I saw the sector plans during the summer. By November, the final allocations had been made jointly by me and sector executives, based on each SBU's potential contribution to companywide revenues and earnings." GE uses a system that it developed with McKinsey and Co. This system grew out of the Boston Consulting Group's growth–market share matrix, which classifies SBUs into growth, stability, or no-growth businesses. Yet the GE–McKinsey matrix is based not on numbers alone, but on a range of other assessments relating to a business's "attractiveness."

Yet even in an organization such as GE, where planning bubbles up from the lowest levels, an occasional instance of top-down strategic decision making crops up. This is consistent with the belief that chief executives do not function, as it were, on just one of two speeds, high or low, but rather adapt their behavior to the situation. And it makes room for an important variable often missed by those entranced by the numbers: the role of human personality.

The merger of GE with Utah International, a mining company, was just such a case. Jones had a vision of what he called "the new GE": a company strong in international markets that could benefit greatly from the acquisition of a high-growth company. Jones said he needed something to "shake domestic executives out of their provincial mindsets." For Utah's part, its chief executive, Edmund W. Littlefield, wanted to spread the risks of operating primarily abroad, where the company had been increasingly threatened by expropriation, particularly with its Peruvian iron mines. Moreover, Utah had been threatened by increased taxes and accelerating economic nationalism in the country where it had its largest holdings, Australia, causing Littlefield to look for a partner. The acquirer would have to be flush with cash, for he had plans to expand in both Australia and Brazil.

And so the largest merger in history—at that time, at least—came about, ironically, against the grain of Jones's treasured planning approach. Jones engineered the deal in a series of secret sessions with Littlefield, an old friend, contrary to his usual practice of using the strategic planners to scout and evaluate potential targets. According to one of Jones's key deputies, Robert R. Frederick (later president of RCA), a lot of GE planners' noses were bent out of shape by the fact that they had not been informed about this potential merger from the outset. Alas, Jones's attempt to get into the takeover swing of things against the grain of his personality turned into a disaster. Mineral prices plummeted and Utah International soon became a millstone around GE's corporate neck. Eventually, Jack Welch, Jones's successor, had to sell it off at a distressed price, and absorb the loss. Ironically, Welch was, in most ways, just the opposite of Jones: aggressive rather than contemplative, extroverted rather than introverted, a doer rather than a planner. Not surprisingly, Welch eliminated much of the elaborate planning apparatus Jones had built. In the concluding chapter, I shall examine the role that individual psychology plays in this significant change in manpower strategy.

HAROLD GENEEN AND ITT

When I spoke with Harold Geneen, ITT was a $17-billion conglomerate that functioned in a wide array of businesses, from manufacturing telecommunications and electronics equipment to defense and avionics equipment, automotive and industrial products, consumer appliances, hotels, baked goods, financial services, and insurance. More than 60 percent of its manufacturing and telecommunications revenues came from abroad; its financial and insurance operations, however, occurred overwhelmingly in the United States.

Geneen held the reins at ITT from 1960 to 1978, when he took on the title of chairman. During that time, he oversaw the company's growth, from roughly $600 million in sales in 1959, to $11.3 billion in 1977. When one looks at the firm's current structure, the fact that it was originally designed by Geneen to function according to an overwhelmingly bottom-up system is not immediately clear. This is because when Geneen took over, after first establishing a European headquarters in Brussels with regional offices elsewhere, his concern was to design a "central core management" that would provide the autonomous units with top staff-level guidance and planning. He initiated a detailed measurement system. Reports were telexed to headquarters from all units on a weekly basis; more comprehensive reports were required each month. Every unit prepared detailed five-year plans on an annual basis. Geneen's policy of constant meetings—over two hundred per year—ensured that the results were constantly analyzed, reviewed, and compared against budgeted forecasts, a process that has become far more common in large, diversified firms than it was when Geneen instituted the practice.

The implementation of these measures by Geneen is consistent with some of the literature which holds that the development of centralized control over decentralized decision-making units occurs as a response to increased uncertainty in large, geographically far-flung firms, with a diversity of products. Although Geneen set up a new structure designed to push the decision-making responsibility downward by requiring him to delegate power to others, the way in which the structure was used served only to reinforce Geneen's own power and authority within the firm (a fact that we shall soon see when I discuss the San Diego cable plant decision).

Geneen's new structure brought an unaccustomed formality to the planning process at ITT. His meetings, an organizational structure burdened by a back-up network of "product line managers" having no operating responsibility, but who instead were used by Geneen to check up on operating personnel, produced a strange amalgam of top-down and bottom-up planning. On the one hand, Geneen believed that his policy on meetings led to a "unique, open management style," one in which each manager could air his or her views and receive feedback from peers. However, managers who were present at the sessions have indicated that Geneen controlled them tightly, failing to explore points in which he had no interest and creating the kind of atmosphere in which individual creativity was often stifled in the desire to manipulate assumptions and hard data in order to please Geneen. Occasionally, the methods he used to create such a climate included humiliating managers in front of their colleagues and holding meetings that would drag on for up to fifteen or so hours.

Max Richards, in *Organizational Goal Structures*, describes four types of "coalitions" that form to develop and use power in organizations: executive, bureaucratic, expert, and political.[2] In the case of ITT, Geneen was clearly the dominant force, a one-man executive coalition who could coerce and influence those further down the ladder. As a result, for Geneen, the top-down approach—even with a bottom-up structure—was very effective. However, the fact that this approach took its toll in fear and trembling from Geneen's underlings makes its validity as a blueprint for other organizations questionable.

To illustrate Geneen's management style, let us look at an example of a project on which Geneen made a decision that was not supported by his staff. It concerns the company's decision to enter the domestic cable market, and, as told in Thomas Burns's chronicle of ITT, *Tales of ITT: An Insider's Report*,[3] the frantic scramblings of Geneen's staff to first fight against the proposal, then to back it up with fictitious numbers. As Burns describes it, management was well aware that the case of the cable plant had much more to do with Geneen's personal desire to prove he could compete in telecommunications with AT & T and GTE in the United States than it did with any strategic purposes. In the past, he had shown himself to be stubborn about getting rid of acquisitions that foundered, such as Champion Lamp Company and Levitt & Sons. Over the years, corporate staffers, the cable division, and even consultants from Arthur D. Little had repeatedly vetoed the proposed $20-million cable plant. Nevertheless, Burns suggests that there was a political incentive: Geneen backed the plant to cater to a local San Diego congressman. After the cable group had assembled the usual data which painted a bleak picture of the cable plant, the head of the Defense Space Group approached Burns with "last minute revisions." And when the business plan was presented at the meeting the next morning, the sales and profit projections had all been revised upward.

Further evidence that managerial democracy went only so far was present at that meeting. There Geneen sat, next to the San Diego congressman. And, unlike his usual modus operandi, Geneen chose not to question the report at all, approving the cable plan and recessing the meeting. The plant turned out to be an economic disaster.

Setting, and Hitting, Strategic Targets

Strategic planning nearly always begins with some notion of a goal or a target. Will a company try to reach certain benchmarks of financial performance—say, a certain return on investment, or a certain earnings growth? Or will it build its strategy around market share in a number of selected markets? Or in the case of smaller, technologically oriented companies, will it simply try to get a product out the door, like a new computer, or a drug through the Food and Drug Administration? All of these are examples of targeting, and the way they are arrived at is intimately connected to the way the corporate organization operates in real life.

Targeting sounds simple, but it can be devilishly complex. For example, when Kodak bought a small California maker of magnetic media, Spin Physics, it also joined the Microelectronics and Computer Technology Corporation, a consortium. At the same time, it was starting joint ventures with three biotech companies—Amgen, Cetus, and Immunex—and watching its equity investment in Sun Microsystems, a maker of advanced workstations, and Interleaf, strong in electronic publishing. All of that requires a tremendous discipline and flexibility to hold in harness.

We have already seen how predominately top-down chief executives such as William Norris or, despite the decentralized, diversified organization, Harold Geneen operate. Few chief executives were as explicit and as forceful about articulating their targets as Geneen was. Not surprisingly, they were very basic financial benchmarks. In fact, one of the earliest things Geneen did at ITT was declare to the organization at large that he wanted return on investment to grow at least 10 percent a year, and that he wanted steady quarterly increases. In time, Geneen produced some forty-four straight quarters of earnings growth. "My own little philosophy on setting targets is that if you want to make a year's budget, or performance, the first thing you do is make the first quarter's budget, and goddamit, that's the one you have to be tough about. Somehow or other it's universal; everyone is going to lose the first quarter, because January is a funny month. Everyone ships everything in December, in order to make last year's total larger, and so January is shy. So you have to work harder that first quarter. If you make the first quarter, then you make the second quarter, and believe me, if you've gone that far, you make the year. If you lose the first quarter, you say you'll make it up in the second, but you don't. So that's our target: make the first quarter, come hell or high water."

Geneen was also fascinating about the psychology of the targets themselves. "I always asked my managers to stretch their targets, and we never shot anybody that couldn't make it," he said. "But we were shooting for 15 percent, knowing that we could get ten, *expecting* to get 10 or 11 percent. But certainly, I wouldn't want them getting used to thinking that they could get 8, when they could get 12 percent by trying to get 15. This business of targets gets to be a matter of tolerance."

By all accounts, Geneen was unique for setting targets so strictly from above in a multidivisional company. In such companies, the complexities are usually too great for a chief executive to rule so autocratically. "It depends upon the style of the person, of course, the style of the company," said Joseph Flavin of Singer. "I suspect that the best plans bubble up to the leadership. To use my past two companies, Xerox and IBM, both of these were strictly in one-industry businesses. You [the chief executive] should know those businesses cold. But the former, Singer was *not* in one business, but in a number of businesses, so there's no way as CEO that you can know enough about each one to truly do all the separate strategies for each. There's no way. You can set objectives and goals in a financial sense for each of these separate businesses. But if you plan the strategies for them from the top, you're going to be wrong. There's no way to be right."

Other chief executives agreed that companies could not necessarily plan as precisely as Geneen did. Edwin Smart, the chief executive of TWA, spent a day describing to me the complex turnaround he had initiated there. Smart was quite emphatic that to build a strategic plan, he needed targets. But he also emphasized that in turbulent times, dollar-denominated targets such as those Geneen has used—financial goals, in other words— were suspect. Said Smart, "When you talk about strategy, you're really talking about several different areas: marketing, personnel, facilities, capital, and profit and loss. Too often, a long-range plan is dedicated to just one of those, and usually it's dedicated to profit and loss and usually it turns out wrong, because the dollars over a four- or five-year period are wrong. We needed a plan [that worked] in principle, which is the greatest need of a long-range plan because of the long-range character of capital." A few moments later, he elaborated, "We needed a plan which would tell us how to be better off than we would otherwise be—not exactly how much better off, not exactly how much money we would make or lose, but would give us confidence in knowing that if we did these things . . . we would make more than we might otherwise have done." Smart's point: strategy making is less a question of hitting a bull's-eye than of hitting the side of the barn.

For most companies, the process of setting targets and of building a viable strategy worked far more incrementally than it did at ITT. William May, the former chairman of American Can, described the process there: "Every year, we used to have these strategic planning meetings, where the board would sit and the management would all be there and each individual would get up in each sector and talk about where he thought things were going, what he thought future opportunities were, what he thought the future problems were, and how he was going to cope with them. And then he would indicate in broad terms what he thought the physical and financial requirements were and what the results of that investment in that direction were going to be. Then, the next month, generally October or November,

229

we'd move to the next scheduled procedure in the planning process. It was a set routine all year long. Any important issue was presented to the board by the guy who had responsibility for it. He knew more about it, could answer the questions better, and I would just be parrying the questions if I tried to do it myself, or if the president tried.

"The guys down here would be thinking concepts, thinking products or market and investment opportunities," said May. "By the time it got to a higher level, it was getting pretty hard with specific investments, returns, discounted cash flows, things of that nature. By the time it got to the board, it was quite hard, because these were month-by-month decisions that were made throughout the year. The board had been approving things throughout the year. Obviously, you don't approve all your expenditures and all your growth and your markets and everything in January, and then limit them for the rest of the year because things change. But in November, the managers would come in and sort of dream with the directors as to where things might be going and what was the long-range opportunity."

One of the more quietly crucial times in corporate life comes when either external factors or internal demands require a change in strategic targets. Over time, companies may change their targets from simple survival to high growth to increasing returns. As William Norris of Control Data said, "In the beginning, I just wanted to do something important—really important—in computer technology. And of course, we had to survive." In time, Norris shifted to an acquisition strategy fed by high internal growth: "I saw a lot of opportunities for buying tiny companies for stock in order to fill some gaps in a hurry. It worked. . . . We really did not contemplate the rapid growth that we finally undertook, and in fact, some of our people were really very opposed to that. They wanted to keep the company small. Lots of advantages in smaller relations. But there was no way we could stay small after the stock went up. That forced us to grow, and grow fast."

The trouble with choosing any single target is that other key goals usually have to be sacrificed. In the chapter on turnarounds, we saw how Roy Ash, a brilliant manager at Litton and Hughes and at the OMB, could not repeat that performance at AM International, trying to do too much with limited resources. May, of American Can, was particularly articulate on the balancing act that is required. "There are some areas," he said, "where return on investment might jeopardize your long-range planning and long-range performance. In other words, sometimes you invest or sacrifice at this moment for something that's going to happen three or four years out. That's hard to do, because of the peripatetic nature of management. The guy often doesn't see himself in the same job in three to five years, so he says, 'Why the hell should I sacrifice performance and all this potential today for something that my successor is going to get the benefit of in four or five years?' " Let it suffice to say that no target exists alone. Instead, they are as interdependent as the strands of a spider web: pull one, snap another, and the entire structure shudders.

For William Verity, of Armco Steel, targeting involved a long, hard process of diversifying away from flat-rolled steel products. For Verity and his staff, targeting provided the necessary discipline to build a full-fledged strategic plan. "There were times when our commitment to this new strategy meant we didn't do as well as our competitors [who remained in steel]. So there were very real costs—human costs—for a considerable part of the time. . . . I found that you had to target in stages. The first thing we did was to get rid of recognized losers. That wasn't very hard. The second thing is that we forced these businesses to look at what it was they wanted to do. Once they decided that, then we had to get rid of what they didn't want. That isn't so hard. Third, and this is a more sophisticated step for us, since we're just a bunch of country boys anyway, was to learn that there are businesses that ten years out aren't going to be so good. You hate to get rid of them; there's one that's a fine company now, but its future is bleak. So we're selling some of those. We are really trying to take assets available to us and use them the best we can to get a 12-percent return on total assets. Each business has a hurdle rate of return on its assets, which we periodically check and then raise higher."

While Verity's methods are far different than Geneen's, one should note that Armco's actual targets are not all that different than Geneen-era ITT's. Particularly, note Verity's stress on the need to initiate and implement a strategy in manageable doses—to fit the strategy, in other words, to the manpower. This human factor in the grand designs of chief executives is a critical aspect of strategic decision making.

Manpower Problems: The Canker in the Rose

Building an organizational structure, however important, is really only half the battle in actually implementing strategic plans. The actual face-to-face relationship between chief executive and management is the grease that

231

oils the corporate wheels. Without it, the finest plans bog down, the cogs and wheels of implementation either turn more slowly or grind to a halt. Perhaps because of its very amorphous nature, building a successful manpower strategy may be the most difficult strategic task of the chief executive. Not only is it difficult to define and implement a successful one over time, but it is perhaps the toughest task of all to cultivate it consistently and successfully over time. Often, the canker of a failing manpower strategy can fester within even the most outwardly successful of operations. While managers can detect a failing new venture strategy by the inability to meet certain set financial goals, issues of morale and motivation move further underground in an established firm, and it takes a manager who is very sensitive and who listens very carefully to pick it up.

There is good experiential evidence that manpower strategies at many major corporations have declined. Many chief executives complained to me of the lack of loyalty shown by managers these days, a lack always boldly compared to the glorious days of the past. "We joined the company fresh out of high school or out of college, and rowed the oars of that company all the way throughout our whole career," said Wallace Rasmussen, of Beatrice, who had joined the company right out of high school (he never graduated from college). "It wasn't like it is today. No one who wanted a CEO's job jumped off the boat." Indeed, job hopping, the most obvious manifestation of that decline in loyalty, does seem to have increased. That loyalty has been strained as well by the behavior of top executives—particularly chief executives. What are middle managers to think when they discover that their leader has donned a golden parachute in the event of a takeover? Or how are they to react when they discover that the chief executive is raking in not only a handsome salary, but tons of stock options, not to mention the use of a car, a corporate jet, and other perks that go beyond the bounds of efficient operations? Or why should managers eschew job hopping, when those above them in the hierarchy have arrived at the company horizontally, from competitors or other industries?

Indeed, chief executives and their staffs can often be blind to what is going on beneath them. One is reminded of Marie Antoinette: "Let them eat cake." Allow me to offer an example from personal experience. In the summer of 1985, I was called in to work on a special project involving two divisions of Citibank that had recently been split. A tremendous number of consulting surveys and amount of analysis had already been done by Allan Kennedy, a former McKinsey consultant. From hundreds of employees in the two divisions, Kennedy had amassed data that revealed a

232

great deal of frustration about their jobs, their future, their work mates and managers, the promotion and review process, and the bank as a whole. My own interviews concerning that survey repeated the same phrase: Citibank is "too political." Fear of the politics at Citibank determined employees' attitudes toward pay and promotion, toward the possibilities for future advancement, toward their own self-respect, and toward the way they reacted to directives and strategy from above. "Around here, it is who you know rather than what you know or do that matters," one employee told me. "It's who your friends are, who your guardian managers are, who is in good with whom."

Here was the canker. What was so surprising about these results was how different they were from both outside perceptions of Citibank's corporate culture, particularly in the banking industry, and from top management, which regarded their selection and promotion system as being the best, the fairest, and the most advanced in banking. Managers of the two divisions I was involved with had even had the slogan, "We're number one in employee work environment" printed on buttons, which employees felt required—a bad sign indeed—to wear. The same slogan was plastered on countless signs posted in Citibank's hallways and bulletin boards. This yawning gap between perception and reality profoundly shocked the top managers. For years, they had been bragging about their manpower strategy and how effective and fair it was.

The realization of the problem resulted in months of meetings and the hiring of numbers of consultants. It was a fascinating process to watch. At first, top managers refused to believe the evidence. At first, they dwelled on a handful of positive comments the surveys had unearthed, such as "I'm pleased to be working for the largest bank in the United States." I must have heard that read aloud a dozen times by managers. But the grim reality soon washed away the few positive nuggets. Indeed, it soon became clear that a large percentage of employees refused to fill out surveys for fear of reprisal, despite the promises of confidentiality. That emerged gradually as they embarked on in-depth interviewing. One manager told me in private: "They wouldn't keep half of us if they knew how we really felt about the system. The top guys here are simply conning themselves into believing what they're forcing on us is working."

Creating an Environment

How do you create a good environment for people to work in? Rasmussen, of Beatrice, had a few opinions on the matter. We were discussing mergers and acquisitions, when suddenly he began to explain how he judged another company—say, a potential acquisition. "The best way to tell how management feels about their employees is to look into the rest rooms. You can tell quickly: if they're messy, walk away from them . . . and if you watch management speak to an employee and they smile, you can believe you can have good relationships with them. If they walk into the dining room and not say a word, forget it. The first thing you have is a union problem. Another good place to look is the garbage disposal, to see how much waste there is . . . [or] we look at the cars they're driving. Employees often buy fancier cars than management. It shows they are well paid." This is the sort of observation and intuition that is not taught in the business schools.

It all begins at the top. Fully fifty-five of the eighty-nine chief executives I interviewed stressed that choosing, motivating, and holding top executives was their most important function as a chief executive. In the next chapter, we will see how important a succession strategy is for the continuing prosperity of an organization; manpower strategy, as I have defined it here, includes a far wider range of issues. "Of all my skills, if I have any, as an executive and an organizer, the most important is . . . my ability to pass on responsibility together with authority," said one entrepreneur. "The two have to go hand in hand. I'm a good picker of people I think, and I know how to work with people. But I'm not the final voice, I'm not the final mind. My mind can be swerved one way or the other quite easily, hopefully on the basis of good, sound logic, but sometimes not. We all make mistakes." Indeed, this chief executive fumbled badly and repeatedly when it came to choosing his own successor.

As we shall see in the next chapter, a major role of the chief executive is recognizing talent, retesting it, and bringing it along. That is a subject John deButts was quite eloquent on. "I keep a secret list right here in my desk," he said. "I keep it secret because sometimes high-potential guys are very low down in the company when they start, and I don't want to distort their growth pattern by anointing them too early. It's also secret because knowledge of who is and who isn't on the list causes all kinds of resentments and animosities." But deButts, like a number of other chief executives, emphasized that just as they had a list of potentially strong managers, so should other managers have a similar list of those in their area. "I have taken a very personal interest in forcing more and more training sessions, and job shifts, and shared responsibilities, to make sure career development is taken as a top priority," said deButts. "If they don't have a quick answer ready for me when I ask about career development, they get a black mark. If they don't have a clearly spelled-out list of back-up managers for every single one of their managers, they get a black mark. If their suggested back-ups are from outside their departments, they get a black mark, for that clearly indicates they've no internal career development of their own."

But deButts's hands-on interest is often the exception. Many chief executives delegate manpower decisions as if they were some unsavory dish at a ten-course meal. Some CEOs build their executive team from scratch; others inherit an ongoing team; others pick and choose, molding a team over time; many drift, allowing inertia to take its course. Said Wallace Rasmussen, "When you know you have a winning team, your objective is to keep the winning team. It's much harder to keep the winning team than it is to build one." Nevertheless, after Rasmussen's tenure, his successor, James L. Dutt, tried to shake up what he viewed as a self-satisfied and somewhat stodgy company by decimating the ranks of top executives.[4] In time, Dutt was sacked himself, and the company was taken private in a leveraged buyout. Dutt's strategy, if it could be called that, was clearly a disastrous manpower problem. But it points out the fact that, right or wrong, chief executives adopt the manpower strategy that fits their own personalities and that of the company. If you take the reins of IBM, you already have a good team, so there is no need to go outside. But if you take over a failing company, as a turnaround artist will, you may be forced to go outside for a new executive team.

As we have seen time after time in this book, what chief executives say does not always reflect what they have done or are doing. The same applies here. Manpower strategies are very fashionable and often discussed, but rarely implemented. Harken back to the signs and slogans at Citibank, and to the reality they failed to acknowledge. In most companies, manpower strategies are far down the list of priorities, though there is always a lot of talk—in public statements, interviews, annual reports, and the company manuals—about what a wonderful job the CEO is doing to ensure those strategies. While some chief executives do hold annual retreats, hire human resource directors, or say they consult regularly with the rank and file, most manpower decisions are still made only *after* other strategic decisions, and then, as often as not, by a personnel director or a middle manager. As a result, the work force, including the bureaucracy, is often violently out of sync with the CEO's general strategic plan. Want to build new ventures? The work force may be as entrepreneurial as a turtle beneath a rock. Want to develop new technology? Managers would rather leave at five o'clock to go home and wash the car.

Saying one thing and doing another creates particularly serious problems. Again, remember the Citibank case. While management was telling the world how wonderful they were, the workers were quietly in revolt. Those contradictions eventually fester; turnover increases; hiring good new people becomes more difficult; few are willing to work that extra hour, or do much more than their job descriptions; initiative, imagination, and passion wither. The situation is not all that different from that of the revolving-door syndrome to be discussed later. Both are manpower problems. Both drive an organization to become bureaucratic and less entrepreneurial. When that happens, the chief executive can only blame him- or herself.

Success or Failure

Manpower strategy is hardly cut and dried. First, the type of manager chosen for a division, a product, or a project must be matched to the type of strategy to be implemented. An accountant should not be running a marketing team. And an entrepreneurial manager may not be the best person to run an established business, or a traditional manager a new venture. Second, some form of incentive, usually monetary, has to be designed to motivate managers. The emphasis on such a salary or promotion scale is to target and to achieve long-term goals. Simple as that sounds, it has proven to be a major stumbling block. Indeed, it can often be counterproductive. Managers will often emphasize short-term profits at the expense of long-range goals, simply to win a bonus or raise.

Third, some form of monitoring system has to be set up. Information and directives have to flow down from the top and back up again, freely, quickly, and clearly. "You name it," one chief executive told me. "I've seen it go wrong when you put the wrong executive into the wrong job and you don't check up to see exactly how things are going wrong. You can't leave it for even a quarter. Get right on top of it. I've known CEOs who let their new executives have a year's worth of rope to hang themselves and the company. That's just insane. Those CEOs kid themselves that they're delegating responsibility. Keep tight control. That's my motto."

There are a lot of ways that strategic planning can run amuck, most of which fit under the rubric of "personnel" or "people" problems. Planning is often viewed by line managers as paper pushing or chart designing, and is criticized for being unrealistic or dismissed as being inconsequential. Then there are the complaints of old-line managers, who say that planning is being foisted upon them by a bunch of MBAs who do not know about people, management, or manufacturing. "Hell," groused one older chief executive, "those whiz kids don't have any practical experience in how to run factories or distribution systems." Despite the prevalence of that attitude, the shock of being beaten in the marketplace by products from a foreign country with alien manpower strategies has forced many chief executives to reevaluate their own methods. Thus, the fashion for Japanese methods, from quality circles to lifetime employment and an emphasis on consensual relations between management and labor, as opposed to an adversarial one. "There is no way we are going to be able to automate all our factories and radically integrate new computerized systems and robotics . . . unless we have a brand new way of relating to our work force," said Roger Smith of GM. "That is the primary purpose of the Saturn project—not the car itself. Our goal is to totally revamp our worker-management system . . . that can let us ultimately Saturnize the entire GM organization."

But beware, in their enthusiasm for the new and glamorous, many chief executives fail to see that those much-ballyhooed Japanese management systems require at least as many manpower skills, and perhaps more, as the American model. *Any* successful business strategy requires a well-executed manpower strategy. Still, the sheer enthusiasm for Japanese management, which many chief executives understand about as well as they comprehend the complexities of Japanese culture, reflects the sheer confusion over manpower strategies. When in doubt, look for the newest cure-all.

Let us look at one issue that highlights the complexities and the ambiguities of manpower strategy. That involves choosing managers to turn troubled divisions around. At first glance, it seems quite logical to take the best managers and throw them into the breach. Such a policy gets the best managers to places that need them the most, and, theoretically at least,

237

provides a means of testing and evaluating managerial talent. But it is not as simple as all that. First, who are the best managers, and which ones have the skills for a particular problem? "I've found that it usually takes a very different kind of manager to run a dying business than to run a successful business well or a start-up venture well," said William May of American Can. "Those are different kinds of managers, and I had to be real careful not to put the wrong type of guy in to manage the wrong type of unit." May's notion flies in the face of the old nostrum that the good manager can manage anything. Most chief executives chose to hire two kinds of executives, both jacks-of-all-trades and a cadre of specialists, skilled at one particular aspect of corporate operations. The trick, of course, is to create the correct mix of the two types and make appropriate assignments according to shifting circumstances, without creating the sort of conflicts that often result. And that is not easy.

Still, once you find the perfect manager, should he or she not be dispatched as quickly as possible to the trouble site? Perhaps not. A number of chief executives I spoke with threw a different light on the problem. Take, for instance, one chief executive who insistently focused not on the possibilities of such a policy, but on the potential disasters: "Either way, in these basket cases [businesses], whether he's a good manager or just an okay one, the guy fails, tarnishing his image and breaking his spirit. The guy feels—and he usually is—less able to get back on the fast track of this company. What's worse, other middle-level managers are less willing to follow his lead in his next assignment we try to give him. So that's a total exercise in frustration and humiliation and those forced managers hate to go down into that pit of the bad business and try that rescue operation because they figure it's doomed and therefore they're doomed. Or, on the other hand, if the guy makes an absolutely tremendous success of propping up that decaying business and dressing it up for sale to an outside buyer, then the very first demand made by whoever is interested in buying that unit is that we must have that guy or it's no deal. . . . And so you lose the hot-shot manager who's proved himself."

MANPOWER STRATEGIES

Evaluation, Pay, and Promotion

The heart of any manpower strategy is the evaluation of management. And although it may sound prosaic, the typical annual or semiannual review can take on a bewildering variety of forms, depending on the chief executive and the company. However, it is possible to sketch a few lessons that apply in almost all cases. These take on the appearance of the commonsensical; indeed, they agree in large part with *In Search of Excellence*[5]— testimony, I suppose, to the fact that the obvious is often easily forgotten or ignored. Companies that have successful manpower strategies invariably emphasize long-term strategic goals over short-term results. These paragons adopt explicit manpower strategies—evaluations, pay scales, promotion processes—that are well known and publicized throughout the company. All employees are evaluated by more than one level of management at least once a year. Merit increases are not simply restricted to one class, one group, or one type of employee category. There is a clear sense of continuity. And, finally, manpower strategy must come from the top. "I spent days and days each year going over pay and bonus rates for my managers," said George Weissman, the chief executive of Philip Morris. "They're the ones that are building this company."

At Texas Instruments, for example, CEO J. Fred Bucy told me that twice a year, he and his staff sat together in a room, each at a computer terminal, and reviewed each of some two hundred top managers, as pertinent data flashed on an overhead screen. Bucy and his staff not only graded each executive, they then compared executives to each other, trying to build a rough hierarchy of talent. The computerized evaluation was then supplemented by discussions among these executives who knew particular managers. Said Bucy, "The process is painful, arduous, it results in a lot of frustrations and wrangling, but in the end it ensures that everyone is given a fair shake. I deem it to be the most important part of our strategic management system. More important than our famous pricing system, more important than new product development. . . . It makes all our people believe in our system of management."

While one has to temper the enthusiasm of a chief executive like Bucy for his own system—recall how Citibank executives thought their system was wonderful, too—I should add that such a system is particularly necessary in a fast-growing company. Thus, both newcomers and old-timers

239

know the rules of the game and how they are being evaluated. And it provides a source of information for top management into the inner workings of the company. "This procedure forces us to keep current in exactly what's happening in our work force and managerial ranks," said Bucy. "It's all too easy as a chief executive to get sidetracked by crises or big plans, but the most important thing we do is to bring on the next generation of managers to carry on after us."

Bucy, however, is the exception. Most of the chief executives I interviewed left routine personnel matters to their personnel department. While chief executives tend to step in during a crisis, most have no program to reward strategic performance or to reward managers for achieving the desired corporate strategy. That can cause difficulties. For instance, personnel departments, which are, after all, bureaucracies, often set up incentives aimed at group equity, not at the satisfaction of strategic goals. Managers are promoted in lockstep, or promotions are based strictly on seniority; where performance measures are used, these tend to rely on short-term numbers of a division, say, not on the distance traveled to long-term strategic goals. Many chief executives said they had told their personnel departments to correlate their reward structures with some performance component. But the component they almost invariably mentioned was the return on investment or return on sales for the department, as compared to the previous quarter. In turn, I found that many personnel departments left their basic salary-scale decisions, benefit plan structure, and other compensation measurement programs to Hay Associates, a consulting firm specializing in measurements and evaluations of corporate pay scales and compensation packages. It is a testament to Hay's marketing department that many of the chief executives I spoke with had, at one point or another, used Hay. Yet there was rarely any explicit directive that Hay should include specific strategic goals in the design of a package.

The one exception to the chief executive's usual ignorance of personnel questions has to do with salary levels. Everyone, from chief executive to new workers, spends a considerable amount of time mulling over salaries. Even those chief executives who handed over manpower strategy to personnel showed an abiding interest in the pay of their top lieutenants and, I suppose, in their own. Again, Hay is often used as a benchmark. "We always pay in the midrange of the Hay scale for each type of job classification," said the chief executive of a multinational chemical corporation. John Culligan, CEO of American Home Products, a consumer goods company, told me: "We pay slightly above the midrange, but we also have a system of rewarding outstanding performance." "We always try to squeak into the top 10 percent of the Hay rates," said a third chief executive. "I've made that a target for six years now. And I made sure I met it."

Behind such concerns lies a fear of losing a functioning team. "This business is too competitive for me to afford to get out of line with those executive pay scales even for six months," said a chief executive who asked to remain anonymous. "I can't afford to lose my best production, design, research, finance, or marketing men, and waste a year searching for, training, and bringing up to speed a new guy who can perform adequately with this super team I've developed over the years. Have you any idea what the real cost is of replacing even one of those top men? It's horrendous. I'm not just talking about the cost of head hunters and executive search firms, but the dislocation of the entire ongoing business in that man's department while he is preparing to leave, departs, and is replaced. I've known cases where the department was never able to regain the momentum it had before. There really is a thing called personal chemistry and corporate culture, and you can lose it real fast when . . . a real leader departs." Added Joseph Flavin of Singer in somewhat more pungent terms, "I was a hard-nosed manager when I started out and I learned the hard way the cost of losing some of your best managers by failing to anticipate their changing financial needs."

I found it interesting that while many chief executives stressed the importance of being the low-cost competitor, not a single one said that they had set a goal of having the lowest managerial salary scale. That includes even old-line commodity businesses, where salaries do tend to be lower than, say, high-margined, high-technology operations. Indeed, one result of comparing salary levels and the threat of managerial job hopping has been an overall escalation of managerial pay across the board, including that of chief executives. Traditionally, in deeply recessionary cycles, chief executives would dramatically rethink these all-but-automatic pass-along contract increases to themselves and their managers. But except in companies staggering toward insolvency, such a pattern of change simply did not happen in the last recession. Top executive salary increases are often the last to be sacrificed on the altar of expedience.

Paying the Price of Change

Change can be a mixed blessing for chief executives. On one hand, it may be necessary to survive, and it may bring many rewards. On the other, change is highly stressful and requires alterations in manpower strategy that at best can unsettle, and at worst can destroy, morale. Companies with a tendency to change manpower strategies often suffered from widespread and deep-seated dissension among employees. "Two new chief executives have twice changed the damn policy," one chief executive of a subsidiary said to me. "Actually, it's more like four times the human resource guidelines have changed. They've changed so often around here that none of us believe the new one will last, so we don't know which goals or targets are top priority. That's fatal for a division like mine, because I have been preaching productivity increases to my managers for the past three years. When they don't see their own financial rewards . . . it makes my job that much harder pushing them to go the extra mile for the company's new productivity plan. Frankly, this shift in CEOs and their different personnel policies is ruining my credibility with my men. I'm losing some of my best managers to competitors because guys no longer believe I can deliver on my promises to them, which I based on direct promises made to me by the previous CEO and personnel director. That's fatal."

That lament resembles the picture sketched out to me by David Rockefeller, then the chairman of Chase Manhattan, after nearly two decades at the helm. Here, after all, was one of the wealthiest men on earth, heir to a great fortune, secure in his position at the top of one of the most powerful banks on earth. And yet, for all of that wealth and power, Rockefeller chose to talk at length about the difficulties of creating an effective manpower strategy. For example, Rockefeller described the evolutions—and that may be a kind way to describe it; contortions might be more to the point—manpower strategy at Chase had gone through.

"I spent my first summer at the bank in 1955 trying to develop an organization chart for the foreign department," he said. "There had *never* been one. I discovered, trying to put down in chart form what we were actually doing, that it was a perfectly ridiculous structure." A short time later, Rockefeller discovered that the bank as a whole also lacked an organizational chart. Rockefeller was finally named co–chief executive with George Champion, an expedient political decision by the board, but a disastrous strategic one. "Our executive organization was split into two by our desires to take the bank in two totally different directions: foreign versus domestic," he said, a bit later adding, "the whole organization was paralyzed. We sort of marked time during those years." When Champion retired, Rockefeller became the sole chief executive. He named Herbert Patterson as president. "I don't think he was prepared to devote the time and energy to the job that it took," said Rockefeller. "Therefore, it came to 1972 when Herb left, and [Willard C.] Butcher came in as the new president. So I must say that most of our new organization has only happened since then."

Even then, Rockefeller delayed. He was candid about blaming himself for the time it took to put a new manpower strategy in place. "The trouble," he said, "was that at the time I really didn't feel that I had the support of the people. Therefore, we kept marking time for years." That kind of delay, he found, could be deadly. "It was very trying, because in the midst of trying to get our strategic process and planning going, all kinds of things plagued us—real estate and other problems. We've had to deal with putting out bonfires. We both thought we ought to be out of all this and be a new kind of bank. But in some ways, maybe it wasn't bad—it made us tougher and better people, having to deal with so many problems at the same time."

That may be so, but business is not therapy, and Chase has since continued to lag behind its major competitor, Citibank. Why did Rockefeller have so many problems developing a successful manpower strategy at Chase? Some critics attributed it to his own personality and his family's wealth, which tended to keep other executives at a distance. Rockefeller himself questioned this hypothesis. "I was very much interested in developing what we considered to be the proper structure and strategy in the human resources area. We pulled in top, specialized field people—nonbankers—for marketing and strategic planning, corporate communications, computer systems, things of that kind, where the knowledge of credit was not really necessary. We wanted people who knew that specialty profession well, rather than trying to remake a banker to do these tasks. What I can claim is, I have recognized for a very long time the need for this kind of evolution. In the early days when I was in the bank, top management discouraged or flatly resented this kind of thing."

Why the problems then? Rockefeller believes that many of his manpower problems stemmed from the historic culture of the bank. "Where we at Chase were unique was that for thirty years we had as chairman men who were lawyers and didn't understand internal affairs," he said. "Next, our bankers didn't think of themselves as business managers, but instead, just as traditional loan officers. . . . There is no question that until the last few years, lending officers felt it was beneath them to be seriously concerned about problems of management, budget, personnel, et cetera. Why they were so slow in coming to it, I don't know. It's no question, but it's true." He also attributed some manpower problems to the changes he instituted. "Then, we had the problem of expanding overseas and trying finally to catch up with Citibank. This involved an enormous capital expenditure and an expenditure of people, and a demand for our officers overseas as we were opening up all over. We had to rob a lot of our domestic areas. This reduced the quality of the people handling it. This showed that some of the domestic business was neglected; therefore, in the last several years, we've been putting a new effort on our national strategy . . . strengthening the executive organization. I must admit, having been with the bank for thirty-three years, one would like to feel that this is proceeding faster than it has."

Finally, Rockefeller admitted that it constituted a strategic failure on his own part. His words could come from any number of other CEOs. "I don't think I had a really well-thought-through plan along the lines of what we have today," he mused. "It's something that has evolved over the last eight to ten years. I didn't have a clear blueprint. I recognized that there were changes that we were going to make, but truthfully, I can't say that I understood in detail how we intended to move. I can't say to you that I had as chief executive in 1969 a clear blueprint of what the benefits would be. I had a general notion, but I didn't realize that we needed a greater integration between the domestic and the international. I didn't see it as clear as I do today. We had to cut across oceans as well as states. I didn't see the implications that would have as I do today."

Conclusion

In this chapter, I have tried to provide a glimpse at how corporations actually attempt to initiate and implement strategic plans. Consider it, in a sense, a three-stage process. First, a chief executive must build some sort of organizational structure in which information can flow up, usually, and direction can flow down. Chief executives are different, and so are companies, so the way these flows operate can be dramatically different as well. What is important, however, is that there is some interchange between top and bottom. Without it, the chief executive sits isolated in an ivory tower, shouting instructions in a language the people below cannot understand.

Second, once that communication operates, a chief executive has to set some sort of goals. Goals or targets are the armature of the strategic plan. Without them, the plan collapses in a heap. Again, these targets can differ tremendously, from the strict, almost schoolmasterish, financial targets hung up by Harold Geneen, to more general, more complex strategic goals outlined by Edwin Smart. Both kinds of targets can easily go awry: the strict financial target can result in a sacrifice of the short term over the long; the more general can devolve into no target at all, but a sort of hazy memory that, yes, once the company was working toward something.

All of that is preliminary to the real, day-to-day work of the chief executive. As I have said, an executive alone in a tower is useless unless there is some way of communicating with the people who actually implement strategic plans. And there is more to it than simple communication. Rather, it enters the mysterious realm of motivation and morale, what I call manpower strategy. I use the word mysterious advisedly, for this may be hardest to get at properly through rational processes. Certainly, managers aspiring to the top job can learn a few things about treating their staffs, and about using them as a tool for their ideas, which is what strategic planning really comes down to. But there is quite a lot in this area that lies in the province of personality, of the ineffable. How do you define, or create, a leader whom others are willing to follow? How do you make people want to work hard, and work imaginatively? All of the self-help books in the world and all of the business courses on motivation will not make most people inspiring leaders. This is the area—perhaps, really, the only area—where intuition reigns supreme.

That is not to say, however, that one cannot learn from the triumphs and mistakes of chief executives. My personal favorite among these anecdotes comes from the blunt and crusty former chief executive of Beatrice, Wallace Rasmussen, who talks of poking into the garbage of potential acquisition targets, checking out the rest rooms, and observing behavior in the cafeteria—all to try to figure out what kind of management he's dealing with. Well, what Rasmussen is offering is a marvelous lesson in manpower strategy: in short, for all of the lofty abstractions of some chief executives, what really matters is how people act on a day-to-day basis. People count. And chief executives who ignore the human element in their strategizing do so at their own peril.

CHAPTER TEN

SUCCESSION STRATEGIES: THE KING IS DEAD, LONG LIVE THE KING

The most important job as chief executive at AT & T is choosing the right successor for me. —JOHN DEBUTTS, former CEO, AT & T Company

Those chief executives who demand that they personally choose their successors are usually full of their own egos. They are preempting a job of the board of directors.
—NATHAN R. OWEN, chairman of the board, General Signal Corporation

The Past, the Present, the Future

Most CEOs experience a succession personally only twice: when they are first promoted to the top job, and when they promote their successor. And yet there are few issues in corporate life as potentially damaging as that transfer of power between the old and the new. Succession means giving up hard-won power, and whether it is in politics or corporate life, few ambitious leaders find that an easy process. As in politics, however, the perspective of the chief executive toward succession often depends on his or her views toward corporate governance.

Many chief executives, as exemplified by John deButts's statement at

247

the beginning of this chapter, are firmly convinced that succession is solely their responsibility and that a board of directors cannot know the candidates well enough to make an intelligent decision. As in any case of top-down control, sometimes that decisiveness spills over into a desire to perpetuate a name or a system, or to punish enemies. Or, if also the founder of the company, chief executives may wish to hold on long past their effective age, thus damaging their own creation. Other chief executives are more democratic, handing the decision to the board, acceding readily to its desire. Such a practice may hand the reins over to a successor who is inadequate.

There is one area of agreement however: succession strategies are absolutely essential to the continuing prosperity of the company. A carefully conducted succession can ensure that other strategic plans continue to be implemented. IBM is the classic example here; executives rise to the rank of president and the chair of the computer giant with smooth regularity, and the corporate machine roars onward. IBM is an example of a case where a successor can be groomed, over a period of time, so that the long-term objectives of the corporation—articulated by either the chief executive or the board—will continue to be pursued.

Failure to plan at all for succession often can, and does, result in the destruction of an efficient management team and the erosion of a carefully nurtured corporate culture. A succession struggle can take a terrible toll in wasted time and energy, forcing managers to turn from long-term strategy to short-term gains in the attempt to show they deserve the top job, or at least are worthy of retaining their position under a new master.

A succession battle often can veer into more dangerous territory. As the missiles fly overhead, top management may think it is safer to work elsewhere, and begin spending time with head hunters or interviewing at other companies. Indeed, the fear is not unfounded; should an outsider come into the company, the new CEO may bring in a whole new staff with new goals and strategies, in the process, throwing out the old staff—they end up scapegoats for any real or perceived corporate failures and for any immediate gaffes by the new gang. And poorly planned successions may be self-perpetuating. Companies that have been performing erratically often see their earnings and stock price foundering during a succession crisis. As a result, the revolving-door syndrome begins. Chief executives come and go, unable to wrestle with basic corporate problems. The malaise begins to sink deeply into the employee ranks. Surviving managers become cynical, hostile to action of any sort, and as self-protective as timid bureaucrats during a purge. And the downward spiral increases.

SUCCESSION STRATEGIES

A succession strategy, like a personality, is determined by a complex of factors. I have broken it down to five:

1. The personal power of the outgoing chief executive and the board of directors.
2. The strength of the company and its industry in a time of succession.
3. The tradition, or lack of tradition, of the company regarding the means to choose a new chief executive.
4. The aggressiveness of major owners or other insiders to influence the chief executive or the board.
5. The influence of outside pressure groups, such as the government or a major supplier.

How do these factors work in tandem? We saw in the chapter on turn-around strategy how in a crisis situation, planning begins to contract to the very short term. The corporation is certain to suffer, particularly if the previous chief executive was weak, if there was little tradition of orderly succession, or if the company is being buffeted by outside forces. A strong chief executive, backed by a long tradition of successful successions, has a good chance of keeping management working efficiently and imaginatively right up to the day of the testimonial dinner. Above all else, strong executives will often choose their successor from within, tapping the successor for as long as a year or two before the actual succession and giving him or her the time to master the job. The lesson here is that the strong get stronger: good executives who generate consistent profits are often the product of a healthy tradition, and are far less susceptible to outside influences. And the new chief, produced from the same environment, will stand a good chance of carrying the tradition forward. Weakness begets weakness, save in those cases where an extraordinary chief executive arrives to save the day. But that is rare indeed.

It is useful to note the sharp differences in CEO succession between American companies and those in Europe and Japan. Overseas companies, in general, tend to take a longer-term view of strategic management, peering into the future for a generation or so. Because the concept of short-term profits is not the only value of chief executives' worth, they are judged not by how they break with the past—as, sadly, many American CEOs are— but how they fit into their predecessors' strategic goals and management style. While such newly appointed European and Japanese chief executives are not forced to adhere to past strategies, they do tend to navigate within the strong-flowing stream of their predecessors. As a result, successions tend not to be the raucous crises that they often are in America.

CEO Succession Trends

Historically, fashions in CEOs—and in successions—have come and gone. As we have already seen (but it bears repeating), companies in the 1930s and 1940s (during the period of shortages caused by the Great Depression and war mobilization) wrestled with overriding questions of production. For the decade or so after World War II, there was a period of fantastic expansion, a glut of production, and marketing became a valuable skill to have in a CEO. Finally, in the 1960s and 1970s, finance became more critical. These were the years characterized by the rise of conglomerates, the use of hybrid securities to entice equity investors, the sophisticated manipulation of debt. Today, the focus has shifted again, this time to corporate strategists, as companies fight desperately against both low-cost, highly productive overseas threats and takeover threats, and as new technologies come rushing into the marketplace. Overall, periodic surveys by *Fortune* have indicated that chief executives are far better educated than in the past, and that those without business, law, or engineering degrees are often eliminated from consideration. Income and family background have also been rising as important factors.

Within those larger trends, however, are preferences and tendencies expressed by specific companies and industries. IBM, a supreme marketing organization, almost invariably promotes its sales people to top posts. And traditionally, only executives with a background in chemical engineering or geology would rise to the top of a major oil company. However, in such beleaguered industries as steel, where production managers traditionally held sway, financial experts have been rushed into the breach to try to conjure up lifesaving cash and cut costs as far as possible. Likewise, smaller new ventures, from computers to biotechnology, often see a regular succession of skills at the helm: the founding engineer or researcher is often replaced by a marketer as products creep from the lab to the marketplace; as the company matures, financial or manufacturing executives may rise to the top.

In the past, job hopping was viewed as an outward sign of a lack of commitment, and the individual was viewed as harboring disloyal feelings, as a failure as a team player, and even as of loose moral character. In fact, the job hunter and the divorcée were often grouped in the same category of the social pariah. By contrast, today, job hopping is viewed by many as a neutral factor. And in some companies, it is seen as a positive benefit, indicating an executive who has flexibility, varied career experiences, lots of self-motivation, high goals, even high standards of corporate performance. Indeed, job hopping has become a crucial aspect of career promotion at many companies; at some places, just about the only way to advance rapidly is to leave one firm and begin job hopping. Executive search firms—head hunters, in the parlance—are constantly prowling around to pick off the best people moving on the fast track. While some companies—IBM, in particular—still look askance at the job hopper, others hardly care at all. In fact, some companies can only find the skills they need by going outside. Steve Jobs of Apple went out and hired John Sculley, then the number-three executive at Pepsico, because he knew he needed marketing expertise in the battle against IBM.

There are other major changes. For instance, statistically, the traditionally long tenure of the chief executive seems to be over. Part of that may be attributed to increasing pressures on American companies. In a turnaround situation, for example, an outsider is brought in to save the company. And the old CEO is usually shown the door. In fact, turnover at the top has never been so great or so rapid in American business—or so highly publicized—as it is today. However, while financial difficulties can explain some of the turnover, it cannot explain it all. If we look closely at some companies, we see reasonably successful corporate executives fired, like baseball managers who finish second too often, and others who are never fired at all, despite dismal performances year in and year out. All that one can really state with some certainty is that CEO turnover tends to feed upon itself. It has now become easier for companies to abandon their CEO, where in the past, they might have held onto them until retirement. Harsh pressures and harsh ways of measuring performance have transformed even sleepy industries into hotbeds of turnover. And the axiom we spoke of earlier applies: succession crises tend to snowball, leading to shorter tenures, greater turnover, and, often enough, poorer performances.

The Outsider

One of the results of job hopping and increased turbulence is that the role of the outsider has become far more prominent than it was, say, twenty years ago. Traditionally, chief executives were recruited solely from within, despite the crisis or the necessity for a dramatic turnaround. Today, there are many famous cases of outside corporate saviors à la Lee Iacocca, although, as with Jobs and Sculley, outsiders also can be recruited simply to fill a perceived need.

Take, for example, the case of RCA. Difficulties at the company began over a decade ago, when the company founder, General Sarnoff, died, leaving his son Robert Sarnoff as CEO. After a few years of sagging profitability, the board at RCA forced him to resign, replacing him with Anthony L. Conrad. Alas, Conrad soon acknowledged that he had not filed income taxes for five years, and rather than explain, he resigned. He, in turn, was replaced by Edgar Griffiths, a dour financial man who had worked his way up the RCA ladder. Griffiths was adequate technically, but lacked the personality to heal the demoralized corporate staff, who were fearful for their jobs and afraid of initiative. Under Griffiths, the company initially did well and then resumed its decline: RCA's NBC subsidiary slipped badly in the ratings, and a heavily capitalized laser-based home entertainment system got off to a slow start. Moreover, he was abrasive with other executives, refused to lay out a clear strategy, and refused to groom a successor, leading many of his own managers to view him as paranoid.

Finally, Griffiths took early retirement and RCA's board turned to Atlantic Richfield Company's second-in-command, Thornton F. Bradshaw, an executive known for being not only highly intelligent, but also an excellent people manager. He was completely different from his unfortunate predecessors. Bradshaw had been a Harvard Business School professor, a management consultant, and an outside director of RCA. As former Attorney General William French Smith told the *New York Times*, "He [Bradshaw] has a way of causing people to do things without a lot of bluster and autocratic ways."[1] Bradshaw proved to be the turning point for RCA. Although considered an interim CEO, he quickly made necessary changes: he hired Grant A. Tinker—another outsider—to run NBC; he took a writedown on the laser system; he began to establish continuity and stability among the corporate staff. Still, who would succeed him? Management had been decimated during the revolving-door years, so Bradshaw looked outside.

Eventually, he hired Robert Frederick, who had just been passed over for the top spot at General Electric. Frederick could master the electronic technology that was increasingly the foundation of RCA, and he had worked in an environment at GE that was well known for collaborative management. The plan was to make Frederick president now, and then to slip him into the chairman's seat when Bradshaw retired.

The pair of them may have been too successful. RCA began to prosper, with NBC under Tinker rising from the dead and a host of new products appearing in the marketplace. At the same time, Bradshaw and Frederick went on a selling spree, dumping Hertz and C.I.T. Corporation, to raise cash and eliminate units that were dragging down earnings. But it was 1985, and takeover fever was running high. RCA's very success made it a tempting target for—who else?—General Electric. In a sense, Bradshaw not only recruited an outsider, he brought with him his entire extended family. Bradshaw saw the decision with the same lucidity and dispassion as he had the divestitures. "RCA must either sell itself to a larger company," he said, "or make a major acquisition itself." One lesson from this may be the close interconnections between turnarounds, takeovers, and the propensity to recruit for outside executive talent.

Grooming the Prince for Power

Despite the gloomy statistics that indicate increasing difficulties in coping with successions, most chief executives actually manage to pull them off with reasonable success. As a result, most transitions are far smoother than the kind I have already discussed. One common strategy is for the retiring CEO to give the anointed successor an opportunity for on-the-job training, allowing the successor to make many of the strategic decisions without the knowledge of the media, lenders, stockholders, or even the board. Such a strategy allows the chief-executive-in-training to work on key decisions without being exposed to the harsh glare of publicity, and avoids conflicts from other managers, who may be anxious to derail a competitor to advance their own case. This sort of secret transition can take place as much as three years before the actual succession is announced.

That was the experience of William Sneath, the former head of Union Carbide. For two years, Sneath's predecessor, Perry Wilson, allowed him to make a number of key decisions. According to Sneath, Wilson told him to make those key strategic decisions because he would be the one who would have to live with them.[2] As a result, it was Sneath who made the controversial, still debated decision to move the company out of its midtown Manhattan headquarters and into the Connecticut woods near Danbury—although it was Wilson who had to take the heat. Other decisions made by Sneath redounded more to Wilson's glory.

Peter McColough, at Xerox, was another chief executive who was given the reins of power privately, long before he received them publicly. McColough emphasized that to put such a strategy in effect required a board of directors that respected the prerogatives of a reigning chief executive to choose his own successor. "I agree with Johnny deButts," said McColough. "Despite the talk from outside of nepotism, it's crucial for a chief executive to choose his own successor. I don't think the board can do that. I think the board will look at very obvious things: this guy's drunk and shouldn't be a chief executive officer, for example. There's no way they can make that judgment in my book, unless they have no faith in the existing chief executive. If I were on the board and I didn't trust the chief executive officer, I don't think I would want to get involved." McColough argued that the CEO should not offer potential candidates a flat commitment. "I think the trick, really, is to identify the person some years in advance and try to work with him, so that he has some fairly good feeling that he's going to be the chief executive, not that he'll rest on his laurels. You tell him that he will probably be the chief executive officer, the way you see it. You don't make any commitment. Obviously, if he starts stealing from the company or is drunk all the time, then that's different."

The major reason for such a transitional period, McColough made clear, was the inherent differences between the top job and every other position at the company. "It's a very different job," he said. "The top job is very different from, say, the second job. The top job involves a great deal more 'outside activities' which not everyone likes. It is one where you have to set the course of the company in broad strategic terms, have a feel for what's going on, knowing your own industry and technology and the world socially—and I think it takes some grooming, and I think, frankly, it's wise to do it gradually. One of the things I was thankful to Mr. Wilson, my

254

predecessor, for, was that at the time of the announcement of my promotion, I'd been doing the job for some time." McColough became the chief operating officer and president of Xerox in 1966, but, he said, "I was really doing the job a couple of years before that; he [Wilson] brought me along gradually, which I was always grateful for. He never just dumped eighty-five functions on me, but gradually, bit by bit, working together. I think it should be a gradual process, although in the press it always looks like a dramatic process."

The essential differences between the top job and other positions means that the person chosen for the chief executive job is often *not* the best performer operationally among the top candidates. This is a fact that McColough, deButts, David Rockefeller, and a number of other chief executives emphasized: many top operational chief executives are passed over, they said, because of the extraordinary requirements of the top job. Obviously, this rankles some, resulting in the departure of many fine executives—executives like Frederick at GE, for example, who was passed over for Jack Welch—or, if they remain, occasional dissension in the ranks. Moreover, one person's second in command is another's chief. Bradshaw thought Frederick was good enough for RCA, for example. And John J. Byrne, Jr., an insurance executive at Travellers who was passed over, went to the troubled Government Employees Insurance Company, turned it around in dramatic fashion, then moved on to wrestle with the newly public Fireman's Fund Insurance Company.

What do you look for in a chief executive? Said McColough, "The things you're looking for, the attributes, can be quite different [for the CEO's job]. You're not going to pick someone who's bad. But if you have a company where, for example, one of the executive vice presidents is going to succeed to the CEO's job, you may have one who's operationally the best, but you don't necessarily pick him. Do those passed over understand that? I think some do and some don't. Some say, my record of performance is better than Joe's and yet he gets the chief executive's job." McColough's criteria for leadership rest on knowing the candidates extremely well. "Perhaps the leadership skills [of those passed over] are not as great," said McColough. "They may be able to run something well, but their leadership skills may not be as great. It's not so much who can maintain the discipline of the company, really. It's more a question of somebody who has the vision to look out five, ten years, and see where we want to go, who can motivate people, who the rest of the company *wants* to follow . . . who fits into what the company views as acceptable. . . . Some people are just not acceptable, personally. There is something you can't define about leadership. There are some very good executives and some have leadership you want to follow and some are good executives you don't want to follow. I look for a number of things. One, I think, I personally value is absolute personal integrity. . . . That sounds simple, but not everybody has absolute integrity. It's very easy to have integrity of not stealing from the company; but when you really get down to tough issues, to where the company would really not like to do something, that's where I think integrity is absolutely essential."

McColough continued, "I also think that it's essential that people have broad interests. I don't think I'd be particularly pleased to see my successor at Xerox—as Harold Geneen did—as one who only wants to run the business and who does not want to contribute a role in society. You also look for good judgment. Good judgment is different from brilliance, because I have the most brilliant people at this company who don't have very good judgment. I wouldn't want to go away for six months and leave them in charge. There are others who may not be as brilliant, but really have good judgment in people things, direction, and so forth. I think you want somebody that people in the company can look up to in terms of integrity and character, and who can put some excitement into the company. There are some leaders who are just dreadfully dull."

Few top executives are chosen for the CEO position. "I think there aren't a lot of people who can do it," he said. "A lot of people think they can, but I have a lot of highly paid people at Xerox, some of whom are younger and coming along. They think they can do it, but there's not many in my opinion with the standards that we have that can do it and do it well."

Measuring Leadership Potential

Almost all chief executives engage in some form of testing to try to take those hazy qualities sought by McColough and make them a bit clearer. This testing usually involves rotating so-called fast trackers through key positions—from finance, to strategic planning, to international operations, to manufacturing. While virtually no one travels the whole grand tour, most chief executive prospects are expected to travel a good part of it.

Second, potential CEOs are tested for the ability to speak publically. That can include presentations before the board, shareholders' meetings, Wall Street analysts, lenders, major customers, and suppliers, testimony before Congress or regulators, and negotiations with unions, joint venture partners, or foreign governments. Some effort is also made to see how candidates deal with the media. Third, they are loaded—often overloaded—with responsibilities, over a range of different operations in different locations, requiring a range of different management skills. Some potential CEOs may be given responsibility all at once, others receive tasks one at a time, although the more common practice is to throw a range of difficult tasks at a candidate to see how he or she manages.

This testing process can be as tough as Spartan military training. Candidates for the top job are often moved quickly around the country, uprooting their families. If you can't move geographically, you often can't move up the ladder. At IBM, the corporate initials are known as I've Been Moved. In forty-two years at AT & T, deButts moved sixteen times—every three years or so. "If you're going to move somebody around just to fill a job, they're not going to move, and I don't blame them. We don't do that. But when a guy gets to the officer level, he knows he can't go any further unless he's willing to move. I had a company president tell me once, look, he'd been offered a helluva job outside the company and he was thinking seriously about taking it, because he didn't want to be moved by AT & T. I was vice chairman then, and I said, 'You want my job?' He said, 'Yeah, I'd like to have your job.' I said, 'Well, you're not going to jump from where you are to where I am. If you want my job, you've got to go through the chairs.' Turned down the other job flat and he's made very good progress." Still, is it any wonder that many executives—many good executives—drop out of the race?

One who did not quit was Charlie Brown, who succeeded deButts at AT & T. It was not easy; just listen to deButts describe the testing process he installed at AT & T: "Brown was a manager for the Long Island department. I needed a guy to be vice president of the Illinois Bell operation in the city [Chicago], and I was told about Brown and I looked up all his records and told him I wanted to have a talk with him, offered him a job, and he took it. He did a very fine job. So a year or two later, I pushed the operating vice president to executive vice president and put Brown in that job. He did a beautiful job . . . I made him the chief financial officer; he never had any experience [in finance], but at a company as capital oriented as ours, you've got to have experience in finance. You've got to know what makes the market tick and how to deal with it. He scrambled like all get-out; fortunately, I had been chief financial officer, so I could give him a little help. He did a darn good job of it, too. Was I taking a terrible gamble? I wasn't when I was put into the job and I created the finest financial system ever done. I put $1.6 billion in one issue. . . . If a guy has the characteristics to be a good manager, it doesn't really make a big difference what the subject is. He can learn. What you want is someone who can use his head in an administrative way. . . .

"I made him do something with credit; he was being tested. If he hadn't done it, if he hadn't shown these characteristics, he wouldn't have made the next step. We have some of that, too. They go out on a job thinking they have it, and they finally found out they don't. Fortunately, this doesn't happen often. We've tested them enough to make sure. Occasionally, we find people who get up there and they decide themselves they don't. They don't want the responsibility, the pressures—and the pressures grow, the higher you get. A job doesn't get easier as you go up—it gets worse . . . tougher, longer hours, more pressure.

"Then I made him vice chairman, and he did fine. I made him president and he's done fine. I know his weak points—and he has weak points; we all do—and his strong points. I also know the others'. I know Ellinghaus [another candidate]; I picked him up on his second level when I was a young commercial manager in Virginia. I've known him almost thirty years. I picked Brown because I thought he was better qualified, did a total job. Ellinghaus is very strong in some areas. Kashel [a third candidate] has considerable strengths. But Brown's better rounded. And the job requires the better rounded."

For all of that, Brown's selection as CEO was never automatic, just as deButts's own selection had not been. "I never thought I was going to get the chief executive job," said deButts. "I thought somebody else was going to get the job, but they didn't. Recommending somebody else is a difficult decision to make, I'll tell you that. You have to be very careful to be absolutely certain you don't pick someone with your characteristics—and I've seen it happen. I was very unhappy because *Forbes* magazine came out with an article in which they picked Ellinghaus to take over, because his characteristics were very much like mine. Very, very unfair. Unfortunately, the article came out two weeks before I talked to Ellinghaus and told him what I was going to do. . . . He's extremely happy and he was terribly embarrassed by that article. But it would be wrong for me to try to pick somebody who I thought was going to operate just like me. It's a tough decision, and you spend hours and hours and weeks thinking about it."

Still, for all of deButts's arguments that the chief executive should personally choose his successor, he, like all smart autocrats, was very careful to appraise the board beforehand of the direction his thoughts were going. "I started a practice in my first year on the job of having outside directors come to dinner, once a year, where I'd go over with them the people I thought were candidates for top jobs at the company, where they were, what they were doing, everything about them and their potential. They would ask me, 'If you get hit by a truck going home tonight, who would you recommend?' I've told them, with the understanding that six months later it might be somebody else. The names have changed. Some have been added. Some have been dropped, but I've done it every year. And I think it was pretty obvious to the board that by the time I made the recommendation that he [Brown] was going to be the one. There wasn't one word to the contrary from the outside directors . . . I talked to Charlie first and I said, now you think about this Charlie, and let's you and I discuss it, and who else is needed. I was told when I was raised to the top job the day before the board meeting that I was going to be recommended, that I was going to be chairman. And I was told who was going to be president and who was going to be vice chairman. And I decided that was wrong, that was a policy I would *not* follow. It so happens that the guys I was given were very good. One of them had been my friend for many, many years, going back to 1953. But my own belief is that if a guy's going to be a CEO, he ought to have something to say about who is going to be on his team, and in what job.

"That philosophy translates into a rigorous testing program. I have some friends in business who never ask anybody's opinion. They just tell people what to do. I don't believe that's good. I don't think you develop anybody for one thing. The only way to develop people is to give them something to do and let them do it their way, see what they can do. Give them a chance to fall flat. Make it a tough assignment. That's the way I learned to swim. My father threw me off the dock and told me to come back. I hope he was ready to jump in in case I didn't. It makes enormous sense for the president to know that his new boss [the chief executive] wanted him. Don't you think he'd do a better job? Don't you think that Ellinghaus will do a better job knowing that his boss, Brown, wanted him in that job, instead of just having deButts, who's leaving, saying he could have that job? You've got to give people jobs to do and then slack the reins and let them do it."

DeButts's view that the selection of a successor is the job of the CEO permeates the organization. "It's something I insist of all my managers. Yes, sir. We'll set up a president's conference, and I'll make every company president *name the people*, not just in your company, but throughout the Bell System, that you think could be a candidate for your job. I do that with the officers. I make them send me a list. Why? Because if a guy picks too many people from the outside, it's obvious he's not doing a very good job within his own company." His testing procedure is not perfect, however. Said deButts, "I have selected some people that I thought had real potential who fell flat on their faces. We had to take them out of their jobs, and anytime anybody falls flat on their face, I regret it, but you have to move. You have to move fast."

Not all testing regimens are quite as benign as AT & T's. Some can resemble bloody wars, with ambitions colliding and competition intensifying to the point where it threatens to engulf the whole company. Some chief executives will purposely foster succession battles among their next-in-line to test their mettle or to keep them sharp. One of the longest-running of these battles was that staged by Citibank chief executive Walter B. Wriston, between John Reed, who had cleaned up the back office at the bank and run the booming consumer division, Hans H. Angermueller, who handled Citibank's legal and governmental affairs, and Thomas C. Theobald, who ran the banking division. The several-year battle finally ended when Wriston retired and appointed forty-three-year-old Reed to the job. General Electric has also been famous for such duels, as well as for the quick departure of those executives who lose out. Such a practice often leads to a traumatic succession. You do not want a war of such proportions that the company is left a charred and smoking hulk. In the Citibank case, Wriston was careful to foster competition, while keeping antagonism low. And when Reed ascended, he was careful to reach out to the other two former candidates.

SUCCESSION STRATEGIES

The Role of the Board

Despite Nathan Owen's belief that boards of directors should play a major role in picking the successor to the CEO, most boards are little more than rubber stamps. This should come as no surprise: most boards would rather follow management than lead it. Inside directors are often beholden to the chief executive, while outside directors often lack either the expertise or the information to make informed decisions. And when a succession does take place, particularly in a crisis, the new chief executive feels it his or her right to make extensive changes in board membership. Ineffective boards, the rule rather than the exception, make it relatively easy for strong CEOs like deButts to handpick and train their own successors.

Sometimes, of course, a board has to leap into the fray. Or outside forces, from banks to major shareholders, will force the board to move against the chief executive, perhaps choosing a fresh face from outside the company, as in the Dunlop Tire case. But power comes and goes in institutions such as boards of directors, and that can cause a shifting pattern of succession decisions. Consider the case of the brokerage firm of Lehman Brothers Kuhn Loeb. When Robert Lehman, the grandson of one of the founders, died without an heir, the board installed an investment banking partner as a managing partner. He proved unpopular, and in a revolt led by George Ball, a former member of the John F. Kennedy administration who was fronting for a group of large shareholders, deposed him and forced the ascendance of a man with extensive administrative experience, Peter Peterson, a secretary of commerce under President Richard M. Nixon. As I described earlier, however, Peterson was undercut by a rise in the power of traders led by Lewis L. Glucksman at Lehman Brothers and by his own standoffish personality. Thus, when Glucksman made his move, Peterson lacked board support, and left—only to return as a consultant when the firm, wracked by dissension and, like many private Wall Street partnerships, desperate for capital, voted to accept a buyout from Shearson American Express.

There is another kind of role the board often takes on: that of a sort of podium for a retired CEO. At many companies, it is common for retiring chief executives to retain a board seat, offering the fruits of their experience to the company. In some cases, it is purely courtesy or a way of saving face. "To dump him," said one CEO of his predecessor, "would open a

261

can of worms." In other cases, particularly when it is a founder who is retiring, the former CEO might own a major block of stock. Similarly, the role of the retiring chief executive varies. Some see themselves as a corporate memory, providing sage advice based on long experience. Others have wide contacts which they allow the reigning chief executive to use. "We talk and work together," said a major company's current chief executive referring to his former boss, the previous CEO, who continues to sit on the board. "I can confide in him. He gives me a feel for people, and awkward situations, and dangers." Other newly created CEOs, of course, prefer to run the show alone, without *any* input or suggestions from the former CEO.

In most cases, however, retiring CEOs can provide invaluable services from their seat on the board. Take the role that Irving Shapiro, a brilliant corporate lawyer, a former chairman of DuPont, and a long-time personal advisor to the du Pont family. In 1981, DuPont got into a wild takeover scramble with Seagram over Conoco, an oil company based in Houston. While DuPont won the prize, the Bronfman family, which controls Seagram, ended up with over 20 percent of DuPont stock—more than any other shareholder, including the du Pont family. Here, then, was a role for Shapiro who knew the complexities of family ownership, knew the company, and was acquainted with the Bronfman brothers. Shapiro calmed the du Pont family and protected the company interests by extracting a nontakeover clause from the Bronfmans, thus stabilizing the situation. Said DuPont's chief executive Edward G. Jefferson, "I don't think this mess would have been handled nearly as smoothly had not Irving Shapiro been involved in personally calming the troubled waters."

The Shotgun Wedding

Nothing throws into a sharper light the clash of chief executive egotism than a merger or takeover situation. The company that results from a takeover might be a combination of assets, but it is rarely a total blend of management. Specifically, few companies can harbor more than one leader—one reason why deButts's monarchical concept of CEO leadership is far more prevalent than Owen's more democratic approach. Therefore, it is essential for there to be explicit legal agreements that officially designate the roles of executives in a takeover situation and the path of executive succession in the long or short term. Sometimes this means setting up an "office of the chief executive" and designating two, three, or even four executives—all candidates—to fill it. In other cases, companies will actually announce who will become chief executive, say, a year or two in the future.

One of the best known examples of such an announcement followed the merger of Allied Corporation and the Signal Companies, the resulting entity dubbed Allied-Signal. In this particular case, Allied CEO Edward Hennessy and Signal CEO Forrest N. Shumway had both been on the prowl for acquisitions and had been close personal friends for twenty years. The merger, then, was exceedingly friendly. Nonetheless, there was still a considerable amount of jockeying for position that took place prior to the formal announcement of matrimony. Shumway agreed to step aside and allow Hennessy and the more powerful Allied to run the show, *if* Hennessy would transfer power eventually to his second-in-command, Michael D. Dingman.

Finally, Hennessy agreed, and the announcement took place, a sort of corporate twist on the prenuptial agreement: in 1990, Dingman would take over for Hennessy at the helm of Allied-Signal. Why was this done publicly so far in advance? Was this just a means to smooth ruffled egos? Hennessy insists that the public commitment was his own idea. "I want to see an orderly transfer of power," he said. "I don't just want to be carried out of here."[3] But it was also critical, Shumway bluntly declared, that Dingman be given some kind of guarantee; otherwise he "would not move east for anything"—that is, from his native California to Allied's headquarters in Morristown, New Jersey. Ironically, no sooner was the merger consummated, than Hennessy announced that he was spinning off some companies from Allied-Signal under a new corporate name of the Henley Group. The chief executive? Dingman, of course.

Mergers and crises often create the most unusual, and unwieldy, position of co–chief executive. Often, this strange beast arises from a compromise between difficult, irreconcilable positions. It rarely works. When Saloman Brothers, the brokerage firm, merged with Phillip Brothers, the giant trading company, the CEOs from the respective companies were named co-CEOs of the new organization, Phibro-Saloman, Inc. The result, said William May, a chief executive of American Can and a board member of Phibro-Saloman, was "a two-headed cow." As a result, a fierce internal struggle ensued, and riding the coattails of the Saloman unit's far superior financial returns, John H. Gutfreund, a former Saloman partner, took control of the company, pushing aside David Tendler of Phibro.

A similar problem erupted at the brokerage house of Lehman Brothers, which I described earlier. Again, much had to do with varying political and financial fortunes of participants, and the flow of power to and fro. At Lehman, Peter Peterson, the reigning CEO and an investment banker, raised Lew Glucksman, who ran the company's successful trading operations, to the co-CEO spot. Their partnership lasted but a few months, when Glucksman demanded that Peterson retire. He did, but the resulting conflicts between the abrasive Glucksman and his traders and the smoother investment bankers eventually forced the company into the arms of Shearson American Express.

Conflicts need not be so public to be serious. Such a conflict over succession arose when David Rockefeller became a co–chief executive with George Champion at Chase Manhattan Bank. "In 1960, I think it was, when Jack McCloy retired, the directors decided I was too young [to be chief executive]. The other candidate was George Champion. I wouldn't have stayed, however, if he had been made chairman and chief executive, and he certainly wouldn't have stayed if I had been elected. So they made what I think was a very unwise decision to appoint us as co–chief executives—he as chairman, I as president." The problem, said Rockefeller, had less to do with personality than with strategic priorities. "We had vaguely defined responsibilities. He was absolutely tops as a banker across the country, and I had experience in the international area as well as other things, but I didn't have anything like the professional credit experience he did. The difficulty was that we had very different concepts of where the bank should go, and if you're aiming like that, it is difficult to come out where you want to be.

"He was brought up in the Chase National Bank and he thought it ought to be the biggest and the best domestic wholesale bank. Everything else we did ought to be peripheral from that. I felt that we ought to be an international bank based in New York with an important stake in domestic business, but with a close relationship between the two. We needed an international network to accommodate the domestic business. Therefore, during the eight years we had this joint venture, if you want to call it that, every time I would propose something, his test would always be, 'What will it do for our domestic business?' We had an opportunity, an unbelievable opportunity, to buy one of the major leading [Canadian] banks, and we spent two years studying it. The objective of the study to Champion was how it would help our domestic customers. If you put the study in those terms, you came out with a different result. Finally, Canada was becoming nationalistic and the whole thing blew up. I only mention this to show you that totally different points of view only produced a lack of policy."

Sudden Death

A plane crash. A deadly fire. A heart attack. Suddenly, shockingly, the company is left without a chief executive. And suddenly the board of directors has to make the decision about a new leader. In such cases, the board has far more power than usual to pick an executive who will pursue a particular type of strategy and who is far more willing than usual to ignore the desires of the late, lamented CEO, and the board installs someone of their own choosing and predilection.

When Charles Bluhdorn, the aggressive and freewheeling founder of Gulf & Western, suddenly died of a heart attack, the board bypassed his anointed successor, an executive by the name of David Norman Judelson, and instead picked Martin S. Davis, another high executive, but one with a very different personality from Bluhdorn. Davis was primarily a financial man, and he quickly moved to rationalize the hodgepodge Gulf & Western had become under Bluhdorn's frantic—and, it has to be said, often successful—deal making. Davis quickly sold off many of Bluhdorn's pet companies, including the ownership positions in many companies that Bluhdorn had played with as if they had been his private investment portfolio. Wall Street certainly agreed with the move. Wall Streeters traditionally dislike and distrust the uncertainty, the frequent arbitrariness, and the tendency to operate over the short-term of an autocratic conglomerateur like Bluhdorn, or like the octogenarian Armand Hammer of Occidental Petroleum, often, as a result, discounting the stock. Thus, when Bluhdorn died and Davis was appointed CEO, Gulf & Western stock immediately rose, just as analysts believe Occidental Petroleum stock will rise when Hammer departs.

Davis was able to make these changes successfully because both the board and Wall Street agreed with him. He also admitted that he was not the same sort of man as Bluhdorn, who, he argued, was the only man

265

around who could keep so many balls in the air at the same time. Instead, Davis streamlined the company, consolidating it into three lines of business, down from the twenty to twenty-five lines under the Bluhdorn regime. This dramatic departure from the past would have been all but impossible if Charles Bluhdorn were alive, but with his sudden departure, both the board and Davis saw the opportunity for a change—and they took it.

But while opportunities do exist when a founder dies, it can also be a period of tremendous stress for the company. Many companies wither and die when a charismatic leader departs the scene. This loss frequently sends small firms—although it can happen to the largest of companies as well— into a downward spiral of uncertainty and doubt as they struggle for a new identity.

The King Lear Syndrome

Perhaps the most vulnerable moment for most companies comes when a strong CEO, founder, or corporate architect faces retirement. Such founders, as I call them, are invariably highly self-confident, even egotistical individuals who are proud of their own achievements and who are chary about leaving the company in the hands of a mere manager. Often, such individuals have wrapped themselves in a cult of personality—not unlike Mao Tse-tung, who also experienced succession difficulties—and have surrounded themselves with sycophantic "yes men" who only reinforce the founder's sense of infallibility. Some have driven away many of the best, most independent managers. Let us look at four such succession problems created by founders.

BREAKING THE GRIP OF THE PAST: FORD MOTOR COMPANY

Ford had the dubious distinction of undergoing two succession crises— the first, following the founding by Henry Ford; the second, after the re-founding by Henry Ford II. The chaos that overtook Henry Ford's death in 1947 is legendary. As we saw in earlier chapters, Ford refused to alter his strategic emphasis on just one car model, the Model T, for all consumers. That short-sighted strategy was exacerbated because he surrounded himself with weak executives who were eager to please Henry at all costs. Said Arjay Miller, "After old Henry bought out all other shareholders and made his billion dollars, he really didn't care about making more money. He should not be judged, therefore, by normal standards. For example, I believe he did not like to pay taxes. I'm convinced he knew that some of his top executives were stealing from the company, but he didn't care. That was how he rewarded his favorites. By keeping salaries low, employees avoided paying high taxes. At the same time, theft losses kept company profits and taxes low. For a long period of time, Ford Motor Company reported only break-even profits."

When Ford died, the company was being terrorized by the inimitable Harold B. Bennett (old Henry's right-hand man) who wandered headquarters brandishing a gun. And rather than turn company ownership over to Ford's son, Edsel, a capable manager who had helped Henry found the company, the old man handed it to twenty-three-year-old Henry II, his grandson, who had no idea of how to run the company. It was almost as if Henry had wanted the enterprise to fail after his passing. Indeed, when Henry II arrived at the office, the company was adrift, and management was confused and demoralized. "When young Henry Ford II came in," said Miller, "he was determined to rescue the company, clean out the thugs and all of the embezzlement, and, you know—he was a proud man—build it into a good company. . . . He knew he needed help."

Henry II was open to new ideas and was eager for help. It was just after World War II, and a closely knit team of extremely bright young Air Force officers were waiting to be demobilized. The leader of the group, Tex Thornton, saw Henry II's photograph on the cover of *Life* magazine and wrote to him to apply for jobs for the group. Henry met with them, discovered they were about the same age as he was, 24, and all but turned the company over to them. "Henry Ford II was a very good judge of people," said Miller. "He could discriminate among individuals, and was not afraid to give young people responsible positions." Indeed, hiring that group—which included Miller—was his single greatest decision. For the "whiz kids," as the group came to be called, was loaded with highly talented executives: Thornton went on to found Hughes Tool and Litton; Arjay Miller became president of Ford; Robert McNamara, the most famous of the lot, went from the presidency of Ford to serving as secretary of defense under Presidents Kennedy and Johnson, and then, in the 1970s, headed the World Bank. (Roy Ash, another Litton cofounder, was head of the Office of Management and Budget under President Nixon and of AM

International during its collapse. He did not go to Ford, but went to the Harvard Business School instead.)

The whiz kids who went to Ford were brimming with self-confidence in themselves and their management ideas. As Miller told me, "We arrived, young and brash, and not knowing anything about making cars. So we decided, let's first find out what the opposition (General Motors) is doing, and then see if we can make improvements." They quickly decided not only to learn from GM, but to steal Alfred Sloan's venerable segmentation strategy, consigning Henry Ford's one-model strategy to the scrap heap. Perhaps if they had not been so brash, or so young, or so ignorant—or had a leader, Henry II, who was just as callow—they could not have broken the grip of the past.

Ironically, Henry II seemed to have learned little from his earlier difficulties. As he grew older, and as succession loomed, Henry II began to act with the same capriciousness as his grandfather had. In the late 1960s, he fired Semon "Bunky" Knudson, the heir apparent, Arjay Miller's successor, and a former GM executive. Knudson was eliminated in large part at the urging of a brash, young up-and-comer by the name of Lee Iacocca. Then, of course, it was Iacocca's turn to be eliminated. Ford sowed the seeds of a confrontation with Iacocca by setting up a three-man executive office, including Ford himself, Iacocca, and an executive vice president, all but unknown outside the company, named Philip Caldwell. While Henry II retained first-among-equals status, he also made it clear that Iacocca was third in the pecking order. A few weeks later, Ford fired him. Meanwhile, the American car industry entered a time of great danger, beset by foreign imports, undercut by skyrocketing oil prices which made driving an expensive hobby—for those who could even get gasoline. Finally, urged on by the board, which had slowly gained some independence from Henry II's willfulness, Ford was convinced to give up the reins to Caldwell. And today, Ford Motor Company seems to have regained its old vigor.

REFUSING TO LET GO: WILLIAM PALEY AT CBS

William Paley built CBS from a handful of fledgling radio stations into the largest communications company in the United States. But, Paley at eighty could not let go. He knew he should—he had begun appointing successors as far back as 1960—but he could never find one he could live with, a problem, one suspects, more with Paley than with his candidates.

268

SUCCESSION STRATEGIES

First, he promoted his long-time number two executive, Frank Stanton, to the position of heir apparent; then, after years of loyal service, he was let go. Then, in 1976, Paley looked outside and found Arthur Taylor at International Paper Company. Despite years of substantial growth at CBS under Taylor—or perhaps because of it—Paley began to distrust him; Taylor seemed almost *too* eager for the CEO job, and too ready to make changes in the exquisite machine Paley had built. So, Taylor was dismissed. The third willing victim was named John Backe, who, like Taylor, lacked television experience—he was brought in from CBS's publishing subsidiary—and again, like Taylor, did rather well at CBS. Ah, the kiss of death: Paley fired him as well.

By now, Paley was getting up in years, and his glamorous, brilliant wife Babe was undergoing a long, ultimately unsuccessful battle against cancer. Nonetheless, he tapped another executive to be his successor: Thomas Wyman, who came from, of all places, Pillsbury Corporation. Paley may have been weakening, and the board may have been growing a little restless at all of this coming and going, but the feeling continued that as long as Paley walked the halls at CBS, anyone else's title as chief executive would be naught but words. Sure enough, Thomas Wyman ultimately was let go as CEO of CBS in 1986 and William Paley returned as chairman.

Since 1975, the situation has altered considerably. Television, like cars, has matured as an industry; market share for all of the networks has been falling, a result of VCRs and increasing cable penetration, and advertising revenues have come under pressure. CBS has also been threatened by takeovers, first from the Christian Crusade, a group led by North Carolina senator Jesse Helms, then, somewhat more seriously, by cable news magnate Ted Turner, a "Paley-like" entrepreneur in his own right. The Turner attempt roused Paley from his position on the board to defend his creation. Paley was ferocious in denouncing Turner's plan, and took part in the CBS board meetings which pushed through a radical restructuring plan. But although Turner's attempt failed, CBS was left in a much weakened state, and Wyman eagerly embraced a white knight of sorts, in the form of Laurence A. Tisch, the wealthy founder of Loews Corporation. Tisch, with his large chunk of CBS stock, joined forces with Paley, succeeded in removing Wyman, and ultimately became CEO himself.

Did Paley's CEO succession machinations hurt CBS? I think they did. As I said, the industry was entering a treacherous era. Many of CBS's top executives fled the company as the revolving door spun. CBS tried to diversify, but for the most part failed, first buying, then selling the New York

Yankees, first starting, then closing a number of very expensive cable operations. And, most ignominiously of all, CBS temporarily lost its dominance in the ratings in the late 1970s. In short, the decades-long succession crisis sapped the company and made its effect felt on the bottom line.

GENEEN AT ITT: THE MERITS OF THE CLEAN BREAK

Harold Geneen was such a dominant CEO at ITT for so long that he became a de facto founder. He too, however, found it difficult at first to step back into the shadows and let a new generation of executives run his creation. Geneen first gave control of the company over to Lyman Hamilton, an ITT executive, although he retained tremendous power as a board member. And so, from his board seat, Geneen eventually engineered Hamilton's demise. Geneen's second choice, Rand Araskog, then faced a dilemma: should he act naturally, making the kinds of changes he thought necessary and facing interference from Geneen; or should he play it conservatively, hoping to survive? Araskog waited. Only when Geneen made it clear that he was stepping aside—moving onto other projects of his own and no longer controlling every major decision at ITT—did Araskog begin the massive sell-off of some eighty companies, most bought by Geneen.

The lesson: power does not respect titles. Giving up the office does not mean giving up the power, which is really what a succession is all about. Araskog could act as a true chief executive only after Geneen really left.

PRESERVING THE LEGACY: LEONARD H. GOLDENSON
AND THE AMERICAN BROADCASTING COMPANY

All of this is not to say that all founders hang on to companies until they shuffle into senility, or that they end up destroying the companies they built. Not all founders are like King Lear; many spend years preparing the way for a successor, then step firmly into the shadows to let the new CEO work. Let us look at a more successful transition by a founder.

By early 1985, Leonard H. Goldenson, the founder and chairman of ABC, was the last of television's pacesetters. Over a period of thirty years, Goldenson had transformed a little string of fourteen stations into a major network. It should come as no surprise, then, that succession was on his mind when ratings disappointingly plunged during the 1984–85 season.

SUCCESSION STRATEGIES

Goldenson was seventy-nine years old and was not ready for another long, hard climb to the top. Rumor had it that he was also dissatisfied with his number two in charge, Frederick Pierce, who many people thought would take over the company. But the ratings decline, a weak stock price, and the turbulent conditions in the industry and economy all apparently convinced Goldenson to look outside, not just for a CEO, but for someone to whom the company could be sold.

So, discreetly, Goldenson began to look. In an age of takeovers, it was not all that difficult. What Goldenson found was a young, aggressive communications company called Capital Cities Communications Incorporated, founded and run by a man named Thomas S. Murphy, who ran a very tight operation with very low costs and very high margins. Murphy was as close as Goldenson could get to selling the company to a younger version of himself. "I wanted to see American Broadcasting Co. in very strong hands," he said. "I felt the merger of these two companies would do that. I built this company from scratch. When you've built a competitive network that has done, in my opinion, great public service, you want to be sure it is preserved in perpetuity. I feel great about the fact that if the merger goes through [as it did] this organization is protected, and will be able to carry on the traditions we have been able to build at ABC. That to me is a great point of satisfaction."[4] Whatever happened to Fred Pierce? He remained in the top ranks of the new company and then after the merger was consummated, quietly departed.

Conclusion

Chief executive succession strategy may be the most poorly understood aspect of strategic planning. The vast majority of chief executives I interviewed admitted that it took them a year and a half to three years before they really understood what the job was all about. This suggests that chief executives were simply not well prepared for the top job by their predecessor, although it also indicates how very difficult, and unique, that job is. Moreover, since the average tenure of the chief executive in America has declined from eight and one-half years in the 1950s to five and one-half years in

271

the 1980s, the pressures of the job have increased. Chief executives have less time than ever to get to know top managerial candidates, season them by rotating them through major responsibilities, and finally choose one.

Although many chief executives claimed that choosing their successor was an absolutely crucial decision for them, and one they agonized over, the training of most successor chief executives has been, by all accounts, quite poor. Partly, this has been because outgoing chief executives have been reluctant to give up the reins of power, or reluctant to commit themselves to one single successor early enough to train him or her for the job. As evidence of this, I cite the fact that many chief executives told me that they did not know they were to be made CEO until one to six months before the public announcement was made. Remember how John deButts recounted how he had not expected to be chosen at all, and how the decision had caught him by surprise. Other chief executives, such as Martin Davis of Gulf & Western, were installed literally overnight—in this case, upon the death of the company founder, Charles Bluhdorn.

This failure to adequately prepare executives for the top job arises from the unique nature of the chief executive position. There are at least three essential activities practiced solely by chief executives. First, they must assume responsibility for all divisions, all functions, all personnel, all financing. Executives who have served as division heads or operating managers have learned to handle some of these high-pressure responsibilities, but taking all of them on simultaneously and learning to juggle them is something that can be mastered only while on the job itself. In a number of cases where total responsibility was thrown at a candidate for the top job, I found that it often resulted in failure and subsequent removal not only from the running, but from the company itself. That is a waste of managerial talent.

Second, chief executives have to interact extensively with outside groups; they must give lengthy presentations before community groups, the press, syndicates of lenders, Wall Street analysts, political bodies such as Congress. Third, almost every aspect of business has become more complex. Chief executives have found that they have had to become instant experts on merger and acquisition negotiations with everyone from the head of a target company to investment bankers, lenders, lawyers, and government regulators. And that is not considering the intricacies of takeover defenses. The chief executives I interviewed admitted that they had been prepared for only one or two aspects of the internal management job; and, more astonishing, 90 percent of them said they had not been prepared at all to deal with the external environment, which they realized now was fully 50 percent of the job.

As a result, many chief executives start their job as if they had suddenly run into a pitch-black room. The major consequence of these ragged transitions, moreover, is that their initial period in office tends to be characterized by irrational planning, tunnel vision, and general defensiveness— all of the characteristics of poor strategic planning I discussed earlier. Then, because tenures are shorter, CEOs have far less time to catch up before a successor is panting at the door. All of this has led to a state of affairs where chief executives feel less emotionally committed to continue the successful strategic legacy of their predecessors, and feel compelled to start afresh. While few chief executives I spoke with admitted to starting from absolute zero, quite a few did say they found the company drifting or heading in the wrong direction when they took over the helm.

Although it is fairly well understood how a series of crisis-ridden successions can derail corporate strategies, I do not believe that the real impact of the lack of preparation on corporate performance has been appreciated fully. As with many issues I have dealt with in this book, this issue is not as clear cut as one may suppose. Critics argue that a lengthy education of a candidate for the top job by the chief executive is only one way for the executive in power to make sure his or her influence lives on. "He was on a total ego trip," complained one chief executive I talked with about his predecessor. "He was trying to hold the company in his grip after his retirement and even from beyond the grave." Such situations undoubtedly do take place. But an education need not imply a mind chained to the past. In fact, such an education at the very top of a company should free the CEO-to-be to think in a broader, more imaginative way. Finally, a certain amount of influence "beyond the grave" is hardly a bad thing. Strategic planning is not only a team concept in terms of executives at a company at a single point in time, but a link between the present and the past. And the way to retain that living link is to establish a viable, stable succession strategy.

CHAPTER ELEVEN

THE AGE OF UNCERTAINTY

Not every word I have spoken in the past has turned out to be 100 percent accurate. . . . What I learn from (our) less-than-glorious forecasting experience is that it's hard enough to get the big picture right, let alone the details. In fact, the more one strives for ultimate precision, the more likely he is to make an error before he gets there. . . . In the case of U.S. energy forecasters, hardly do we make a new calculation when events prove us wrong.
—C. C. GARVIN, JR., chairman of the board, Exxon Corporation

In the first half of this decade, we went through the wringer. In 1980, the little girl with the lemonade stand down the street made more profit than all of us—GM, Ford, Chrysler, and AMC—together. The four of us lost four billion dollars. The kindest thing the economists said about the industry was that it had "reached maturity," which means not much of a future.
—ROGER B. SMITH, CEO, General Motors Corporation

It has been said that he who lives by the crystal ball soon learns to eat glass.
—ZOLTAN MERSZEI, president, Occidental Petroleum Corporation

The Trouble with Excellence

In the last decade or so, even some of those "excellent" American companies identified by Peters and Waterman in their book *In Search of Excellence* have tasted failure in many different ways—marketing gaffes, succession crises, technology that did not work or did not sell, ill-conceived new ventures. It has been a time when the traditional self-confidence of American business and management as a shining example to the world—which it

275

truly was in the years after World War II—was shaken and replaced by a new realism and, not coincidentally, by a new interest in foreign styles of management. Nonetheless, despite commendable initiatives to regain competitiveness on a worldwide basis, an actual turnaround by U.S. business has so far involved more talk than action; in fact, ironically, the rise of strategic planning has been accompanied by a decline in American productivity—although it would be simplistic to suggest that one led to the other. In the 1960s, productivity in the United States was growing at a 4.2 percent rate; that fell to 3.1 percent in the 1970s; and today—or at least in the 1980s—it has fallen still further, to about 2 percent. That convinces me that the situation will get worse before it gets better, although lower oil prices and a healthy stock and bond market do ease the way. It is still a tough world, and that means that life for a chief executive is often—to steal from Thomas Hobbes—"nasty, brutish, and short."

One could call this the age of uncertainty. The world has speeded up; tenures of chief executives are shorter, job hopping is increasingly prevalent, money races through the world financial system at dizzying speeds, the rate of technological development seems to escalate exponentially, fads and fashions, with their impact upon marketers, come and go on a seemingly daily basis. While some business executives have adjusted to this speed-up, most others have taken refuge in a number of strategies that, if it were currency trading (which also changes constantly), would be called hedging, or spreading the risk. The analogy is a useful one: currency trading, in a sense, is a foundation stone of modern financial strategy, and it too is extremely short term in duration. Like currency traders, chief executives have looked to the short term to ensure maximum flexibility, not only in financial matters, but increasingly on questions of production, personnel, technology, and marketing.

The problem, of course, is that any form of hedging is really pursued to guard against down-side risk—to ensure the status quo. Alas, in a world of change, the status quo is rarely enough. Thus, we see the phenomenon of even much-praised corporate paragons—the kinds of companies featured in *In Search of Excellence*—absolutely blindsided by circumstance. In many of these cases, the gap between theory and practice, initiation and implementation, or sheer talk and effective action, yawns before one's feet, threatening, in extreme cases, to swallow up the company. Granted, closing that gap can be fearfully difficult. When I spoke with John deButts of AT & T in the late 1970s, years before the divestiture, he was already talking about the necessity to alter the culture of the company and, in particular, to build a competitive marketing team to sell the company's state-of-the-art technology. When Charlie Brown succeeded deButts, and unbundled AT & T from the operating companies, it was with the notion that he could engineer a thoroughgoing face-lift of the company—and he all but echoed deButts in his assurances that the company was making great strides, particularly in the marketing of computers and information services. Unfortunately, as we have seen, by 1986, AT & T's information services still appeared dead in the water, and the company was feeding off the profits thrown off by its long-distance service. By that time, Brown was retiring, leaving the job to James E. Olson, the new chairman and chief executive. All of which raises the question: while Brown's divestiture decision was daring, was it also wise? Talking about upgrading marketing skills is one thing; actually competing successfully with the likes of IBM is another. It may appear to be heresy, but one has to ask: if you are unable to compete, why get in the game at all?

Other companies that we have touched upon here and there have experienced similarly painful confrontations with recalcitrant realities. Let us turn to Harold Geneen's creation, ITT, which in the 1960s and 1970s was the exemplar of the conglomerate and a training ground for a whole army of executives. As we saw, Geneen did not give up power easily, continuing to try to oversee the company from his position on the board. Finally, however, he left the company to one of his former executives, Rand Araskog. Araskog has struggled to restructure the empire that Geneen built. As businesses turned sour, he unloaded them, in turn pouring money into an area that he thought would provide the kind of growth Geneen championed: international computer and telecommunications services. In a sense, Araskog was turning back the clock, taking the company back to its roots in international communications.

The keystone of that technology was the digital switch, a merging of the digital computer and the traditional telephone switch, which sells for a hefty $3 million or so and is the basic building block of a modern voice and data communications system. Alas, like AT & T, strategic implementation has failed to fulfill a quite rational strategic theory. Through years and years of research and development, and more than a billion dollars of invested capital, ITT has struggled to get its newest creation known as System 12 up and working and into various telephone companies and postal exchanges worldwide. Early on, the company had a technological edge with a design for a distributed architecture that, in theory, looked as if it could be a world beater. And so, ITT went out and sold the still-

277

uncompleted system, furiously closing deals in regions of traditional strength, particularly Western Europe. Then came the crunch. To really generate growth, ITT realized it would have to sell the system in the United States, comprising some 30 to 40 percent of the world market. That meant reconfiguring the software to fit into the vagaries of the Bell system. The company, dispersed worldwide, launched at least three different efforts, one in Belgium, one in West Germany, and one in the United States, each going off in a different direction. Trying to get them together was an organizational and technological nightmare.

Would Geneen, if still at the helm of ITT, have suffered similar woes? That is all but impossible to say, but it is clear that he would have been forced to sell off many of the same companies that Araskog did, and that he would have been forced, by the pace of technological development, into either leaping wholeheartedly into a digital world or backing out of telecommunications entirely. That having been said, the failure of System 12 can clearly be laid at the door of poor technological management, which Geneen, with his omnipresent "no surprises" reporting system, might well have been able to anticipate. Certainly, ITT's telecommunications strategy was eminently rational; unfortunately, the actual implementation of it— what might, in other contexts, be called management—fell far short of what was required for success. As a consequence, ITT foundered and became increasingly vulnerable to a takeover by raiders such as Irwin "Irv the Liquidator " Jacobs. Although ITT's earnings were up in 1986, the company is today a shell of its former self and not the technological giant it once was.

Unlike the failures of AT & T and ITT, most failures cannot be ascribed to just one strategic miscue, such as marketing or technology. Most are systemic problems that infect all areas of strategic action. Consider Beatrice Companies, the Chicago-based diversified food and consumer products company. As I said earlier, Wallace Rasmussen, as rough and blunt as an old bear, had run the company for many years until he finally stepped down in 1979. Rasmussen pointed to Beatrice's enviable record of twenty-six straight years of earnings gains (it finally ended in 1983), although earnings per share had begun to slip. His successor, James Dutt, had what he called a vision for the company: to increase earnings per share by culling out failing properties from the 430 different profit centers and 90 products; to build a national marketing force to sell a number of regional brands nationally; and to convince consumers that the heretofore obscure corporate label of Beatrice meant quality.

THE AGE OF UNCERTAINTY

On paper, Dutt's strategy could have come from the Harvard Business School case book. But implementation along a variety of fronts proved to be more problematic. First and foremost, Dutt was widely known to be autocratic, driving away top executives at the traditionally decentralized company and starting the revolving door spinning wildly. From 1982 to 1984, for example, Beatrice's La Choy Oriental-foods business had three presidents; in 1984 alone, Tropicana Products had three. Those who remained at Beatrice tended to be Dutt loyalists, afraid to question the wisdom of the master—whose photograph, by the way, hung in every major Beatrice facility worldwide. Second, Dutt had trouble implementing that ambitious marketing plan. He spent some $30 million during the 1984 Olympics advertising the corporate name, and another $70 million sponsoring an automobile racing team, both in the hopes that it would bolster the sales of separate products. There were no signs that it did. Third, his acquisition strategy proved to be his undoing. In 1984, Dutt acquired Esmark out from under a leveraged buyout sought by Esmark executives, including chief executive Donald P. Kelly (ironically, Kelly had just engineered the takeover of conglomerate Norton Simon Inc. out from under a leveraged buyout [LBO] sought by *its* chairman, David Mahoney), and Kohlberg Kravis Roberts & Co. (KKR), a New York–based firm specializing in LBOs. Dutt offered $2.5 billion for Esmark, then raised it to $2.7 billion—some twenty-three times its earnings—a price that Wall Street generally thought was too high. As a result, the stock price tumbled. Even worse, Dutt borrowed nearly all of the money for the takeover, at rates from 12 to 14 percent. By selling off $1.4 billion worth of operations, Dutt lightened the load, although it was still a steep 108 percent of equity—versus 38 percent before the acquisition.[1]

Dutt might have gotten away with all of this if earnings and earnings per share had risen. But they did not. Interest payments of some $382 million dragged down earnings; and because money was funneled into advertising, new products could not get funded. Again, Dutt either fired or forced out many of the top executives of similarly decentralized Esmark. Finally, the board turned on him, forcing his resignation and replacing him with the experienced, amenable William W. Granger, Jr., a long-time Beatrice executive. But by then, the company had been seriously weakened, exposing it to the watchful LBO mavens at Kohlberg, Kravis Roberts and the temporarily retired, though equally watchful, Donald Kelly. KKR and Kelly failed once to take Esmark private; they would not fail again with Beatrice, although they did have to adjust the $6.2 billion offer downward in order to get $3.5 billion in bank loans. In essence, Kelly, who will run the now private company, had managed a coup like that engineered by Edgar M. Bronfman and Seagram: the ostensible loser of the takeover skirmish scoots in the back door to take the ultimate prize. And what kept that back door open? Beatrice's strategic failures.

Has Beatrice finally come out of the woods? Not so fast. As we have seen innumerable times before, once a company begins to experience difficulty, it becomes more and more difficult to bring it to safety. Each battering weakens it further, making it vulnerable to future difficulties. So, with Beatrice, which has been loaded down not only with Esmark debt, but with LBO debt, Kelly finds himself faced with a difficult turnaround situation—although without the pressure of Wall Street to be concerned about.

Sometimes, the causes of failure are so diffuse that they can hardly be pinned down at all. Failure seems to lurk behind every decision, every initiative. Such has been the case of Eastman Kodak over the past decade. In many ways, Kodak has been, since the late nineteenth century, a model of how a company can dominate a single market for generations. But then, in the 1970s, it began to crumble—slowly at first, then more rapidly. For years, Kodak successfully sold easy-to-use cameras and high-quality film to an enormous mass market of shutterbugs—a market it had all but created with George Eastman's early automatic cameras. When Edwin Land of Polaroid introduced the instant camera, Kodak all but ignored it until that market grew large; then, in 1976, Kodak introduced its own instant camera, though Polaroid continued to dominate that segment. That was a pattern that would continue to haunt Kodak: too little, too late.

For example, in 1982, Kodak came out with its low-priced, small Disc cameras. Certainly, a Disc could fit into a pocket, but the quality was poor, and Discs lost out to the easy-to-use thirty-five-millimeter cameras sold by the Japanese. A Japanese company, Fuji, began to make inroads into Kodak's huge film business. An attempt to diversify into copiers—going up against Xerox—resulted in some early success that eroded when Xerox beat Kodak to the punch with an improved second generation. An attempt to diversify into medical X-ray film ran head-on into government attempts to contain costs in hospitals. Some $800 million spent on a large blood analyzer called Ektachem produced a fine system technologically, but was late in the game and was selling into a market that, by 1979, was hardly growing at all. An attempt to get into the newspaper and text-editing business in 1981, by buying a company called Atex, fizzled out when many of the key executives and scientists left. Then, in 1985, came the greatest shock of all: a patent decision declaring that Kodak had infringed on Polaroid's patent on the instant camera forced it to withdraw its cameras from the market, at a huge cost, and to pay Polaroid an enormous settlement fee. The result of all of this was that profitability slumped, Kodak—which for years had offered a form of lifetime employment (it had no unions)—began layoffs, and while the company still had a clean balance sheet, cash flow was meager, and thus funding for new businesses was not as plentiful as it once was.

The problems afflicting Kodak could symbolically represent those of American companies in general: a long, comfortable run shattered by change. A company that prided itself on technology and marketing, beaten time after time by faster-moving competitors. A paternalistic company that finds that its traditional methods simply do not work at smaller, more entrepreneurial ventures. It is indeed a new, very tough world, and one in which many companies wander as if they are strangers.

Psychological Style and Strategy

What lies behind these corporate failures? Well, as my discussions with chief executives progressed, it became clear to me that they were tending to focus on a few major strategic areas. I found that chief executives gravitated, time after time, to three major complexes of strategic decision, areas that hold their attention above all others: in the choice of their successor; in a takeover attempt or defense; and in the decision to seek opportunities and markets overseas. Not surprisingly, it is also in these three areas where chief executives' personal predilections—their cast of mind, prejudices, desires—come closest to the surface to play the largest role in actual decision making. These, in other words, are areas where psychological make-up mingles with the rational processes CEOs can bring to bear on a problem.

Perhaps the best example of that is in the decision to go international. We have already seen how some top executives—James Mortensen of Young & Rubicam, David Rockefeller of Chase, Peter McColough of Xerox—viewed the international markets as areas of great opportunity, while others, Harold Geneen in particular, though he is hardly alone, viewed them with some alarm. The decision to go abroad, I found, almost invariably grew out of chief executives' own travels, contacts, or personal interests. Even the particular countries they chose to locate in and the way they chose to enter them—co-ownership, subsidiary, exports—was closely allied with their own personal desires.

It comes as no surprise, then, that international markets are littered with failures. The symptom of such a failure is the boom-and-bust syndrome, the frantic expansion, followed by the desperate attempt to retrench. For example, the big money-center banks, including Rockefeller's Chase Manhattan, charged overseas in the 1970s, trying to "sell" the petrodollars flowing from the Middle East. The enthusiasm for lending to Eastern Europe and South America was enormous. We now know the unfortunate result of that enthusiasm, that naivete: entire countries skirted the edge of default; loan portfolios had to be propped up with larger and larger pools of reserves; a few domestic scandals, such as Penn Square and the shakiness of giants such as Continental Illinois, threw the whole mess into bold relief— and the banks were forced to cut and trim overseas operations. While I would not want to leave the impression that the overseas expansion by American banks was caused *solely* by the fond memories of a few chief executives for a vacation hideaway in, say, Brazil, I would argue that it is an area where psychological make-up, which includes the confidence to try to swim in foreign waters, does play a more prominent role than usual.

Let us now turn to an area that is even more suffused with the chief executive's psychological make-up: management style. Management style for a chief executive is like a suit of clothes; no matter how flamboyant the clothes, or how low-key, they become a kind of visible representation of a CEO's self-image, of the way one wishes to be viewed by the world. Though one should not exaggerate the importance of clothing, some chief executives do consciously manipulate this more than do others. Allen H. Neuharth, the chief executive of Gannett Corporation, wears only clothes of black, white, and gray, telling the world that he not only likes those colors, but that he is different, less stodgy, more active, more bold than the run-of-the-mill CEO. The pin-stripe suit and the grey flannel suit, while far more common, offer their own intimations of how chief executives want the world to see them.

Chief executives build management style from the inside out, from the interactions of their own psychologies with the external world. Throughout this book, I have tried to present a panorama of chief executives talking about a variety of subjects. In many cases, one can sense their psychologies simply by their speech: gruff Wallace Rasmussen, analytical Roy Ash, combative Harold Geneen. Let us try to go a bit further now. For instance, for the fifteen years that he ran ITT, Geneen was widely suspected of having a spy system in place throughout the company. Geneen's informants supposedly fed information to him that allowed him to catch his managers in lies, fabrications, or inadequacies, and that allowed Geneen to determine potential trouble spots in his far-flung empire. Often, Geneen would spring his informational bombs on his managers at the legendary monthly meetings he instituted, conclaves with up to one hundred managers that could last all night. In these meetings, Geneen grilled his managers unmercifully as to the problems and prospects of their areas of responsibility, exposing them, if need be, before his peers. "Geneen's meetings could be absolutely brutal interrogation sessions," said one of his top managers.

Were these meetings necessary, or were they a form of megalomania? As we saw earlier, Geneen argued that they were necessary to control the vast enterprise he was building, that the meetings and the spies were simply two aspects of his larger, conglomerate strategy which I described earlier. "Those meetings made us into the company," he told me. "They made us into a single, highly profitable machine." Needless to say, Geneen's view of his own management was not always shared by his subordinates. While he saw those meetings as quasicollegial—a sort of forum for sharing problems—many of his managers looked upon them as interrogations to be dreaded. "Geneen was authoritarian, dictatorial, and absolutist in his demands," said one ITT manager. "I dreaded those meetings," said another. Both of these executives went on to become CEOs of their own companies. Today, said one, "I'm careful as hell not to terrorize top management guys or spy on them all the time the way Geneen did."

What came first, the style or the strategy? Probably the style, if only because other chief executives undertook the conglomerate strategy without recourse to what his critics called "management by terror"—although few, to be fair, were as successful as Geneen was. He, of course, did not see it as terror. Said Geneen, "I'm sure I dominated some of the meetings, but not with the thought that anybody didn't have the right to disagree with me. I'd appreciate it if he had a point that was exactly right." At another point, he said, "One day one of the guys came to me and said, 'You know that if I didn't have to attend these meetings, I'd have a lot more time to work. . . .' I said, 'That's right, but you know something, since we've been

283

making these decisions with you as part of them, we haven't heard so much about all those damn fool decisions that New York makes anymore.' So he thought about it for a minute and said, 'That's right.' We were able to keep a very nonpolitical, open atmosphere where anybody could argue with me."

One can view chief executive psychology with a more rigorous perspective that stems from psychoanalysis. Traditionally, CEOs were viewed through the lenses of traditional analytic approaches, either Freudian or Jungian. Some analysts have looked at CEOs such as Geneen in terms of their drive for power, their need to dominate, their ways of using power, as well as their ability to cope with failure—all within the framework of Freudian analysis. Thus, psychologically, they were viewed in standard Freudian ways: childhood problems, problems in their relationships with their parents, sexual difficulties. More recent psychological analyses have offered a bit more insight. This approach, which follows some of the theories of Swiss analyst Carl Jung, tries to draw some conclusions by looking at the type of personality—extrovert or introvert—as they work in different types of corporate organizations. Hence, the development of the so-called Meyers-Briggs Type Indicator to assess exactly where business leaders fall in terms of psychological types.

Let us take a brief look at that approach. Jung declared that extroverts are motivated by external factors, say the unwritten rules of the phantom club, and actively try to influence people and events. In contrast, introverts hesitate to deal with their environment. They want to have the time to contemplate before they act. Jung also distinguished between people motivated by sensing and those who are more intuitive, and contrasted decisions based on rational thought that arise from logical analysis and those based on feelings that grow from an individual's personal values.

One can draw parallels between these general types and strategic planning. Extroverts are most often chosen, by the board or by the outgoing CEO, because of a felt need to alter some aspect of the organization, to seek new markets or products, or just to shake the cobwebs out of a sleepy work force. Turnaround artists are, by definition, extroverted. Other, more introverted chief executives may be chosen simply because of their innate conservatism, which, in the context of the company, may be viewed as a strength. These are caretaker chief executives who are often better at managing by consensus or fine-tuning the bureaucracy. Take, for example, Reginald Jones of General Electric. When he was tapped to run GE, it was a large, multiindustry company that performed fairly well in a number of mature markets, from light bulbs to appliances. The company, however, was experiencing a bit of a mid-life crisis: a price-fixing scandal that sent several executives to jail, and GE's sound defeat, and subsequent retreat, from the mainframe computer business. Jones provided the salve to bind those wounds. As we have already seen, he instituted formal strategic planning and built up one of the first strategic-planning units of a major corporation. Jones was psychologically suited for such an operation: dignified, refined, very bright, but able to delegate enormous amounts of authority. GE moved into new areas, but carefully, after much thought, and efficiently. Business was good.

But times changed, and toward the end of his time—he retired in 1982—Jones clearly sensed that the strategic requirements were changing as well. Like a middle-aged man who finds himself yearning for a different life, Jones, in his acquisition of Utah International, tried to adapt to the new turmoil breaking over the corporate world. While the Utah International acquisition proved a failure, Jones and the GE board had the wisdom to select not a man just like himself, but one as different as night is from day: Jack Welch. Here was a man to wake GE up and get it moving again. Welch nearly eliminated the planning group, shifting planning to line managers. He cut the work force by 20 percent, closed dozens of plants, sold off lackluster divisions, invested over $8 billion in computerization and robotics, forged ahead in financial services, and bought NBC.

Welch became as well known for his extroverted personality as the introverted Jones had been for his. "He demands action immediately," said one right-hand man. "Welch doesn't wait for second opinion like Jones did." Admitted another GE executive, "Our managers would schedule appointments with Jones long in advance and make presentations while he sat quietly listening, not interrupting. But your encounters with Jack are often when he walks in the door." Welch's "hard-charging personal style can raise a manager's hair," said one executive. "Jack is aggressive," said another, "but when someone is running a show well, he keeps out of it." Welch has become famous for working in his shirt sleeves and his twelve- to fourteen-hour days. He pounces on executives in meetings, calling for fresh ideas and imaginative ways to, say, cut costs. He has a legendary temper. In contrast, Jones had a patrician's air of slow deliberation and unflappability, the ultimate rationalist. Not surprisingly, Welch's team calls him "Jack"; with Reg Jones it was always "Jones" or "Mr. Jones."

Usually, the differences between psychological types is not so strikingly clear. Most chief executives are a mix of the two, extroverted in some ways and introverted in others. Charlie Brown, of AT & T, for instance, is soft spoken, even diffident. And yet, his decision to break up Bell has to be viewed as one of the most daring—in our typology, extroverted—in U.S. business history. The same applies to Roger Smith of General Motors: very quiet, almost shy in terms of outward appearance; but as a strategic planner, he resembles a corporate swashbuckler.

Despite this complexity, I think some general conclusions can be drawn from the typologies I have laid down—while remaining aware of the risk of indulging in reductionism. Extroverted chief executives, who were described by Meyers as "men who try to run as much of the world as may be theirs to run,"[2] place an emphasis on acquisition and expansion, often integrating vertically, using aggressive marketing programs and reacting quickly to changes in the environment—sometimes, perhaps, too quickly. These CEOs love to use financial leverage, to take risks, to bet the company. By contrast, the introverts are less likely to attempt product innovations or major diversifications, less likely to use leverage to acquire new companies, and more likely to concentrate on cost control, as opposed to growth, often buttressed by sophisticated management information systems. These chief executives are often no great fans of the risks involved in research and development, and, at times, may find themselves boxed in by new developments, relegated to producing commodity products, and competing to be the lowest-cost producer. They are, as Miles and Snow[3] characterized them, "defenders."

That, of course, is but the tip of the iceberg when it comes to the psychology of chief executives. Using the Jungian typology, I have scattered some further thoughts that became apparent to me during the extensive interviewing.

THE EXTROVERT

While inevitably garnering the most publicity, a CEO extrovert can create as much harm as good. Extroverts, for instance, are often contrarians in the Wall Street sense; that is, they will feel that the best policy is to go against the herd, a feeling based as much on the rational calculation that all things change as on a personal drive to distinguish themselves and to prove everyone else wrong. As Armand Hammer, a classic extrovert, said,

"In business, whenever I see everyone rushing in one direction, I know it's time to move the other way." Certainly, while a number of Hammer's initiatives at Occidental have been successful—for instance, his decision to deal with the Libyans for oil—others have been disastrous. As a result, Wall Street tends to discount Occidental stock. And contrarionism can itself become a fad, and create its own herd. If everyone is a contrarion, what do you do then?

That contrarion nature, which in a better light can be viewed as independent thinking, can create opportunities. The extrovert then tends to be the kind of chief executive—we can see it in Jack Welch—who is willing to jump on those short-term openings without the benefit of careful, rational analysis and planning. There is Armand Hammer striking a deal with Lenin for pencil factories when no other American businessman would touch him. And there is William McGowan, voluble, a brilliant self-promoter, daring to challenge the almost unimaginable breadth and depth of the prederegulated Bell System. These chief executives often gain the reputation of being impatient with slower-moving colleagues, and to run roughshod over environmental, organizational, or capital market constraints. In recent years, in particular, we have tended to turn such traits into myths, to idolize anyone who breaks through established barriers. We slap the tag of entrepreneur on them, even though most, like Welch, have never really started their own businesses. Consequently, while we hear about the successes of the extroverted chief executive, we hear less of their failures. At ITT, Harold Geneen was warned by virtually everyone not to try to compete with AT & T in the cable business. But Geneen went forward anyway. And Ash at AM International certainly saw himself as trying to foster the entrepreneurial spirit.

Contrarions also tend to think of themselves as gamblers, and again, as with most gamblers, it is easy to take flight from reality. Taking risks when the odds are carefully calculated often shades imperceptibly into risk taking for the sake of risk taking. When they succeed, these chief executives think of their actions as demonstrations of their leadership and vision, and conjure up visions of the phantom club by speaking of how other CEOs are watching them, following them. However, when they fail, they are untouched by the experience: because they are so certain about the inherent correctness of their approach—theirs is a form of corporate self-righteousness—they believe that they are looked upon as a paragon, no matter what happens. Some extroverted CEOs even view their companies as the instrument for the construction of their own legend. And that means living at least part of the time in a fantasy world, never a particularly desirous component of good strategic decision making.

There are, of course, less serious manifestations of this phenomenon, which, in politics, would be called the cult of personality. There is Dutt with his photograph in every major Beatrice building, just like, as *Fortune* wrote, Mao Tse-tung.[4] Others like to appear on television commercials as company spokespersons. More commonly, many chief executives I spoke with provided me with sanitized versions of their lives and achievements. Lee Iacocca, for instance, was kind enough to provide me with numerous of his statements over the past ten years, so that I could understand the process of strategic decision making that went into the turnaround at Chrysler. These first-person accounts were exciting and compelling descriptions of his personal acts, feelings, strategies, and methods, as was his best-selling book.[5] The only problem: they were not necessarily always accurate, as I discovered by talking with other participants in the Chrysler turnaround.

Let us look at one illustrative example. In the early days of the turnaround, the U.S. government hired consultant Booz Allen to analyze which cuts Chrysler should make to survive. The government, of course, was an interested party because of the loan guarantees it had provided Chrysler. While Iacocca was arguing that only $400 million in cuts had to be made, Booz Allen weighed in and calculated that a much higher figure, $1.2 billion, was necessary. Iacocca objected strenuously to these outside consultants, and criticized their estimates. Nonetheless, in the end, his staff worked closely with Booz Allen and eventually slashed over $1 billion. One would not know this by reading Iacocca's biography, or from the twenty-some speeches he delivered. Not only was Booz Allen never mentioned, but often neither was Gerald Greenwald, his deputy, who had played such an important role during a crucial period when Iacocca's wife was dying. Such a case of monument building, while extreme, is hardly unusual. Extroverted CEOs tend to be as political as, well, politicians.

Finally, some extroverts often seem to act more on whim than on analysis. Henry Ford II, as we saw, acted on impulse by grabbing the whiz kids, and in later years, anointing, then dropping, successors. Again, the results are often wildly divergent. The whiz kids, of course, helped rescue the company from decline, and provided leadership over the next two decades or so. But the failure to plan for the succession caused the company to founder in crucial years. With Henry II, who was born into wealth and used to the power and glory of his famous last name, such autocratic whim seemed an ingrained part of his personality—whether it was his tempestuous personal life, his on-again, off-again political involvement, or the supposedly cavalier way he treated his work force, there was a tendency to zig strategically as he was zagging psychologically.

THE INTROVERT

When I began to look over my list of eighty-nine chief executives, I expected to discover that most could be characterized as extroverts. Instead, I found that over half of them, if not complete introverts, had many of the introvert's traits. I have already mentioned Charlie Brown and Roger Smith. While those two *acted* like extroverts, their outward personalities were those of the introvert. Alas, others tended to be not only withdrawn outwardly in terms of personality, but cautious to a fault strategically. Why was I surprised? Because, as I said in my discussion of extroverts, the conventional wisdom characterizes chief executives as aggressive world beaters, clawing their way up the corporate ladder, or—excuse the muddling of metaphors—sprinting on the fast track. Obviously, appearances do not always provide a window into personality, not to mention strategy.

In retrospect, it should be no surprise that many chief executives fit into the introvert mold. While metaphors like fast track imply a bruising race of flying elbows and feet, most corporations are actually bureaucracies in which performing a set of tasks is more important than wild imaginative flights. That is not necessarily a bad thing. As I said earlier, most established companies do quite well by tending to lucrative markets they dominate. "If it ain't broke, don't fix it" applies both to the behavior of many companies and to the executives they promote to the top. The best of these technician chief executives can, like master mechanics, squeeze the last bit of horsepower from the corporate machine.

Traditionally, most companies sought consensus builders, a trait, logically enough, shared by introvert CEOs. In a sense, consensus managers work just the opposite of contrarions: they try to get the herd moving in one direction. That means planning, meeting, position papers, compromise. It can also mean stagnation, uncertainty, timidity. "I never wanted to get too far out in front or out of line with what other companies in our industry were doing," admitted one introverted CEO to me. "I never found it paid. Look at the problem Apple had when it developed a bunch of computers that were incompatible with IBM." One of the fascinating things I discovered while interviewing was the dawning realization coming over many introspective and bureaucratic chief executives that the era of hostile takeovers was upon them, and that bolder, more aggressive strategies were required. To some, it came as quite a shock. "It's gotten a lot rougher," sighed one chief executive. "I'm not sure my basic personality type is all that suited to this hostile takeover era. Because the problem is, today you have to be prepared either to fight them or join them. You can't just get on with making your products and running your company the way you used to. You have to be constantly looking over your shoulder." Let us not forget the pitfalls of introverted CEOs, like Reginald Jones, trying to instantly adapt to a new era.

THE ENTREPRENEUR

Where does the entrepreneur fit into all of this? Well, the entrepreneur—pictured in the media—is clearly closer to extroverted than introverted. Entrepreneurs, however, tend to be loners, taking a few of the traits of both extroverts and introverts: the extrovert's aggressiveness and risk taking, the introvert's concentration on a single product or technology. Someday, of course, most entrepreneurs hope to wake up to find themselves atop a large corporation, transformed, like a Steven Jobs or a William Norris, into a corporate chieftain. Such chief executives, generally speaking, are notoriously willful, even stubborn. They are often not fans of diversification and tend to put high-quality products over profits. They are usually not famous for cost control. As Miller and his colleagues make clear, they trust their intuitive insights concerning people, phenomena, and events, regardless of established authority or popular beliefs.[6] The result is that their stubbornness and narrowness can be positive or negative, as we have seen in the careers of both Jobs and Norris.

Egotism and Competition

Despite the typology, most chief executives are competitive animals. It is part of the nature of the beast. That competition, stoked by ego, often spills over into strategic initiatives that may better resemble personal vendettas or monument building than rational corporate strategies. At a certain point, chief executives find it difficult to discern where they begin and their company ends. Winning becomes both a gain for the company and a personal triumph to be savored. Many takeovers are pursued or fought against not for rational ends, but for the ego satisfaction of the chief executive. Both Harry Gray of United Technologies and Edward Hennessy of Allied have reportedly been rivals since Hennessy left United Technologies. And Donald Burr of People Express is said to have competed with his former boss, Frank Lorenzo, of Texas Air, by engaging in a broad acquisition strategy, picking up Frontier Airlines, Brit Airlines, and Provincetown Boston Airways. Burr denies this: "People call up asking, 'Does Don really want to be Frank?' That's nonsense. All I want to do is win."[7] (By the end of 1986 Burr ironically had to merge People Express into—yes—Texas Air to save it from insolvency.)

Not everyone is so circumspect. Iacocca spent much of his autobiography attacking Henry Ford II. Insiders and investment bankers admitted that long-lasting rivalries between successive CEOs of the two large cigarette companies, Philip Morris and R. J. Reynolds, led to their simultaneous decisions to purchase cigarette companies abroad in the 1960s and 1970s, and giant food companies in the 1980s. The business press and Wall Street analysts speculated that Philip Morris had lost out in the battle for Nabisco to R. J. Reynolds. And a number of investment bankers argued that this rivalry caused Philip Morris to pay at least 10 percent too much for General Foods. "Sure we have a competitive rivalry between Philip Morris and Reynolds," said George Weissman, Philip Morris's former CEO. "However, we never lost out in the battle for Nabisco to R. J. Reynolds. Nabisco was obviously among one of the earlier considerations when we looked at the food industry, but we never made a move for it, and concentrated on more basic segments of the industry resulting in our bid for General Foods. The question of having paid 10 percent too much for General Foods is your judgment. Based on the way all food stocks moved between the time of our purchase and August 1986, we are just in line with the market." Weissman concluded by saying, "In fact, over the years since I have been in the tobacco business, we have been friends with many of the R. J. Reynolds people, and there is nothing personal about the rivalry between R. J. Reynolds and Philip Morris. It's a competitive situation."

What are some of the strategic effects of these rivalries? Well, it is widely recognized that the strategic options of chief executives are directly affected by their competitors' changes in price, technology, quality, or marketing approaches. For example, even shy individuals—in our typology, intro-verts—find themselves involved in personal rivalries with competitors, not unlike the battles between Pepsi and Coke or between Burger King and McDonalds. When industries are flush and everyone is making money, such rivalries are often jovial and involve the fight over market share points. But when an industry finds itself in deep trouble, corporate rivalries can become deep personal vendettas, resulting in irrational initiatives—expensive advertising campaigns, deadly price wars, an absurd cold war of spying, even a counterproductive takeover campaign—that sacrifice long-term health for short-term gratification. Such vendettas often open the door for a third competitor, say a Japanese company, to walk in and take over the market.

Like many of the other traits I have discussed, rivalry and competition are deeply ambiguous in the corporate context. On one hand, you want a chief executive with a healthy dose of egotism. On the other hand, competitiveness is a passion, not a rational process, and as such can carry the company to regions where no sane mind would have led it. CEOs who are obsessed by beating out a rival are as far into a personal fantasy as CEOs who are ruled by whim or entranced by the monument they are building to themselves.

Coping with External Forces

That, then, is a brief glance *within* the chief executive. What of the forces impinging upon CEOs from the outside—the external pressures, the sudden shifts in the economic environment, or the state of technology? As I said earlier, the sheer rapidity of the change and the depth of the uncertainty force many chief executives to seek refuge in the realm of the short term—the quick fix, the acquisition, the short-term financial instrument—no matter that the price tag on these expediencies is often very high.

Still, while the short-term approach is understandable, and in some cases necessary, it can spawn loss of direction and orientation. The price of infinite flexibility is confusion. Such a chief executive is like a sailor without a rudder; trying simply to survive each passing storm, the sailor's overall situation becomes worse, rather than better. In the end, knee-deep in water, exhausted, confused, the sailor tries to survive in a constant state of crisis. The widespread term "environmental turbulence" has been used by many strategic planners and analysts to describe the present period of acute uncertainty. The result of these analyses is that the corporation is more vulnerable than ever to external environmental threats, and that collectively, these forces have severely restricted corporate independence and self-reliance.

There is an ironic process at work here: as chief executives try to maintain their corporate equilibrium and protect themselves against external threats, they often find themselves backing into other threats, like the man who escapes from a mugging only to get run over by the getaway car from a bank robbery. Thus, chief executives seeking to avoid the risks of concentrating their assets in businesses that are vulnerable to external forces often stagger into businesses they know nothing about, resulting in the necessity to divest. And we have seen how companies trying to make themselves invulnerable to takeover piled on the debt and became vulnerable to insolvency; or how those that tried to pare down their debt became vulnerable to takeover.

This catch-22 is omnipresent: to avoid union problems, companies agree to escalating wage and benefit increases—and watch their profitability plummet. But when they choose to challenge the unions, they face the threat of a productivity-sapping strike. Going abroad for manufacturing offers similar risks: not only are there foreign supply problems, the threat of nationalization, and foreign economic policies, but companies can be whipsawed by currency fluctuations. For instance, in the early 1980s, many American companies moved facilities overseas to take advantage of the strong dollar; then, as the dollar fell in 1986, they were faced with uprooting those facilities or riding out the storm. The syndrome even applies when companies try to manipulate outside forces coming from Congress, the regulatory agencies, or the Pentagon. Firms that felt vulnerable often hired small armies of lobbyists, made political contributions, or even offered a bribe here or there to attempt to turn back the pressure or to turn it toward their own ends. That, in turn, has resulted in the passage of campaign contribution limits, antibribery laws, and disclosure regulations for politicians and civil servants. And there are so many lobbyists chasing so many special interests in Washington that they often cancel each other out.

How do external pressures affect strategy making? First, by derailing

293

previous strategies. Second, by forcing chief executives to constantly draw up new plans to meet new contingencies. Third, by drastically reducing the amount of time needed to develop a consistent, long-term plan, which leads to a reliance on consultants or the adoption of either fad or cookie-cutter strategies. Thus, two crucial patterns develop: chief executives get into the habit of fire fighting—remember David Rockefeller's comments about Chase Manhattan; and these problems absorb so much time that CEOs tend to have less time to manage their business. "We were so swamped with asbestos cases and Chapter 11 issues that . . . it's hard to run the business," said John McKinney of Manville. "It [the Tylenol crisis] absorbed 100 percent of our time for the crisis period," said James Burke of Johnson & Johnson. "For the rest of my career," declared Warren M. Anderson of Union Carbide, "I know that I will be judged on how this [Bhopal] affair is handled."[8] Although Anderson later added, "I used to spend 100 percent of my time on Bhopal, now it's maybe 10 percent,"[9] the crisis did continue to impose a heavy burden of time and energy on Anderson and Union Carbide management, so heavy that the company found itself vulnerable to a takeover threat from the GAF Corporation and its CEO, Samuel Heyman—not an untypical turn of events.

No single institution poses as bewilderingly a variety of pressures and influences on corporations as the government does—hence, the often wild talk of dismantling government regulation entirely. While pharmaceutical companies, defense contractors, and aircraft builders have to live particularly close to the house of government, all corporations, whether public or private, have to deal with the vagaries of the tax code, OSHA (Occupational Safety and Health Administration) regulations, import and export rules, and a thousand more rules and regulations. Nonetheless, despite the power of government-generated incentives and disincentives, chief executives must balance them with a variety of other factors both internal and external. One day, Thornton Bradshaw at RCA was asked by students in a class of mine to comment on his reaction to the new 1984 tax program, with its incentives to invest in research and development. "RCA will probably not take advantage of those tax incentive programs," replied Bradshaw. "At present, we simply don't have the cash to invest in research and development. We have no choice. We're in a cash squeeze." Thus, we find that different chief executives will view the tax incentive plan differently. "Some don't need the tax exemption right now," said another chief executive. "Other firms in the industry who made profits this year could be in a better position to take advantage of it. But for this year, we can't."

External pressures also wreak havoc over the long-term. Take, for example, the foreign import threat. The first time around, many American electronics companies, full of confidence, fought back bravely, and lost. The second time around, many of them literally abandoned the fight—sometimes even before foreign competitors had begun production. In essence, the year of foreign competition was extremely effective in scaring U.S. companies from markets they may well have held. Once burned, many U.S. manufacturers extrapolated failure across a range of products, brutally constraining their own strategic options. A similar type of overcompensation applies as well against hostile takeovers, government regulatory actions, oil shocks, and even interest rate escalation and inflation.

This is a not uncommon psychology which might be called the Munich Syndrome, for the appeasement strategy of British Prime Minister Neville Chamberlain just prior to World War II. Munich, like Vietnam, provides a historical paradigm that helps us make sense of complex historical realities—whether or not it is applicable. Some psychologists have focused on the time that these overcompensating reactions take place, compared to the time of the original shock. Others have studied the psychological fear or confidence that different boards or chief executives display when confronted by these threats the first, second, or third time, as a means of studying learning behavior or psychological reinforcement patterns. It is common for management to always fight the last war, to cope with the last fear or problem, or to overreact because they have failed to judge correctly the scope of the current threat.

These external crises would have less effect if there were not a fundamental weakness among these companies. We saw how succession poses more of a risk in companies that are already weakened by crises. That same law applies to companies in general. A strong, healthy company can survive and triumph over some foreign competition or over a competitor with a technologically advanced product. But a company that is already decaying from within may collapse in a heap. One can conjure up a number of examples—International Harvester, the integrated steel companies, AM International, to name a few. And there are others who survived the steepest of challenges, such as Manville and Caterpillar.

Finally, a sign of continued uncertainty about the external environment and how to deal with it can be seen in the shifting roles of specialists who monitor environmental changes. From the 1960s to the early 1980s, these groups grew rapidly, particularly at such companies as Mobil, Exxon, General Motors, Ford, Dow Chemical, American Express, and Citibank. For many companies, these units were integrated directly into strategic planning. However, when corporations began breaking up strategic-planning units around 1983 and integrating those functions into line management, there was a tremendous amount of confusion about where these people would fit. In some cases, where companies retained an issue analysts group, they have been relegated to simply passing along files of information from the press, from Washington lobbyists, or from various trade associations. At other companies, the responsibility for scanning the external environment was broken up and handled separately by headquarters groups such as the treasurer's office, the legal office, personnel, or lobbyists in Washington. For example, it is now routine for the treasurer's office to monitor a whole range of interest rates and financial instruments, changes in currencies, even changes in the political situations abroad.

Likewise, most major corporations have increasingly brought legal work in house and enlarged their legal departments. During their divestiture, AT & T's legal department was one of the largest in the world, with over a thousand lawyers. By building in-house legal departments, companies found they could slash costs and take on a wider array of tasks.

The result of all of this is that information on the external environment is coming to chief executives from a greater number of directions, making it their task to synthesize it all into a coherent, rational world view that allows them to build a long-term strategy with some confidence.

Facing the Future: New Rules, New Game

What lies behind this sudden turbulence that has wrecked so many proud corporate vessels? That is an enormously complex question that really requires a volume to itself. It is more than just the ascendance of power-hungry planners and bullying corporate bureaucracies intent on upholding the status quo. It is more than just the obsession with finance that ruled so many companies for so long. It is more than foreign competition, repeated economic shocks, and government regulation. And it is more than just a rise in takeovers, an increased financial volatility, and a decreasing degree of corporate loyalty. It is even more than just tunnel vision, bounded rationality, or a propensity for muddling through.

These are the symptoms, the phenomenology, of a deeper economic and business reality. Allow me to focus in on what I believe are a few major, interrelated components that make up that reality, that have, in the apt phrase of Austrian economist Friedrich von Hayek, triggered "gales of constructive capitalism": first, globalism, and the blurring of international boundaries that accompanies it. Second, the computer, and its basic unit, the semiconductor, which has allowed former production verities to be overturned and opened up the field to competition.

Let us begin with the computer. William McGowan of MCI summed up the staggering scale of the change. "I've talked with CEOs around the country—at meetings, conferences, one-on-one. And believe me, they know some profound changes are taking place. They know the information age is coming. They see the traditional distinctions between telecommunications technology and computers and information blurring. They see their phones acting more like computers, their computers communicating across the country, even around the globe. And they can't help but see the explosion of information this marriage of computers and information is bringing them. But a lot of CEOs still don't understand just how completely the information age is going to restructure the way they—and their competitors—do business. So we need to point that out to them" (and, he might add, sell those products to them).

McGowan has a point. He takes the example of Tandy Corporation, with its chain of some eight thousand Radio Shack outlets. Each store is linked to Tandy headquarters in Texas, allowing planners—and the chief executive—to keep a running tally of inventory, of sales, of what is selling and what is not. Humana, the hospital management company, has similarly linked its hospitals to a central computer in Louisville, Kentucky, allowing management there to actually know what is going on in each unit without the bother, expense, and tons of paper required to implement a detailed reporting system. Imagine what Geneen could have done with such a system.

The computer used in this way can also generate real efficiencies in the marketplace. Inventories can be kept smaller, products can be manufactured on the basis of need, advertising and marketing can be evaluated more quickly, and operations can respond more quickly to changes in consumer demand. Companies can also begin eliminating layers of middle managers whose role is really to take data from below, package it, and send it to those above. Finally, McGowan argues that many companies can save millions simply by storing information more efficiently. "Most companies today pay $18 per year for a square foot of office space. And a lot of that goes for filing cabinets. We pay to air condition the filing cabinets in the summer and heat them in the winter. Can you imagine? Millions of tons of paper being heated and air conditioned . . . not to mention copied and distributed and mailed and opened and ultimately, laid to rest, probably unread."

All of this sounds so wonderfully simple, but getting management to alter old, ingrained habits is never easy. Technology is a tool that must be mastered; it is not some magical alchemist's stone that transforms lead to gold as if by magic. Take the disappearance of paper that should follow automation. Often, the real-life case has been just the opposite: a proliferation of paper as managers urgently made hard copies of everything they thought important; and, since they had access to far more data, more things *seemed* important. In the best of all possible worlds, more data should result in decision making that is faster and accomplished by fewer executives—and hence, a sharp increase in productivity. So far, those increases have been spotty. Thinking aggressively, making decisions, going out on any limb is something most executives would rather avoid. By breaking down barriers, the computers throw executives back upon themselves; in fear, they erect walls and procedures, new bureaucracies. Finally, there are limits to the magic that sheer data crunching can provide. Computerized econometric forecasts still are not all that much better than their human counterparts who sniff the wind and play by intuition; and strategic planners often miss the key human element in a situation by depending too heavily on the data spewed forth by a machine.

So there are caveats to this revolution heralded by McGowan. But he is clearly correct in his broader analysis. Let us take it a step further, for computer technology is also working to alter the very structure of the industrial economy. Since the early days of the Industrial Revolution in England, there have been a small number of iron laws of the market, the most famous of which is the economies of scale. We saw it in its various guises not only in the discussion of Henry Ford's volume strategy, but in Texas Instruments' practice of pricing down the experience curve. Economies of scale, of course, is based on the idea that the more units of a product one makes, the lower the price and the greater the productivity.

It rests traditionally on the seemingly inescapable fact that to sell a new product meant to build new machinery and a new factory. Thus, the more goods sold from that factory, the longer a period of time the cost of building it could be spread; and so, each unit produced a greater increment of profit.

But the automated factory is altering that rule. Using computer-aided design and manufacturing (CAD-CAM), small companies can more cheaply gear up to produce products that can compete on price with those of large companies. And they can refit the assembly line almost overnight from making, say, televisions to making Walkman radios, computer CRTs, or VCRs. That, in part, explains the ability of Far Eastern competitors, like the Japanese, the South Koreans, Taiwanese, and Hong Kongese, to make many products, such as textiles and electronics, into commodity goods. And it underlies the Japanese near-obsession with the robot as a manufacturing tool. Not only can robots, properly designed, fulfill the routinized tasks of the line perfectly and for long periods of time, they also can be reprogrammed or reconfigured to make, say, sedans one day and station wagons the next. And, as the saying goes, they may break down, but they don't go out on strike.

But automated systems for manufacturing are only half the battle. To make it work requires a wholly revamped system of inventory which, not surprisingly, the Japanese have pioneered. Called *Kanban*—Japanese for "card," which specified the amount and time a piece of inventory was delivered—it involves getting just enough inventory to the plant to fulfill the day's production run. While Kanban sounds simple, once implemented, it alters traditional relationships with suppliers, slashes the amount of warehousing space, reduces wastage and spoilage, and most important, alters perceptions of what the optimum production run, order size, or work force requirement is. It forces an entire rethinking of the concept of economies of scale.

Bruce Henderson, the founder of the Boston Consulting Group—which did not use to be terribly concerned with operational questions, but which has, of late, changed its ways—has become a fan of Kanban for American companies. Henderson argues[10] that the "competitive and strategic advantages of Kanban are enormous. In many traditional factories, there is a habitual practice of making somewhat more than what is needed to protect against shortages, defects, lost material, or miscounting. For the same reason, there is also a tendency to requisition slightly more from stores than is actually needed. These overruns are the source of compounding costs.

Such problems can escalate into production crises if shortages cause attempts to cannibalize some orders to get other higher priority orders delivered. Whole factories with thousands of employees have been forced to shut down for periods as long as a year. The difficulties often followed this pattern: supplies of a single major component were stopped because they often had defects. This caused production to slow considerably for lack of that major component. But other material continued to be delivered with the hope that production would catch up. Some orders were completed by cannibalizing other orders that were on hold. Soon, the plant was choked with material. The identity and location of material in the plant became uncertain, and production came to a halt when the plant had too much unmatched material."

Under Kanban, argues Henderson, companies can dramatically reduce the cost of warehousing, checking, counting, and rejecting parts. "But most important," he says, "is the huge time savings that results from reducing the set-up and scheduling delays so the factory becomes a continuous production plant with batches of near-perfect parts arriving each hour on schedule exactly when they are due to be fed into the assembly line or production process. The results are dramatic cost and time savings at each stage of the production process. As these techniques are further developed, the effects of Kanban-type production will be highly leveraged. Normal forty-hour-per-week, full-capacity utilization may be expanded to 80, 120, or even 148 hours per week with virtually no increase in assets and a modest increase in labor hours." One example: the Buick plant in Flint, Michigan. While the plant cost more to build than a more traditional facility, it returned great improvements in productivity. "The whole factory layout was changed to permit delivery by suppliers directly to the production line. Suppliers were used who were a hundred miles or less from Buick City, and delivered directly on tightly scheduled programs. Many were provided with manufacturing facilities immediately adjacent to the Buick factory.

"Under the new program, six dies could be changed simultaneously by the regular work crew in less than fifteen minutes. Previously, these die changes had required ten hours and multiple crews of various specialty trades. But under the new system, production is stopped on one frame, the die changed, and production is resumed on a different frame, all within fifteen minutes; and the work is done in an orderly, unhurried manner by the regular workers on the machines." Again, allow for caveats. To make Kanban work requires having leverage over your suppliers. Smaller operators find it more difficult to implement. And while Kanban does afford productivity increases, it is but one part of a larger context of changes—from factory automation to the elimination of antiquated work rules. Treat Kanban as this year's fashion, and it could result in an enormous waste of time and money. Instead, treat Kanban as a tool.

How is this technology contributing to the globalization of the world economy? Well, I have already mentioned how nimble overseas enterprises can go toe to toe with massive American companies. But other technologies—high-speed telecommunications, computers, and the kind of manufacturing techniques I spoke of earlier—can give production managers the kind of flexibility we have found in financial matters: the ability to move operations to adjust for changing wage and currency values, to alter the mix of products or their design through direct links from headquarters. Hence, we have seen the appearance of the "hollow corporation," a U.S. company that contracts out for low-cost manufacturing done elsewhere. That sort of phenomenon plays into the hands of multiindustrial corporations. Industries dominated by multinationals—companies active in a range of operations in a range of nations—find that they can "treat their business lines like part of an investment portfolio and may be very dispassionate and uninvolved in its continuance," said William Rothschild, formerly a strategic planner in charge of global strategies at General Electric. "They may have other options, and if attacked, they may merely retreat, sell off, and put their resources elsewhere. Thus, they may be easy to dislodge and it may be easy to take share from them. Professional managers may be assigned and their time horizon may be shorter than specialists'.

"Today, the world is quite different. There are more global and multiindustrial companies. In these countries, the leaders are multiindustrial, multinational corporations such as Hitachi, Toshiba, Philips, Siemens, and a few quasispecialists such as Fuijitsu. In the future, the situation is likely to become even more multiindustrial, and this will change investment, profitability, and the rules of winning." Zoltan Merszei, former president of Occidental and the Dow Chemical Company, put it into an even wider context, with greater demands on chief executives: "Our entire economic order has changed. We now live in a global economy . . . as a consequence, we must think of our competitors, our suppliers, and our customers as other countries, rather than just other companies. Americans think American—they need to expand their perspective of the world. If they want to sell to Europeans, their probability of success is much higher if they value European needs from a European perspective."

Blending Strategies in a Complex World

In the beginning of this book, I warned that there would be no simple cure-alls to the plight of the corporation in an uncertain world. By now, I hope that that point has been driven home. It is not enough to build a wonderful, caring corporate culture if you do not pursue intelligent strategic ends; you end up with a heart without a head. Likewise, all of the strategic planning in the world will come to naught if there is no follow-through, if the man-power of the company cannot or will not initiate the plan; this would be the head without the heart. This complex balancing game extends to in-dividual strategies. An inflexible long-term financial strategy can strangle a company, while an intensely short-term strategy can leave it without direction and constantly in crisis. Too much corporate attention can smother a new venture; too little can starve it. In an age of rapid techno-logical development, companies have to have some window on what is going on in the lab; but simply throwing money at some scientists and engineers without a clear idea of a company's goals is like throwing money out the window. Technology without marketing or finance produces little; similarly, a marketing strategy without a new product to sell or without money to buy advertising is a futile attempt.

That balancing act plays an especially vital role in the interaction of planning (what one might call initiation) and operations (or implemen-tation). As we saw, strategic planning achieved enormous popularity in the 1960s and 1970s, with the rise of financial strategy as the primary focus of most chief executives and the apotheosis of the conglomerate. Power shifted from the production line to corporate headquarters; the responsibility for planning increasingly centered on burgeoning planning staffs which gained more and more power. The economic shocks of the early 1980s—partic-ularly the crisis of confidence brought on by foreign competition—began to force the pendulum back. Suddenly, numbers-oriented, analytical, headquarters-centered strategic planning efforts fell out of favor; planning functions were again forced back to operations, decentralization became the rage. General Electric's decision to replace Reginald Jones with Jack Welch was symbolic. But there were other signs as well. The Boston Con-sulting Group began looking closer at operations instead of focusing pri-marily on conceptual strategies. Roger Smith, who pioneered strategic planning at General Motors, became a convert to decentralization, particularly with the Saturn program. *Business Week* heralded the change with a September 1984 cover story called "The New Breed of Strategic Planner: Number-crunching professionals are giving way to line managers."

Is there anything wrong with this shift? Of course not. Uncertain chief executives *had* allowed strategic-planning departments to grow out of control. They *had* robbed the operational units—which were, after all, closer to the customer, to the production line, and to the lab—of input into decision making. But while it is certainly a good sign that such a change has been made, so also does one sense that it will eventually go too far. Most chief executives—in fact, most executives in general—are quick to sense a fad. As a result, the herd has begun to thunder after the elusive benefits of decentralization. Sooner or later, you know they will wake up with a pounding hangover. At times like that, contrarions look like geniuses. For the kind of intelligent, far-ranging foresight that skilled strategic planners can provide, simply because they are not involved with the daily problems or the entreaties of single customers, is lost.

No one ever said running an American business was easy, particularly in this age. And while the uncertainty provides an explanation for this tendency of chief executives to grasp at simple-sounding prescriptions for health, it does not provide an excuse. Chief executives sit at the point where forces collide; they provide the fulcrum upon which the corporation pivots. Those forces are increasingly complex, making extraordinary demands upon CEOs and requiring very special men and women trained in very special ways. For if they allow one or more of these forces to predominate, the company begins to shake and shiver and smoke like a misfiring engine. Trying to readjust, to regain that equilibrium, is always more difficult than keeping the machine running smoothly in the first place. One miscalculation is often succeeded by a second or a third. The balance is lost and the company begins to fly off in different directions. In the end, the symptoms of decline become apparent to all: the revolving door, the lurking takeover maven, the leveraged buyout, the appearance of the turnaround artist.

"The world," said Greek philosopher Heraclitus, "is an ever-living fire, kindled in measures and in measures going out." To control the mutability of that fire requires boldness and restraint, passion and analysis, both the objectivity of distance and the subjectivity of intimate involvement. In other words, some feel for the divine mean, for the balance point, that the Greeks (for good reason) were so famous for. No one said finding that mean was easy. And indeed, for the most part, chief executives are like men peering through the night—perhaps one should say like the figures

303

staring at the shadows in Plato's cave—unsure of what they are seeing, uncertain about how to react to it, tempted by simplistic advice by a variety of sophists and sycophants. But there is some hope. Times have forced chief executives to reevaluate their perceptions, driving them out of the dark, comfortable room of the past and into the bright, if shocking, world outside. Now, if they will only open their eyes and see.

NOTES

CHAPTER ONE

1. Colby H. Chandler, "Eastman Kodak Opens Windows of Opportunity," *Journal of Business Strategy* 7 (Summer 1986): 5.
2. Michael Macoby, *The Gamesman* (Cambridge: Harvard University Press, 1976).

CHAPTER TWO

1. Gary Slutsker, "I Want to Do What Carl Icahn Does," *Forbes*, 21 April 1986, 139.
2. James B. Stewart and Daniel Hertzberg, "Landmark Victory: Outside Directors Led the Carbide Defense That Fended Off GAF," *Wall Street Journal*, 13 January 1986.

CHAPTER THREE

1. T. Boone Pickens, Jr., "Shareholders: The Forgotten People," *Journal of Business Strategy* 6 (Summer 1985): 4–5.
2. Steven Gates was my research assistant on this chapter.
3. Statement by Harold S. Geneen to the Antitrust Subcommittee of the Committee of the Judiciary, House of Representatives, November 20, 1969, in *Competitive Strategic Management*, ed. Robert Lamb (Englewood Cliffs, N.J.: Prentice-Hall, 1984), p. 406.
4. Lamb, ed., *Competitive Strategic Management*, 401–2.
5. Malcolm Salter and Wolf Weinhold, "What Lies Ahead for Merger Activities in the 1980s," *Journal of Business Strategy* 2:4 (Spring 1982): 66–100.
6. Samuel Richardson Reid, *Merger, Managers and the Economy* (New York: McGraw-Hill, 1968), 46.
7. Jeffrey Pfeffer and Gerald Salancik, *The External Control of Organizations: A Resource Dependence Perspective* (New York: Harper & Row, 1978).
8. Wayne I. Boucher, "The Process of Conglomerate Mergers." Prepared for The Bureau of Competition, Federal Trade Commission, Washington D.C. (June 1980).
9. Robert Emmett, "How to Value a Potential Acquisition," *Financial Executive* (February 1982): 16–19.
10. Lee A. Daniels, "Acquisition Fits Allied's Style," *New York Times*, 16 May 1985.
11. This was not a quotation from J. W. McSwiney.
12. Andrew C. Brown, "The Devil's Brew in the Love Canal," *Fortune*, 19 November 1979, 76.
13. Vincent P. Rennert, "The Raiders," *Across the Board* 16 (July 1979): 12–22.

NOTES

CHAPTER FOUR

1. Lindsey Gruson, "Leading the Drive to Save Lilco," *New York Times*, 8 April 1984, sec. 3.

2. Michael Blumstein, "A Failed Gamble for Palmieri: He Cites Missteps at Baldwin," *New York Times*, 15 November 1983.

3. Donald Bibeault, *Corporate Turnaround: How Managers Turn Losers into Winners* (New York: McGraw-Hill, 1982), 99.

4. "Operation Turnaround," *Business Week*, 5 December 1983, 127.

5. Gruson, "Lilco," 8.

6. William S. Anderson, "Address to Beta Gamma Sigma Dinner" (Wright State University, April 19, 1976) in Bibeault, *Corporate Turnaround*, 167.

7. Jonathan P. Hicks, "Heyman of GAF: Tough, Tenacious. Carbide Fight Is His Biggest," *New York Times*, 18 December 1985.

8. Ibid.

9. Lee Iacocca, "Turnaround Strategies: The Rescue and Resuscitation of Chrysler," *Journal of Business Strategy* 4:1 (Summer 1983): 67–68.

10. Raymond M. Gomez, Director of Corporate Relations, Manville Sales Corporation, Letter to the Editor of *Harvard Business Review* 5 (September-October 1986): 130.

11. Susie Ghareb Nazem, "How Roy Ash Got Burned," *Fortune*, 6 April 1981, 72.

CHAPTER FIVE

1. Proxy statement, Trans World Corporation (November 25, 1983), 6.

CHAPTER SEVEN

1. "How the PC Project Changed the Way IBM Thinks," *Business Week*, 3 October 1983, 86.

2. Alfred P. Sloan, Jr., *My Years with General Motors* (New York: Doubleday, 1963), 65.

3. Sloan, Jr., *General Motors*, 53.

4. Thomas J. McNichols, *Executive Policy and Strategic Planning* (McGraw-Hill: New York, 1977), 23.

5. Michael Macoby, *The Gamesman* (Cambridge: Harvard University Press, 1976).

6. This list appeared in Zenas Block, "Can Corporate Venturing Succeed?" *Journal of Business Strategy* 3 (Fall 1982): 22.

7. "Gillette: When Being No. 1 Just Isn't Enough," *Business Week*, 13 August 1984, 126.

CHAPTER EIGHT

1. C. Don Burnett, Dennis P. Yeskey, and David Richardson, "New Roles for Corporate Planners in the 1980s," *Journal of Business Strategy* 4:4 (Spring 1984): 64–68.

2. Lee Iacocca with William Novak, *Iacocca: An Autobiography* (New York: Bantam Books, 1984), 134.

3. Zachary Schiller and Amy Dunkin, "New? Improved? The Brand-name Mergers," *Business Week*, 21 October 1985, 109.

NOTES

4. Harold Levinson and Stuart Rosenthal, *CEO: Corporate Leadership in Action* (New York: Basic Books: 1984), p. 181.

5. Levinson and Rosenthal, *CEO*, 181.

6. Scott Scredon and Marc Frons, "Coke's Man on the Spot," *Business Week*, 29 July 1985, 57.

7. "Coke's Man on the Spot," 60.

8. "Coke's Man on the Spot," 60–61.

CHAPTER NINE

1. Thomas J. Peters and Robert H. Waterman, Jr., *In Search of Excellence: Lessons from America's Best Run Companies* (New York: Harper & Row, 1982).

2. Max B. Richards, *Organizational Goal Structures* (St. Paul: West Publishing, 1978), 52–64.

3. Thomas S. Burns, *Tales of ITT: An Insider's Report* (Boston: Houghton Mifflin, 1974).

4. Arthur M. Louis, "The Controversial Boss of Beatrice," *Fortune*, 22 July 1985, 110.

5. *In Search of Excellence*, 3–28.

CHAPTER TEN

1. Sandra Salmans, "Bradshaw Brought RCA Back," *New York Times*, 13 December 1985.

2. Robert Lamb, Eleanor Johnson Tracy, Nancy Love, and Ann M. Morrison, "Businessmen in the News: Even a Water-Walker Needs a Committee," *Fortune*, December 1976, 21.

3. Lee A. Daniels, "Acquisition Fits Allied's Style," *New York Times*, 16 May 1985.

4. "Big Media, Big Money: The dramatic takeover of ABC is the latest and largest deal in the feeding frenzy over hot media properties. The Founder Speaks," *Newsweek*, 1 April 1985, 58.

CHAPTER ELEVEN

1. Arthur M. Louis, "The Controversial Boss of Beatrice," *Fortune*, 22 July 1985, 110–116.

2. I. B. Meyers, *The Meyers-Briggs Type Indicator* (Palo Alto: Consulting Psychologists Press, 1962).

3. Raymond E. Miles and Charles C. Snow, *Organizational Strategy: Structure and Process* (New York: McGraw-Hill, 1978).

4. "The Controversial Boss of Beatrice," 111.

5. Lee Iacocca with William Novak, *Iacocca: An Autobiography* (New York: Bantam Books, 1984).

6. D. Miller, M. F. Kets de Vries, J. Toulouse, "Top Executive Locus of Control and Its Relationship to Strategy-Making, Structure and Environment," *Academy of Management Journal* 25:2 (June 1982), 237–253.

7. John A. Byrne, "Up, Up and Away?" *Business Week*, 25 November 1985, 94.

8. "1982 Report Found 'Major' Faults at Indian Plant," *New York Times*, 11 December 1984.

9. Thomas J. Lueck, "A Clouded Future Seen," *New York Times*, 3 December 1985.

10. Bruce Henderson, "The Logic of Kanban," *Journal of Business Strategy* 6:3 (Winter 1986) 6–12.

APPENDIX

CEOs AND DATES INTERVIEWED

Roy A. Anderson, Lockheed Corporation, May 1982

Roy Ash, AM International Incorporated, October 1976, May 1980, and February 1982

Karl D. Bays, American Hospital Supply, March 1984

Michel C. Bergerac, Revlon Incorporated, March 1982

W. Michael Blumenthal, Bendix Corporation, September 1976 and Burroughs Corporation, October 1981

Thornton F. Bradshaw, RCA Corporation, April 1984

Edgar M. Bronfman, Joseph E. Seagram & Sons, Incorporated, March and April 1983

Charles L. Brown, AT & T Company, October 1981

J. Fred Bucy, Jr., Texas Instruments Incorporated, November 1981 and October 1983

James E. Burke, Johnson & Johnson, April 1983

John W. Culligan, American Home Products Corporation, October 1982

John deButts, AT & T Company, October 1979 and February 1980

Herbert D. Doan, Dow Chemical Company, May 1983 and June 1984

Joseph B. Flavin, The Singer Company, October 1980 and December 1982

Henry Ford II, Ford Motor Company, September 1976

Robert R. Frederick, RCA Corporation and General Electric, September 1979

Harold S. Geneen, ITT Corporation, March and May 1982

Bruce D. Henderson, The Boston Consulting Group, 1976–1986

Alan Hirschfield, Twentieth Century Fox Corporation, April 1982 and Columbia Pictures Company, October 1982

E. Robert Kinney, General Mills Corporation, April 1983

Thomas Lamont, Morgan Guaranty Trust Company, February 1966

C. Peter McColough, Xerox Corporation, June 1980 and April 1982

John A. McKinney, Manville Corporation, May 1980

J. W. McSwiney, Mead Corporation, November 1980

William F. May, American Can Company, 1976–1986

Arjay Miller, Ford Motor Company, November 1976 and May 1982

James E. Mortensen, Young and Rubicam Incorporated, June 1982

William C. Norris, Control Data Corporation, May 1980 and February 1981

Nathan R. Owen, General Signal Corporation, June 1978 and May 1983

Andrall E. Pearson, Pepsico Incorporated, May 1984

APPENDIX

T. Boone Pickens, Jr., Mesa Petroleum Company, May 1985
Wallace N. Rasmussen, Beatrice Companies Incorporated, March 1980
David Rockefeller, Chase Manhattan Bank, October and November 1982
William Rothschild, Consultant to General Electric, 1976–1986
Irving Shapiro, E. I. duPont de Nemours & Company, September 1976
Andrew C. Sigler, Champion International Corporation, March 1982
L. Edwin Smart, Trans World Corporation, October 1976 and April 1980
William Sneath, Union Carbide Corporation, October 1976
Charles (Tex) Thornton, Litton Industries Incorporated, November 1977
William C. Verity, Armco Steel Corporation, February 1977, October 1981, and
    February 1982
David W. Wallace, Bangor Punta Corporation, May 1981 and March 1984
George Weissman, Philip Morris Companies Incorporated, April 1985
Robert Wilson, Memorex Corporation, February 1980

Many other CEOs were interviewed for this project, but did not wish to be publicly
    acknowledged.

INDEX OF EXECUTIVES

INDEX OF EXECUTIVES

INDEX OF CORPORATIONS

313

INDEX OF CORPORATIONS